THE HABIT OF SURVIVING

MARILYN

Bobby's mother was a cook and her sisters did "day work." They worked for white folks and they came in from a full day's work and said "fuck you" whenever it suited them. I was scared to be a "fuck you" woman. I was scared of everything.

SARA

I wanted to know influential people. I looked to the high school assembly. That was where the principal would make public affairs announcements or introduce several programs or guest speakers. Then [one day] someone came on stage and made an announcement about the murder of Emmett Till. This event stirred up a fire in me.

ELAINE

I am faced with a summer with my husband [of thirty-one years of marriage], with whom I have nothing in common and I almost die. And he used to pride himself on being exactly the same person he was when he graduated from high school. One night Louis reached for me in the bed and I say I can't do this or it's going to drive me crazy. The next day I tell him that I want out of the marriage, that I have a job waiting for me in another city and that I'm leaving on the weekend.

GWEN

I remember one weekend in Miami when all three guys visited in the same week. I had slept with three different men at three different places for a whole week. I was so tired. I remembered telling my sister, "I never want to see another dick as long as I live." I had been famous for juggling stuff like this in the past because I didn't want to give them up.

THE HABIT OF
SURVIVING

KESHO YVONNE SCOTT

BALLANTINE BOOKS

NEW YORK

LIBRARY OF CONGRESS CATALOG CARD NUMBER: 91-75993

ISBN: 0-345-37676-5

Cover design by Ken Brown
Cover photographs by Jeanne Moutoussamy

Manufactured in the United States of America
First Ballantine Books Edition: January 1992
10 9 8 7 6 5 4 3 2 1

To my mother, Connie L. Scott,
I dedicate this study.
Your habits of surviving, loving,
and being—although I did not
always acknowledge or understand—
were given so freely, I almost
missed them.

CONTENTS

ACKNOWLEDGMENTS

Most especially I wish to thank the four women who told me their stories and who, through those stories, taught, touched, and guided me—not only to discover my own habits of surviving but also to have the courage to ask myself, What is life beyond surviving?

Many persons have helped to produce this book. Chief among them is my loving-in-all-the-right-ways husband and my telling-it-like-it-is daughters, who left me alone at my computer on many weekends, supplied me with many back rubs, and reminded me that I was brave and loved.

Among my academic colleagues who gave advice and read portions of the manuscript, I am particularly indebted and grateful to the following professors at Grinnell College: Michael Bell, whose Irish sense of humor, professional mentoring, and lessons in "reading the text aloud" helped me through the last days of agonizing rewrites. Michael, you are a blessing from my Higher Power. And Maria Mootry, I thank you for putting in long hours at night with our four kids, for pizza dinners, and for your megatalents in helping me layer the many voices in this text. You are an inspiration and soul sister to me. I would also like to thank Rich Horwitz of the

University of Iowa and Melba Boyd of the University of Michigan-Flint, whose early encouragement in 1986 made me take myself seriously when I asked, "Do black women *really* have the habit of surviving?"

For technical assistance (transcription, word processing, and editing) at various stages of the manuscript, I am especially indebted to Randy Lincoln, Karen Groves, Faun Black, Angie Story-Johnson, Lisa Mulholland, and Carol Kalbaugh at the University of Pennsylvania. I am also indebted to Sandy Stein, my student and dear friend, who provided research and editing suggestions, along with love and acceptance throughout this journey. Thanks, too, to Grinnell College for magnanimous support.

Finally, I want to thank my editor, Leslie Mitchner, at Rutgers University Press, for her consistent encouragement, imaginative suggestions, enduring understanding, and persistence in urging me to keep a balance among my truth, my honesty, and my vision for black women.

THE HABIT OF SURVIVING

Having been a Black woman, you learn not to depend on anything. You get into the habit of surviving.
　　　　　　　　—Lena Horne and Richard Schickel, *Lena*

When Black women told the stories about their real lives and actual experiences, they prove the power of art (history) to demolish stereotypes; and if power (at least the beginning of it) is the ability to name one's own experience, Black-Eyed Susans was the first step toward power, for it celebrated the legend of Black women, weaved dreams into myths that allow us to recover and name our own past.
　　　　　　Mary Helen Washington, *Black-Eyed Susans*

Self-perception can be as deceitful and stereotypical as those projected on a person or on an entire community. Exposing forces generating distortions inside or outside the contextual reality of our vast interconnected fabric of human relationships and envisioning us as complementary, autonomous spirits is the thematic desire of the visionary artist. Unless we purge the insidious fears and cowering illusions within, the larger monster will never be dismantled.
　　　　　　Melba Joyce Boyd, "The Salt in the Sugar"

INTRODUCTION

The link between experience and consciousness that is revealed in life histories enables us to see that consciousness is not simply the act of interpreting but also of constructing the social world.

—Doris Kearns

THIRTEEN years tall, I stood in the living room doorway. My clothes were wet. My hair was mangled. I was in tears, in shock, and in need of my mother's warm arms. Slowly, she looked me up and down, stood up from the couch and walked towards me, her body clenched in criticism. Putting her hands on her hips and planting herself, her shadow falling over my face, she asked in a voice of barely suppressed rage, "What happened?" I flinched as if struck by the unexpected anger and answered, "They put my head in the toilet. They say I can't swim with them." "They" were eight white girls at my high school. I reached out to hold her, but she roughly brushed my hands aside and said, "Like hell! Get your coat. Let's go."

My mother taught me two powerful and enduring lessons that day. She taught me that I would have to fight back against racial and sexual injustice. Striding down Greenfield Avenue and across the Southfield Expressway with me crying and following behind, terrified of how she was going to embarrass me even more, she taught me that my feelings did not matter, that no matter how hurt I was, how ashamed, or how surprised I was, I had to fight back because if I did not, then I would always be somebody's victim. She also taught me a lesson I did

3

not want to learn: She taught me exactly when my private pain had to become a public event that must be dealt with in a public manner. That day my mother offered me no personal comfort for my momentary shame and embarrassment; instead she made me see my pain as not mine. Though she spoke no words directly, she made me realize instinctively that my experience was not some expression of tenth-grade girls' jealousy—not a silly, private adolescent version of "They don't like *me.*" My experience, she taught me, was directly related to facts I could not control—my blackness and my womanness. This was her lesson.

I did not know then that my childhood had ended and my initiation into black womanhood had begun. Neither did I know that I had experienced my mother's habit of surviving. I just knew that standing up for myself was what I had to do because it was the way black women had to be. We had to stand up in public for what was right, and stand against what was wrong. That was our role and our achievement. It was as Lena Horne had said in an interview: "If anyone should ask a black woman in America what has been her greatest achievement, the honest answer would be 'I survived.' "[1]

BLACK WOMEN'S ISSUES

Black women in America have waged battles against what has been called the "largest cultural Goliath" in human history— American dominant/mainstream/hegemonic culture—and some have won.[2] Even for these women, however, reflecting on past experiences at some point becomes necessary for establishing meaning and direction in life.

Writing about black women and reflecting on my own legacy from a self-conscious political perspective has given me inspiration in my own life and in my scholarly efforts. It has also challenged me—and I hope my work will challenge others—to search for commonalities among all women's lives, and to embrace them.

Among the issues I address in this book are the politics of black women's everyday lives, the roots of scholarly black women's perspectives and activities, and the social and ideological problems specific to the lives of women of color. I also focus on the contributions black women have made to the construction of knowledge and to literary creativity.

> *The best we can offer is a partial rendering, a subjective portrait of the subject from a particular angle of vision shaped as much by our own biography—our attitudes, perceptions and feelings toward the subject—as by the raw materials themselves.* [3]

PERSONAL POLITICS AND SCHOLARLY PERSPECTIVES

The impetus behind my interest in this study is extremely personal. As a black radical feminist socialized by the liberation movements of the sixties and seventies, I have found myself at times an anomaly among my friends and professional peers. Like many black women, I did not come to feminism through the white women's intellectual movement. I imitated my foremothers: my mother, my grandmother, my great-grandmother, whom I'd known until I was about six. (My feminism also grew in response to struggles inside and outside racially segregated political organizations.)

The second wave of the white feminist movement (an essential root of it, anyway) emerged from the expulsion of whites (including white women) from the Student Nonviolent Coordinating Committee (SNCC). This action forced white students (and many liberals) to develop their own political ideology of oppression, to create all-white (nonintegrated) political organizations (for example, Students for a Democratic Society, SDS) and to confront the chauvinism and sexism of white men. By contrast, I became a feminist by choosing to do political work in specifically all-black nationalist organizations (like the Black Panther Party), which were traditionally sexist. The twin evils of racism and ethnic chauvinism inside progressive multiracial leftist organizations made it difficult to commit to working with whites. (Remember the experience of Bigger Thomas in *Native Son* who worked with the socialist in the ghetto of New York.) The trade-off (as I saw it) was either to fight racism in white-dominated organizations (where whites did the leading, the thinking, the writing, etc., and blacks did the confrontational work or were organizational showpieces) or to develop a personal strategy to fight (simultaneously) against externalized racism in society *and* against sexism within all-black organizations. The popular belief in our black feminist tradition has been to rank racism as the worst of two evils (or as the more important struggle) and to tolerate black male sexism for the sake of the political organization.

Nonetheless, I was an anomaly, even among other black women, because of my travels in and beyond this country's borders, travels that expanded my political concerns and that allowed me to acquire a cross-cultural, international perspective. Eventually, I became a well-educated professional woman, financially and politically independent. And, finally, I was a straight, single parent, whose political growth depended on role models and allies who were lesbians of color.

My sense of myself was confirmed by others who saw me as being "different" from the majority of American women, yet somehow "typical" of black women. I began to realize how peculiar I seemed when I discovered that I was as alone as I had earlier imagined. In the black community, I was called a "tuff mama." Other labels were applied to me as well. I was called a "dynamic woman" because I juggled careers, parenting, sometimes marriage, and political activism. I was labelled a "new woman" or "superwoman" in academic circles; and sometimes I was given other names, far less complimentary. All these labels implied that I was liberated, but, I asked myself, "liberated from what and to what?"

Sex, Self, and Society for Black Women

I knew that the experiences of black and white women in America had developed historically in different directions and patterns. While many white, middle-class career women have experienced work as liberation from traditional sex-roles (grounded in domesticity), black women—like other oppressed and poor ethnic women—have for generations been forced to work outside the home so that their families could live and develop economically. Any emotional autonomy black women might have has paradoxically and necessarily evolved out of slavery and the historical extensions of racism, sexism, and ongoing economic oppression. Black women have almost always operated outside of traditional and middle-class white sex-roles, thus transcending and "recoloring" their blackness—changing a "negative" into a "positive." Any attempt to study black women involves the interplay among three intertwined areas in ethnic, racial, and class studies: sex-role socialization, construction of self-identity, and social movements.

The women in my own family and community seemed to be poised on a "tightrope," suspended between different but overlapping worlds—the worlds of being black and being woman. Their experiences were colored by their own cultural invention—their creation of themselves and their personal stories. Their personal stories are self-conscious testimonies— what they have wanted to tell—about themselves as victims and as survivors who exist on the margins of American culture. In the process of "storytelling," each woman has exposed how black female identity is socially constructed. Thus in creating themselves through their stories, the women of my family, and all black women, have also helped to create expanded definitions of what it means to be black, female, and American.

Any study of black women living under American racism demands a research perspective that embraces race, sex, and class. Moreover, researchers carrying out such a study must beware of misrepresenting the cultural values and practices of black women's actual behavior and self-perceptions. Such a study must allow us to see how black women both shape the world and are shaped by it. It must acknowledge that black women create their own black feminist theory. They come to feminist theory and practice out of the oppression they experience as people who are poor and black and women. I contend that black feminism has evolved historically over centuries, outside traditional white feminine roles, white social institutions, and white feminist cultural theory.

When I began my own journey to acquire knowledge from white feminist texts that connected sex-role socialization, self-identity, and liberation movements, I could not help but notice that the lives of black women had gone largely unremarked or had been undervalued. Since white feminists' interest in theory tended to ignore the importance of cultural context, I consulted other histories written by and about black women. Paula Giddings's book *When and Where I Enter* is based on an Afrocentric perspective of black women's history. In it I found reasons why such terms as "a liberated woman" have different meanings for different races. I began to explore the Afrocentric perspective further through the writings of radical black feminist Barbara Smith, who introduced the concept of the "interlocking web of oppression" (which directly affects the lives of Afro-Americans).[4] I was then able to connect Giddings's and Smith's work with Suzanne Pharr's concept of homophobia as a weapon of sexism that affects the ability of all women to understand the interrelatedness of race and sexuality.[5] Oppression and heterosexism are the chief components of American culture that entangle both black and white women's stories. And if I was going to untangle new truths, according to Catharine A. MacKinnon, I needed a "personal contextualization of [black] women's lives, making them invaluable for deepening cross-cultural comparison and preventing facile generalizations that evaluate women's experiences or oppressions."[6] Only through personal histories of difference could I hope to reflect Ellen Cantarow's notion that "there is a democratic idea at the hearing of oral history: because the people who have lived through particular events are the ones best qualified to talk about them."[7]

HOW OPPRESSION AND SURVIVAL ISSUES INTERRELATE

Finally, my research perspective and angle of vision were further focused by the works of Rickey Sherover-Marcuse, Suzanne Lipsky, and Barbara Love on internalized oppression and survival. They defined and described some "habits of survival" as manifestations of oppression. Sherover-Marcuse suggests that habits can be positive as well as rigid, destructive, or ineffective; and that they are based on feelings, attitudes, or behaviors that are internalized by the oppressed person in reaction to the knowledge of her or his own mistreatment.[8]

Suzanne Lipsky takes the examination of survival to another level; she develops the idea of "survival as a skill." She suggests that behavior patterns (developed by black people to help them survive racist oppression) are part of the Afro- and American socialization and acculturation process.[9] Moreover, she insists that every oppressed group receives oppressive conditioning, and that responses to this conditioning are misidentified as part of the black culture. According to Love, black people learn that appearing to function well in America often requires them to accept the dominant society's prejudices against them.[10]

Synthesizing the ideas of all these writers into a new way of seeing, I was able to make a connection between habits, learning, and skills that led me to a deeper understanding of the choices survivors make. I could begin to see that we as black people (and especially black women) had some good habits and some bad habits, and that both played a role in our survival. I could finally make a theoretical leap from survival by means of group practices in everyday life (and in my own life) to the design of an oppressive society to exert control over not only the material world but the hearts, minds, and spirits of oppressed people, especially black women.

RATIONALE AND METHOD

My challenges in developing the research for this book were, as I see it, twofold. First, I needed material that would enable me to write about black women's "habits of survival" as well as their roles as creative agents for social change (which Gerda Lerner calls "survival as resistance"). Second, I wanted to examine critically the full range of what Lerner calls the "warrior mode," in all of its pain and glory.[11] The definitions of these key terms go a long way toward explaining the rationale for the book.

I use the phrase *habits of survival* to refer to the external adjustments and internal adaptations that people make to economic exploitation and to racial and gender-related oppression. Such habits, first and foremost, are responses to pain and suffering that help lessen anger, give a sense of self-control, and offer hope. They can also be responses to unexpected happiness—ways of keeping "good times" going. They work, so oppressed people use them over and over again to defeat pain or prolong pleasure. People teach these habits to each other, often by example. They become as automatic as dance steps that we practice and perfect. Like dance steps, they provide a social etiquette, a way of moving through the world, and "proof" that we are in control. Eventually, the habits cease to be mere responses. They acquire the status of cultural prescriptions. In fact, they harden into ingrained attitudes—routines of thought, feeling, and action—that over time become unexamined and unquestioned traditions. In the end, they become so familiar and seem so deep-rooted in our culture that we say of them "it's just the way we do things."

As expedient and often unexamined ways of behaving, habits often have been negatively cast. However, many habits of survival—the habits of mind, will, feeling, or action—have sustained and inspired individuals and whole communities through overwhelming situations. The danger occurs when we invoke old habits in new social circumstances and end up acting like wind-up toys on a cultural chorus line instead of being our own choreographer—choosing our own moves. When we do this—continually and uncritically use these habits to adjust, to stay within tradition, and to survive—the habits seem to change from being governed by some larger force to being governing forces themselves. Thus habits can become obstacles to personal and group growth.

The "warrior mode" is an example of a habit. It is a "dance step" that many black women do that, I believe, has us confused about the reality of our opportunities to make choices. The term *warrior mode* designates an attitude, a style of approaching life, in which one perceives existence as a continuous battle. This mode derives from black women's belief that they, as mothers of black culture, should be responsible for the world. In this mode, we can never let down our guard (even to ourselves). In the warrior mode, many black women's individual and group responsibilities are distorted, personal and political boundaries are blurred, and personal and community priorities are unbalanced. The irony is that warriors almost always use survival tactics taught to them by the previous generations. These tactics are like old dance steps that don't fit the new beat: they do not help black women synthesize new steps; they do not help black women defend themselves against new contradictions in their present reality. In this way, the warrior mode is an additional obstacle—along with all the "isms"—that black women have to overcome.

The challenge to black womanhood in the twenty-first century is to go beyond cultural prescriptions. We need to discover how we can function in an oppressive culture, change it, and live beyond mere survival. To make these discoveries, we need answers to questions: How do we liberate ourselves *from* the external and internal tentacles of oppression as well as liberate ourselves *to* a new and flexible idea—the role of ourselves as "choosers"? How do we make up a culture to empower ourselves as we go along? Survival is not enough. Liberation is the next step. Liberation as a process requires that habits be identified, acknowledged for their pluses and minuses, and relegated to the realm of the conscious and chosen. Choice is the key to liberation. Choice is how we emancipate ourselves.

My examination of black women's habits of survival in America centers on the life stories of four women between the ages of forty-six and fifty-two, all of whom were born in the thirties, raised in the forties, and married in the fifties. All of these women—Marilyn, Sara, Elaine, and Gwen—are successful, both by dominant white and by Afro-American cultural standards. Central to both standards is the idea of success as the acquisition of higher education, increased personal and family economic opportunity, and cultural assimilation of white values—in short, the practice of biculturalism, so that one can fit and function in both white and black worlds.

All of the women I interviewed are politically conscious, mature black women whose stories not only illustrate how they have survived "out in the world" but also reveal their interior worlds. Their reports provide both a direction and a model for studying black women's lives within the matrix of race, gender, class, and history.

Over a period of three years, I taped and, with each woman

helping me, transcribed the interviews: Marilyn's and Sara's in 1986, Elaine's in 1987, and Gwen's in 1989. That year I also interviewed my two daughters, who are called Jameka and Monté in this book. All of the interviewees' identities have been masked in order to protect their anonymity and that of their families. Their names, the names of their significant others, and such details as names of cities and identifiable sites have all been altered.

To open each interview, I asked each woman the same question: "Will you state your name, place of birth, and present occupation?" From that starting point, each woman described her life and related her feelings and attitudes about family, men, feminism, politics, God, and why she wanted to be involved in this book. On the last point, each woman expressed her trust in me and her hope that she could personally grow. And, in fact, as the material increased in volume and as interpersonal intensity developed between us, we created a safe place for catharsis and trust. Each interviewee and I experienced the feeling that we had known each other for years. Over the many hours we spent together, the women's voices varied from loud and boasting to warm and vulnerable. They laughed with silly humor, and they shared their most intimate pain and their tears.

The taping, finally, amounted to more than 156 hours, and the unedited transcription totaled over 720 pages. In preparing this large quantity of information for this book, I have taken care to let each woman's words stand on their own. The chronologies that you read here are practically verbatim. I have, however, punctuated the narratives and edited out repetitive details as well as tangential information in order to focus on the women's survival stories. In doing so, I have made every effort to protect what I perceive to be these women's powerful and varied voices and intonations—or, as they would say, their "girlfriend, I tell you—" styles. As editor and "girlfriend," I have included the material from each interview that I think best characterizes the speaker as an individual and as a black woman who has survived. In a few cases, I have altered the opening sequence of events somewhat to prevent monotony in the recitation of life chronologies. Thus some narratives begin with a significant event from the woman's life. These slight changes in form do not affect substance, however. In each case, I have presented the speaker's storytelling pattern as it evolved, unfettered by my influence.

My role during the interviews was to listen carefully, take notes, and interrupt only to remind the speaker of what had taken place at the last taping session. This approach was gratifying to all of us and ensured that these women's stories were told in their actual words. And their words best describe their strategies for life.

In addition to editing the interviews to give them structure, I made an effort to select material that would highlight similarities in the women's lives. For example, I included information about families from the South who moved north and settled in the Midwest (rarely depicted in contemporary media). I also edited to show differences, for example, between the lives of women who remained married and those who did not. Further, I edited the narratives in such a way as to facilitate the interaction of my own voice in critically evaluating American culture where it intersects with these contemporary black women's histories. Through this critical analysis, I hope to emphasize parallels among the lives of the interviewees and connections to the lives of generations of black women who share similar legacies.

Marilyn, Elaine, Sara, and Gwen collaborated with me to create these interpretations of their lives. Through their interviews, they have shown me their own particular realities and have also built a bridge for me between their cultural context—growing up in the forties and developing their own survival skills—and my own. This biographical bridge is the by-product of our "invented lives" and provides an intimate portrait of the full range of our habits. Mary Helen Washington believes that the bridge extends the tradition established by black women writers as literary forebears. She says, "So it seems what we're doing is piecing it together like a quilt. You know, everybody who picks up one little piece tells us what that meant adding to that quilt, and each one of us is adding a stitch or adding a square or adding a color. What we're trying to do is produce out of our own needs the writers and the writings that will take us to the next step."[12]

As a collaborator, I am both participant and observer in these women's reconstructions of their stories. James Clifford argues that this kind of collaboration has ethnographic authority because "to understand others arises initially from the sheer fact of our co-existence in a shared world."[13] Their stories spiral outward, encompassing black families, then community, then white power structures, and then nationhood, and, ultimately, our identity as spiritual beings. I am grateful to have shared these women's "tight spaces" between the society, the family, and the self.[14]

LIFE-HISTORIES AS CONTRADICTIONS
OF STEREOTYPES

These self-reported life-histories directly challenge inaccurate stereotypes inside as well as outside the women's movement. In my analysis of these narratives, I strive to demonstrate how these black women, at least—and I believe they are representative—have been historically committed to antiracist and nonsexist human relationships among people of all colors, sexes, and classes. These interviews reveal the muted stories and ongoing struggles of an unsanctioned black women's movement and resistance, or what Audre Lorde calls "the many roots to the tree of anger: of silenced black feminist voices."[15] Even before the mass political and social upheavals in the 1960s, these lives were describing and supporting what Bell Hooks calls the complex triple-consciousness of the Afro-

American woman (as warrior against a racist and patriarchal system).[16]

Further, I also hope these oral histories speak directly to the white woman's movement about when, where, and why black women will enter a collective sisterhood. They challenge the emptiness of the struggle to achieve the American dream for all minorities. They demonstrate not only a kind of feminism and racial pride but also a testimony of our historical presence, representing a tradition of protest against all forms of human oppression. Finally, they are biographical histories of black women's antioppressive tradition, reestablished by giving definitive value to womanhood.

OVERVIEW

Chapter One of this book is a cultural history of black women who were raised in the forties and influenced by the "promises of postwar modernism" that followed World War II. As Barbara Tuchman comments, "biography is not quantitative, but it has its historical place."[17] This chapter describes the historical place: the black woman's American homeland, which has been rendered virtually invisible in the historical annals of the United States, the male-centered Afro-American culture, and the history of white women. Also detailed here are the struggles, both heroic and tragic, of black women's public lives as they have adapted to racial oppression and sexual discrimination.

Chapters Two through Five each focus on one woman's description of the conditions of her life and the patterns of her survival. Each of these chapters opens with an overview of the woman's experiences and closes with an interpretive analysis of her life. In Chapter Two, Marilyn's story reveals her as being both enriched and impoverished by the habit of surviving through "private, rebellions and overt self-denial." Demonstrating the negative power of intraracism, she sees herself as "a piece of yellow thrown away." Her story is the struggle to find acceptance of her talents within her own family, community, and country.

Chapter Three is the story of the habit of surviving by "never looking out of control." Sara describes the rewards and punishments of upward mobility and eventually acknowledges the "no-win" situation that comes from thinking you can control everything in a racist society. Sara's story is the struggle to accommodate her own personal needs as she carries out her responsibilities of leadership and service to her people.

Chapter Four is the story of Elaine, whose habit of surviving takes the form of hiding her brilliant mind behind her role as the "sacred mother." Her words about a healthy family life reveal a sterile marriage where she never had room to learn to be intimate. Elaine's is a story of struggling to take time to "smell the flowers" and hear oneself think while loving others.

Chapter Five is Gwen's story of "acting, dressing, and looking right" in order to fit into, to step outside of, and to challenge male-centeredness in her family, work, and community life. Her words recount a life of surviving through inner resourcefulness and of suffering painful disappointments in the belief that answers for women can be found in just looks and men. Gwen's story is about how pernicious the warrior mode can be when it escalates from a temporary stance, necessary for survival, to an involuntary, permanent posture.

In Chapter Six I look at black women's habits of surviving as learned routine steps danced by a chorus line. Using the dance metaphor, I examine tactics for adapting to a racist, patriarchal society, and I analyze the steps of these women's "dances" in the contexts of black family life, the community, the larger society, and each woman's personal identity.

Chapter Seven describes my own dance in a generation shaped by the moral and political struggles for civil and women's rights, for economic black power, and against U.S.

imperialism. My dance—my habits of surviving—reflects the malaise that comes with trying to balance "having it all" and "keeping the revolution going." It reflects the terrible rending of personal and psychic identity that can occur when prospects open very wide and possibilities seem unlimited. My story is the story of learning when, where, and how to let go of some survival skills—skills not unlike those of the women I interviewed—and accepting that to survive is not to be liberated from ongoing confrontation with new questions and choices. In this chapter I also find that the gap between my own generation and an earlier one is not quite so great as I had once imagined.

The Conclusion ends the book with a gentle caution to black women about blind spots *in our view* of our legacy and a look at the next generation, described by my daughters, who are already acting out lessons they learned from (and asking new questions of) their mother. Their voices are already asking, "How do I be a black woman if it means I have to save the world?"

Having heard myself in my children's words, dreams, fears, and criticisms, I am not sure I should be congratulating myself for completing this book. At best, I think I can experience it as another "habit of surviving" in the context of my own *internalized* oppression. It has worked for me as a kind of telescope for seeing myself outside of my oppression, where I—and the women who share my legacy and future—continue to strive to be whole.

CHAPTER 1

THE PREVIOUS GENERATION

WHEN Marilyn, Sara, Elaine, and Gwen told me their stories of surviving, I found it nearly impossible not to assume a great deal as I listened. My mother used to say, "Separate the *ass* from the rest of the word and that's what you've made of yourself." Her words echo for me as I think back on the interviews. I kept assuming alternatives for these women that did not exist. I found myself getting angry, listening to incident after incident in the women's lives. I wanted to attack the real and imagined enemies of these sisters. Sometimes, I even wanted to attack them for their seeming complicity in their own exploitation. "If it were me," I'd think, "I'd take my 1980s ball-busting black-feminist style and . . ."—you know the rest.

In the end, I managed to keep quiet while I tried to make sense of these lives and landscapes that were so very foreign to me. Over and over they would say, "Well, Kesho, what do you mean, birth control, or marry for love, or ask him to do the dishes, or choose my own career, or file a discrimination case, or . . ." and I'd say, "I'm sorry, I forgot. That isn't the way it was in those days." I would sigh, rearranging the knots in my stomach, as I listened to their explanations of how sexism, racism, and classism tripped them up before they knew what had happened.

Although I had studied Afro-American, women's, and American history, the women's personal stories about racial segregation, sexual discrimination, life in government-subsidized projects, and their experiences during and after World War II, created for me a new feeling of familiarity with a world openly hostile to blacks and women—a world quite distant from what I had known as an adult in the eighties. After each interview I would get a migraine headache. I felt heavy, anticipating each new avalanche of information, of finished interviews, and of transcription as I worked toward preparing the printed words. There was pain in the telling, the listening, the recording, and the writing.

Between sessions, I would have nightmares about being trapped in their time and fighting to get out—like Dana, the main character in Octavia Butler's novel *Kindred,* the story of a black woman in the seventies who involuntarily time-travels back to the antebellum South. Like Dana, I wanted to perceive myself as strong, confident, and intellectually superior to the women of our past. I believed I was more "together" than all four of them. I quickly recognized that I was assuming not only that I was part of a progression but that I had "arrived"—and that I had definitely overcome *their* fears of "talking back to white people." At the same time, I knew I could not have survived—there is that word again—their trials. And I did not have to or want to. I tried to create an intellectual distance, a safe haven, that I savored in the evenings, when I was secure in my own world, my own time, my own mind.

Undeniably, however, I felt strong kinship with the four women. Their stories made me angry. I heard echoes of my own mother's voice in their words. And then I remembered the "Mary McLeod Bethune stories" from both of my grandmothers. When they pronounced her name I felt that I had to sit up straight and suck in my breath. They kept telling me about her selflessness and all she had done for the race. They kept telling me to be like her.

Mary McLeod Bethune wrote to her friend Charlotte Hawkins Brown in 1947:

> My eyes sparkled with glee and my heart vibrated with joy . . . to see your . . . Award for Interracial Advancement. God bless our women. They are reaching forward speedily . . . Harriet Tubman, Sojourner Truth, Margaret Washington— all of those who were sowing seeds when it cost so much more than it does now, must rejoice in the Glory Land over the great harvest that is now coming to Negro womanhood in America and throughout the world. . . . The harvest is bound to come but it is heartening to those of us who have tried so hard, to live sufficiently long to garner in just a little of the harvest while we are still alive.[1]

The lines in this letter tell me what the clear cultural mandate was for black (Negro) women in the forties.

The champion for change for black women growing up in the forties, Bethune understood the complex and harsh price black women paid for helping the race. Like W.E.B. Du Bois, she believed that "we cannot abolish the new economic freedom of women" as workers and that "the future woman must have a life work and economic independence."[2] She was imbued with the idea of a "mission" that connected her missionary work, the establishment of a school of higher education for girls (Bethune-Cookman College), her ceaseless fundraising for educational causes, her colored women's club work, her child welfare work, and her antilynching and antirape crusades. Bethune's passions—race, women, education, and youth—were to become part of the national agenda as the country entered World War II and created a new context for black feminism.

The experiences of black women in the forties are linked with those of all Americans and cannot be separated from the historical context in which they took place. Yet, if there were similarities in the changes all Americans went through, there were also differences. The major shifts in American political, economic, and social life dramatically altered black women's personal lives, intimate relationships, private activities, and self-perceptions.

During the forties, two central questions haunted our society: How could the economy be restructured to provide Americans with decent jobs and also maintain stability and economic growth? And, how could the country best protect and promote American interests abroad in an unstable and threatening world?[3] World War II launched us into a global catastrophe, but it also turned the unemployment problem of the Depression into a labor shortage and propelled the economy into a new era of production and prosperity. The war effort led to the government's implementing the New Deal so as to maximize production, to equip soldiers and allies, to sustain the civilian population, and to create revenues to finance new economic enterprises.[4] The government responded to the military crisis by taking charge in new areas—asking its citizens to sacrifice and limiting the choices of what people could buy, where they could live, how they got to work, and whether they could change jobs. The New Deal also created a Congress of Industrial Organization (CIO) policy on race relations that pushed white employers to lower racial barriers against blacks in order to meet wartime production needs.

A major shift in the government's handling of discrimination resulted from the efforts of A. Philip Randolph, organizer of the Brotherhood of Sleeping Car Porters, says historian Howard Stikoff. Their organizing efforts yielded the threat of a massive demonstration in Washington. The government responded with Executive Order 8802, forbidding discrimination on the basis of race, creed, color, or national origin in the nation's defense industries. In 1941, the Federal Employment Practices Commission was established to implement the executive order. This mandate, however, did not include the word "sex." It was assumed that the race provision would protect black women. The 1940s black liberation strategy of the National Association for the Advancement of Colored People (NAACP), Congress of Racial Equality (CORE), and the National Urban League consisted of "double victory" campaigns to combat racism at home and fascism abroad.[5] Black political pressure, enforced by federal mandates, left many employers no choice but to hire blacks—until the first sign of peace in 1945. Racial barriers returned after the war, however, and the memory of them surfaces in the work of later writers such as Maya Angelou. Her observations of the treatment of black war heroes suggests that they "hung on the ghetto corners like forgotten laundry left on a backyard fence."[6] "Thus we lived through a major war," Angelou wrote, "but the question in the ghettos was, can we make it through a minor peace?" In many cases ex-soldiers, like Shadrack in Toni Morrison's *Sula*, remained shell-shocked as well as displaced.[7] For black men, then, the advantages and advancements were short lived.

The most significant change in the workplace during the forties was the massive entry of women into the labor force. The war-induced economic boom created unprecedented opportunities for women. Propaganda activities of the War Board emphasized women's central contribution to victory in the home and in the workplace. The mobilization of women for war work was said to improve their lives and status. Media campaigns were designed to make women aware not only of their important roles as mothers, wives, and homemakers but also of their value as workers, citizens, and soldiers. These extrafamilial roles increased public consciousness, created real economic opportunities for women to earn higher incomes, and opened up chances to enter fields of employment once exclusively dominated by men.

World War II created higher wages for women in real dollars and in relationship to men. It elevated women's status as workers and as consumers. Public ideological debate raged about what women's primary role should be during the war. Women actually came to symbolize freedom and democracy, and this status, in turn, gave them legitimacy as workers.[8]

But the experiences of black women inspired separate strategies for change and created histories that were separate and unequal to those of other Americans. Black women entered the wartime milieu as members of the oldest and largest minority group in the United States. They continued to endure intense discrimination and segregation in the forties, but they also succeeded in turning the country's military and employment crisis to their own economic and political advantage.

Black women have worked for over three hundred years in this country. Discriminated against both as black and as female, they are the most disadvantaged race-sex group. For three centuries, they have been consistently undereducated, underemployed, and underpaid. In the forties, one in three black women over the age of fourteen was in the labor force.[9] Fifty percent were in service and domestic occupations.[10] While, in the main, middle-class white families needed the wife's wages only for discretionary income, nearly all black families needed such income for basic survival.[11]

The war and decisive actions of the NAACP and CORE stimulated modest economic gains for black women. Their own efforts were strenuously supported by liberal whites and were bolstered by international competitive realities as well as new legal efforts by the government to protect blacks' rights to economic equality. While the number of white women in the labor market exceeded the count for both black men and women, black women's employment increased from 1.5 million to 2.1 million between 1940 and 1945.[12] New employment opportunities accelerated black migration from the rural South to northern and midwestern cities. While Zora Neale Hurston's novel *Their Eyes Were Watching God* portrayed the rural southern black women's search for self and the cultural richness in black folk-culture, racial segregation offered no economic opportunity for rural black women. It is estimated that of the 1.5 million black migrants to the North and Midwest, the vast majority were women escaping domestic servitude in the rural South. Such large numbers, of course, flooding the market, had a major impact on wages and opportunities in the North and East.[13]

As black women trickled into defense industries, black newspapers editorialized about white reaction: "The chief opposition to employment of colored women did not come from management or the employees . . . but from white local housewives, who feared lowering the barriers would rob them of maids, cooks, and nurses."[14] While a few black women were fortunate enough to get better jobs in war industries, the majority were locked into the urban ghettos of the forties. For writers such as Ann Petry, Margaret Walker, and Gwendolyn Brooks, the connections among race, sex, poverty, and urban life were central issues. Their works tell the stories of these women, for whom the northern or western trek meant stepping into the new challenge to the black family—institutional racism. While the northern industrial jobs paid more than some domestic jobs in the South, and as day-working domestics replaced live-in European servants, the complications of daily life vexed black women's lives as workers: lack of child care, segregated and costly public transportation, overcrowded and deteriorating housing conditions, disease, long hours, and inconvenient work shifts. In addition, the wages black women were able to garner affected their personal relationships with men. They found that their ability to earn money seemed threatening to the men, who believed the women wouldn't need them anymore.

At the workplace, violent "hate strikes" were instigated by

white workers over the hiring of blacks.[15] And when black women were recruited for the war effort, they worked in racially and sexually segregated shops. They were forced to take jobs in laundries, cafeterias, and white households. The Women's Bureau was created to oversee women's entry into the industrial labor market, but it was far from evenhanded. Through discriminatory practices, it helped reinforce racist and sexist stereotypes. One defense worker publicly took the position that black women did not "even realize that they are doing war work, work which affects directly the country's war production and that every worker we can place in a laundry is worth three new workers in our plants."[16] This overtly racist position only fueled competition for jobs and housing. Urban riots broke out in cities across the country. Overt racism also fueled one of the most successful mass protests staged to publicize the hiring issue. It took place in Detroit in 1942. Ford Motor Company had openly refused to hire blacks in general and black women in particular. The black community's NAACP chapter joined a national delegation to march on Washington. This action forced Ford to hire blacks and women, but these victories weren't always what they seemed. Black women got the most dangerous and grueling jobs with the lowest pay. They found themselves working in stifling "dope rooms" filled with nauseating glue fumes (Audre Lorde claims this might have been the cause of her breast cancer), while white women worked in well-ventilated sewing rooms.[17] Black women, exclusively, held jobs in the sintering plants, where the air was filled with ore dust and heated by the blast furnaces. Moreover, black women worked with ammunitions and gunpowder, poisonous plastics and acetone, sealing mud, and hazardous equipment—without the prospect of job advancement or security, with forced night shifts, and with little if any union protection.

Mary McLeod Bethune was quick to react to the overall treatment of black women in the war industries. In a letter to Secretary of War Henry L. Stimson she wrote:

We cannot accept any excuse that the exclusion of Negro representation was an oversight. We are anxious for you to know that we want to be, and insist upon being considered, a part of our American democracy, not something apart from it. We know from experience that our interests are too often neglected, ignored or scuttled unless we have effective representation in the formative stages of these projects and proposals. We are not blind to what is happening. We are not humiliated. We are incensed. [18]

The United Automobile Workers (UAW) did maintain a public commitment to racial and gender equality in labor, but black women took the initiative to protest and to protect their rights by organizing themselves as workers. Such black women as Moranda Smith, Luanna Cooper, Florence Rice, Bessie Coleman, and Octavia Hawkins played significant roles in the labor movements of the forties. As leaders in labor struggles, they received help from black women's auxiliaries to fight for increased wages and better working conditions in the garment, steel, laundry, tobacco, and food service industries. [19]

The battle against discriminatory practices was waged in other areas of work besides industry. Such battles also took place in semiprofessional and professional employment arenas; for example, northern telephone companies. In turning away black applicants, telephone employment offices used such excuses as "we have not yet installed separate toilet facilities," "colored women have not been trained to start a separate shift," "we cannot put a Negro in the front office," and "we do not employ coloreds." [20] Black women's union activists battled such policies and mobilized to protest the court martial of six black Women's Army Corps (WACs) nurses at Fort Devens, Massachusetts. The nurses refused to accept kitchen and custodial assignments while their white nursing counterparts worked in the motor pool and other medicine-related divisions. These antiracist efforts were supported by such black women's organizations as the National

Council of Negro Women and Alpha Kappa Alpha sorority, despite the U.S. Navy Women's Reserve Board's exclusion of black women until 1944.[21]

The distribution of the black female labor force also changed significantly during the forties. Before the war, 70 percent were in service jobs and 16 percent in farm labor. By 1944, that agricultural force was cut in half. The number of black women in commercial services increased some 20 percent. These gains also registered in clerical, sales, and professional categories. Black clerical work increased fivefold.[22] Up until that time 68 percent of all Afro-Americans still lived in the South.[23]

Those black women who remained in the South were also affected by the wartime labor changes in the forties. The South was undergoing a profound agricultural transformation based on the introduction of new kinds of farm machinery (especially the mechanical cotton picker, which rendered the sharecropping system obsolete). Such changes converted a massive number of sharecroppers into cheap hired hands. Most southern industries hired black women only as janitors, sweepers, and materials handlers, because managers would not integrate them into production lines. The working world of the vast majority of rural southern black women was altered by huge tractors and eastern-based national corporations and agribusiness. Many who could not get work had to try to exist on Aid to Dependent Children (ADC) programs. But almost half of the southern states denied benefits to any woman who had a man in her home or who herself appeared "employable." Women living in the North and receiving similar aid were below the established national poverty line. These changes pressed many black women to seek political action before the 1950s Civil Rights movement in order to maintain their long traditions of household and community solidarity. But every advance forward was accompanied by a slide backward. Many white Americans viewed government aid to the poor as creeping socialism.[24]

The anticommunist attitude in the country and the "no-strike" pledge made by over a million workers during the war were supported by black workers, both male and female. Nonetheless, many black women's efforts to get higher wages were tagged and tainted "red." "Redbaiting" was not used exclusively in the South and certainly was not confined to denigrating blacks' attempts to gain more rights. However, predominately white unions, "red" or not, were not responsive to the needs of black workers.

Black women were able to make significant gains during the war in fields of professional and semiprofessional work: education, entertainment, and the arts. For example, the critical teacher shortage opened that profession to married women for the first time, and women in nursing increased by 20 percent. The number of black professional women increased from 4 to 6 percent by the 1950s, especially in the fields of education, nursing, and social work.[25] Many other black women opted for nontraditional jobs in merchandising, reading specialization, medicine, and engineering.

Clearly, the forties was a decisive decade for the education of women, including black women. They received more B.A. degrees from black colleges than did black men, and black schools encouraged them not only to seek greater salaries but to go into occupations that prepared them for greater leadership roles. One consequence of black women's rising levels of education and employment was that many of them delayed marriage. The backlash reaction in some segments of the black community was to blame black women college graduates for the growing tension between Negro men and Negro women. (This pattern of advancement met by stiff resistance occurs again and again.) Bethune countered this negative propaganda about educated Negro women, defending their accomplishments:

It certainly was history-making . . . sixty-seven Negro women marching to the White House in their own right, standing on their feet expressing what they thought concerning their own people and the participation they should have had in the general affairs of the country. I think we have five Negro women lawyers. We presented the very best we had because this country, you know, only knows a few of us, just a few. Some wanted to know if these were the people of Booker T. Washington. . . . They don't know any black man except Booker T. Washington. . . . We want people to understand that there are myriads of prepared Negro women. . . . I was glad to sit aside them and see them stand on their feet fearlessly preparing themselves and their thoughts, not coming as beggars but coming as women wanting to participate in the administration of a human problem. . . . The pressure we have been making, the intercessions . . . they are finding their way. A door has been sealed up for two hundred years. You can't open it overnight but little crevices are coming. . . . Sixty-seven women sitting down at the White House—the first time in the history of the world.[26]

The 1940s was also the decade black women advanced as entertainers and in the arts. Previously ignored by white culture, they provided new role models, although their efforts were partly based on the advancement of white women. As usual, black women received a mixed message. The war failed to portray positive images of black women's roles in the general popular culture. And black publications, even the *Ebony* comic strips, showed black women emasculating black men or imitating white middle-class women's materialism. On the other hand, *Ebony* presented a number of profiles of black women leaders, female entertainers, and ordinary women who attained professional success. In doing so, the magazine stressed the intelligence and diverse accomplishments of black women. The July 1949 issue included an article entitled "Women Leaders: Their Century-Long Pilgrimage for Emancipation of Their Sex and Their Race Is a Historic Battle." This article showed black women in new roles, long ignored by white culture.[27] Mary McLeod Bethune and Lena Horne were frequently featured in *Ebony*. It would appear that the editorial policy of the magazine was ambivalent, eager to promote black womanhood as measured against the white world, but fearful when black women seemed to threaten black men.

Also during the forties, radio featured daytime serials such as "Kitty Foyle" and "Sally Farrell," about women who took jobs in the defense industries. Big-breasted women and pin-up girls like Betty Grable and Rita Hayworth became heroines. Howard Hughes exploited white women's sexuality in films like *The Outlaw*, starring Jane Russell. *McCall's* countered these efforts by creating the "American Girl," and assaults on "heartless career women" were launched within the film industry. Witness Ingrid Bergman's role as the psychiatrist in *Spellbound* and Joan Crawford's as a successful businesswoman in *Mildred Pierce*. Other movies portrayed women as sacrificial mothers, doomed career women, treacherous vamps, or helpless angels. Comic strips also showed women stepping outside of conventional feminine roles. Tillie the Toiler became a WAC; Winnie Winkle married a GI; and Sheena, Queen of the Jungle, added to the composite of women's new identities.[28] Clearly, America as a whole was confused about women's lives and appropriate places in society.

Afro-American women, of course, were not immune to these changes in the depiction of women in the popular media. But, as we have seen with the example of *Ebony*, such changes were often absorbed in highly strained ways and their reception was affected by racial and sexual politics inside and outside the black community. Going back to 1929, a film like *Hallelujah*, directed by King Vidor, gave black actors a chance to showcase their abilities but ultimately reinforced black stereotypes. Louise Beavers and Hattie McDaniel made their careers enacting the sturdy, compassionate, wise family servant, who acted as "de mule uh de world."[29] McDaniel even won an Oscar for her performance in *Gone With the Wind.* Ethel Waters and Butterfly McQueen, like Beavers and McDaniel, had to choose between accepting parts as domestic servants or not working at all. Through articles such as "Eight New Hollywood Films Backtrack to Racial Stereotypes" (Aug. 3, 1948), *Ebony* did speak up, condemning industry trends that almost exclusively cast black actors as maids and menials.[30]

The other stereotyped role available to black women was the glorified "cream-colored bourgeois diva." Lena Horne and later, in the fifties, Dorothy Dandridge, specialized in these roles. They represented the glorified "honey beauties," who lacked the rough ethnic black edges and who possessed physical characteristics of the dominant white culture. They started their careers in night clubs and concert halls before entering the movies. Lena Horne was the embodiment of black beauty and black racial consciousness. Active in liberal politics, she campaigned for Henry Wallace and the Progressive Party in 1948, and snubbed Jim Crow restaurants who considered they were paying her a compliment by treating her as a non-black. Horne rejected Hollywood's attempts to put her in "mammy" roles. She recalls, "They did not make me into a maid, but they didn't make me anything else either. I became a butterfly pinned to a column, singing away in Movieland."[31] She was hailed as the most valued of female performers, and refused to sing when she discovered German prisoners of war seated in front of black GIs when she played the United Service Organization (USO) circuit. When asked once how she was able to persist in the entertainment field, she answered, "Black women have the habit of survival."[32] Horne, who made eleven movies, was not alone in protesting stereotypes of black women in the entertainment industry. Butterfly McQueen, Pearl Bailey, Juanita Hall, Joyce Bryant, and Josephine Baker (who was an expatriate living in France) reacted by negotiating "nondiscrimination clauses," stipulating that black patrons be permitted in their audiences.

Black women rose to national stature in other kinds of cultural roles in the forties. Carol Brice was the first Afro-American to receive the coveted Naumburg Award in music. Other concert singers of that era included Dorothy Maynor and Lillian Evanti, who followed in the footsteps of Marian Anderson. There were also Hazel Scott, Billie Holiday, Ella Fitzgerald, and Sarah Vaughan in the jazz world. Mahalia Jackson elevated gospel music in American culture, while Elizabeth Prophet, Selma Burke, and Augusta Savage stood out in the art world. Katherine Dunham, Pearl Primus, and Mary Hinkson made breakthroughs in dance; and Margaret Walker, Gwendolyn Brooks, and Ann Petry won major awards as writers of fiction and poetry. While Lena Horne served as the pin-up girl and sex symbol for black soldiers overseas, Anne Petry's *The Street* challenged the idea that "the black urban reality" of Richard Wright's *Native Son* was exclusive to males.

In the forties, *Ebony*, from which I have frequently quoted here, was the most popular black magazine and served as a cultural mirror of the black elite's public and private life. The bulk of the heavily illustrated publication was devoted to "entertainment cooking," beauty aids, and clothes. Jacqueline Jones notes in her book *Labor of Love, Labor of Sorrow* what should be clear by now, that *Ebony* had no single editorial policy on women. When *Ebony* did editorialize, however, as in a 1947 piece entitled "Goodbye Mammy, Hello Mom," it could offer a black twist on the postwar feminist ideology that deplored Rosie the Riveter's alleged retreat into the home. This editorial pointed out that throughout history black women, "whether slaves or war workers, had never had the opportunity to devote their full attention to family. But now, for the first time 'since 1619,' wives and mothers were enjoying the benefits derived from their husband's high wages."[33] Again, when the magazine could show black women supporting black men, it was eager to make the case. As a black woman, Zora Neale Hurston critiqued such an attitude. In her book *Their Eyes Were Watching God,* Janie Stark marries three times. First she is treated like a mule; then she is treated as a lady who is "The Queen of the Porch"; finally she is treated as a potential equal.[34] Despite its bourgeois values and black middle-class cultural chauvinism, with sexism and assimilationism thrown in, *Ebony* did serve as a militant advocate of black civil rights—with large doses of sexism and assimilation for the general black population.

Up to this point, we have been looking primarily at women's public roles, but the private lives of women in the forties, especially black women, were also affected by many complex changes. Although the war had expanded women's opportunities, it did not release them from their attachment to traditional sex-roles or from racist beauty standards. In 1941, the early war propaganda emphasized women's roles in the home and family. It wasn't until later that women were allowed to play a part in the war effort. Even as late as 1947, women were said to be replacing men in the workplace only "for the duration" of the war. And war propaganda emphasized that women should retain their "femininity," even as they performed masculine duties. Even when women became essential to the war effort, the media emphasized the eternal feminine motivations behind women's willingness to work outside the home during the military crisis. Patriotism for women in the forties meant taking war jobs in order to bring their men home more quickly and to help the world become a safer place for children. Women who had been thrust into the working world still had to rely on other family members—mostly other women, but also husbands and sons—for help with finances and child care as well as emotional support. Many women found it difficult to imagine returning to their prewar domestic roles. In fact, this was nearly impossible for most, especially for black women, who had traditionally worked out of economic necessity. During the war the federal government's child care program (both nursery and after-school) accommodated relatively few. In any case, many women viewed daycare as an abandonment of their maternal responsibilities and did not use it even when it was available. Finally, women's lives in the forties were undoubtedly affected by the loss of millions of husbands, fathers, brothers, and sons. Many women suffered from loneliness and boredom, and from the anxiety and depression of being a serviceman's spouse, cut off from familiar relationships, and crowded into temporary quarters and communities.

Such conditions of war as these further compounded the already complex lives of married black women. While significant numbers of white women entered the labor force to help support their families and to show their patriotism, black women continued to play their triple roles of wife, mother, and worker. Angela Davis speaks of this triple tradition of black women's femininity from slavery to the present. She writes: "The alleged benefits of the ideology of femininity did not accrue to her. She was not sheltered or protected; she would not remain oblivious to the desperate struggle for existence unfolding outside the 'home.' She was also there in the fields (or plants), alongside the man, toiling under the lash (or time-clock) from sun-up till sun-down."[35] As traditional marriage continued to be the single most important feature of women's lives, black women who married continued to work and to provide more than half the family income.

As consumers, black women used their incomes for meeting the basic home necessities. They seldom had money available for timesaving domestic devices. In fact, many of these women continued to take in laundry, do catering work, or "run numbers" to supplement their working income. Although most Americans (through their increased wages in a wartime economic boom) enjoyed a higher standard of living, blacks, who were 8 percent of the total population, accounted for 50 percent of the population below the poverty level. In 1948, the median annual income for white women was $1,000 compared to $676 for black women.[36]

Both during and after the war, blacks remained segregated

in older urban areas, living under the strains of extended families in the North and South. Black schools, public transportation, and medical services were generally poorer than those available to whites. In addition, older residents of the urban areas resented newcomers who competed for opportunities in the war industries.

During the war, racism, poverty, and values within the black family excluded daycare facilities as an option for most black women. Before the war, most daycare centers were for poor children and, consequently, most blacks associated child care with white charity. Government handouts were not seen as desirable; neither was the idea of putting young children in strange environments that might be hostile. Therefore, most children of black working mothers were left with other family members or trusted neighbors.

The war and the social, personal, physical, and emotional turmoil that followed it took their toll. In 1947, when one of every twenty-nine American marriages ended in divorce, the rate of divorce was much higher among blacks.[37] The inability of some black men to adjust to a working wife was a contributing factor. Divorce, abandonment, and death left many women without financial assistance and with family responsibilities. Black families survived through their extended-family relationships and the strength of the black mother. A model of the powerful black mother is seen in the character of Lena Younger in Lorraine Hansberry's book *Raisin in the Sun.* Hansberry writes that "Lena is unsparing of herself . . . she never loses faith in God, in herself, or her family."[38]

Black women's lives in the forties changed in more private ways, too, especially in the area of birth rates, birth control, and abortions. Although all birth rates rose in what we now call the "baby boom," black birth rates increased significantly during World War II in relation to the national average. The average black family included more than four children in the North and more than seven in the South. The war opportunities expanded the class stratification among blacks. According to E. Franklin Frazier, it increased the "new black bourgeoisie" that was largely composed of clerical workers (and other semiprofessionals) who were trained during the war. Once again, *Ebony* articles highlighted the accomplishments of this growing class but focused particularly on women who gained access to predominantly white but also male occupations. It called attention to "firsts" in every field: Federal Judge Jane M. Bolin; Helen O. Dickens, M.D., member of the society for surgeons; Jean Harris, M.D., the first black to graduate from a medical school in Virginia (later to become Secretary of Housing and Urban Development in the Carter administration); Mary Jones King, a bank manager; Democratic politician Jeanetta Welch Brown; and United Nations delegate Edith Sampson.[39]

While *Ebony* traditionally projected a small selection of the black middle-class as successful role models for all black women, the magazine was caught up in a larger national economic attack on all women. Madison Avenue "hidden persuaders" were trying to convince women of the forties that they could be given "the sense of identity, purpose, creativity, the self-realization, even the joy they lacked—by buying things."[40] Acting out their class privileges, black middle-class women began to act on the message that materialism was a symbol of social status. Black magazines such as *Sepia* and *Ebony* typified this black middle-class impulse and encouraged the imitation of white beauty standards as well as conformity to patriarchal roles and Christian values. Maya Angelou speaks tellingly of such desires in her autobiography: "Her fantasy as a child was to wake out of her black, ugly dream and surprise everyone when they discovered that she had blond hair and blue eyes and had been turned into an ugly black girl by her cruel stepmother."[41] Similarly, in Gwendolyn Brooks's novel *Maude Martha*, Maryginia Washington, one of the boarders in Maude Martha's building, tells a black woman to apply lightening cream to her skin and tosses off this caution: "They ain't no sense in lookin any worse'n you have to."[42] Many black middle-class women conformed to this judgment. These women were routinely relegated to the status and role of the housewife/breadwinner even after completing an advanced education.

Yet, as I have said, it was a no-win situation: Articles appeared monthly scolding these status-conscious middle-class black women for being too domineering, too ambitious, too idle, too materialistic, and too much like white women. In the same media, mixed messages criticized all black women (especially middle-class or aspiring-to-be-middle-class black women) for outgrowing their men rather than holding back, staying subordinate, and supporting the men in the climb up the (white) social ladder. Articles appeared with titles like "What's Wrong with the Negro Women?" "Do Career Women Make Good Wives?" "Do Pretty Women Make Good Wives?" and "Why Black Men Leave Home," which blamed black middle-class women for their men's infidelity.[43] These attacks also blamed black women for black men's desiring marital relationships with white women, while making the reverse a taboo for black women.

Although the black woman's historical and respected status as a wage earner continued to be recognized, her sacred status as working mother began to alter. The vast majority of black working women were not reaping the benefits of new social images and greater economic prosperity brought on by the war, but were affected by the postwar propaganda against all women and especially black women. Paule Marshall, in her story "Renna," writes of a black college woman whose husband and community condemn her success "as a way of pointing to her husband's deficiencies."[44] Marshall's story is about the pain, tension, and disappointment that mar many black male-female relationships.

Many black men were exempted from service during World War II because of family responsibilities. Birth control was less likely among poor and uneducated black women, and, therefore, birth rates were high among this group of people who could least afford to support large families. In the black community, suspicions were aroused about the motives of white birth-control advocates. Such suspicions were not grounded in faulty information. In 1939, the Birth Control Federation of America (BCFA) promoted a Negro Project that called for the passage of compulsory sterilization laws, and such laws were adopted in at least twenty states. The BCFA's report stated: "The masses of Negroes, particularly in the South, still breed carelessly and disastrously, resulting in an increase in Negroes, more so than in whites, causing a larger number of children to be born to the portion of the population least fit and least able to rear the children."[45] One Maryland research study surveying 357 black women in the late forties concluded that only one in five practiced birth control.[46] Condoms, diaphragms, and the rhythm method were less accepted by black women than the use of douches.

Planned births were a strong practice among most middle-class women of the forties and particularly middle-class black women who were balancing continuing education and career goals with the responsibilities of the family. Jeanne Noble's study of 412 college graduates, "The Negro Woman's College Education," noted that 38 percent had one child, 15 percent had two children, 6 percent had three, and 41 percent remained childless.[47] This sharp decrease in birth rates was only within this small section of the black community.

Abortion was not a common practice among black women. Again, past imposition of population controls resulted in strong moral opposition to abortion among blacks. Barbara Christian says that "the result of imposed population controls on black women has been an increase in the tension between reproductive rights of Afro-American women and the awareness of black genocide."[48] Alfred C. Kinsey's Institute for Sex Research noted that in the forties abortion was most prevalent among economically comfortable, urban, highly educated, younger, white women (24 percent of whom were married).[49] Poor women were more often subject to illegal abortions without good facilities. For poor black women, abortions commonly meant a twisted coat hanger and two dozen quinine pills.

The forties launched the great debate over dual careers and family and whether it was possible for women to manage both without adversely affecting their children. If that were not bad enough, a "new social science and psychology" was popularized through Philip Wylie's depiction of the overprotective, overindulgent mother ("momism") in *Generation of Vipers*. This best-seller, along with other similar works, blamed women for failing to cut their sons' apron strings. The author claimed that women were stunting men's mental growth, causing them to suffer mental illness.[50] Simultaneously, in the black community, E. Franklin Frazier, Nathan Glazer, and Gunnar Myrdal introduced, attacked, and insulted the black family with theories of the "black matriarch."[51] Thus through the forties ideological battles raged over child-rearing practices and family norms and how these reputedly did or did not produce socially well-adjusted adults.[52] Many white male experts prescribed that parents relinquish control and become more permissive. Arnold Gesell's government Children's Bureau document, *Infant Care,* and Benjamin Spock's *Baby and Child Care* (1947) outlined new directives to women: Let the child take the lead. These texts dripped with signals that every early experience bore implications for a child's psychological development. The ideal "American family" was encouraged to become child-centered, which, of course, left women with the added burden of balancing the ideals of permissive motherhood with the exacting standards expected of them in other family roles.

These cultural developments and new perspectives had little impact on the majority of black families, however. Black child-rearing practices generally followed the historical traditions of the slave family, in which parents attempted to suppress the children before the slave master had to. These methods were also dominated and complicated by patterns of racial oppression and of racial self-hatred. For example, lower- and working-class black parents often used direct physical punishment and demanded absolute verbal and physical obedience from their children.[53] Most black households used methods that were just the opposite of those recommended by Gesell and Spock. Alvin Poussaint says that blacks, as poor people, choose child-rearing practices that would equip children for future employment and survival in the harsh realities of American racism and discrimination.[54] In this respect, many black households were likely to be domineering and authoritarian environments, sexually hierarchical, devoid of physical and verbal affection, and training grounds for staying within the social limits set by white society for blacks. In *Sula*, when Hannah asks her mother whether she "loved her three children," her mother answers, "What you talkin' bout did I love you, girl? I stayed alive for you, can't you get that through your thick head?"[55] Many black parents remained emotionally indifferent to their children in order to teach the children to keep their own emotions under control.

During the forties, black women were twice as likely as white women to be single parents. Death, divorce, jail, and separation accounted for most situations in which women raised children without husbands. It is estimated that 17.6 percent of black families were headed by single women. Single women between the ages of fifteen and forty-four bore children at the rate of 7.12 per thousand. It was not uncommon for black women to have more than one child before marriage and several with different men after divorce.

New and other modes of female intimacy developed in the forties. Although most Americans viewed marriage as the exclusive path to happiness and fulfillment, 18 percent of women wanted to combine marriage with a career, and one percent wanted to remain single.[56] For black women, a combination of marriage and work was most desirable and expected. The choice was marriage/family/career and not family *or* career.

A social role in the community was also expected. Joyce Ladner's *Tomorrow's Tomorrow* documents this cultural norm among black women who still expect themselves to be mother, wife, wage earner, and social supporter for the race, church, and community. Angela Davis underscored this theme of black women's "centered" position in the black family from the perspective of a later generation.[57]

Black lesbianism was becoming more visible in the forties. For all women, and particularly black women, wider choices of lifestyle and sexual preferences were made somewhat more possible by the economic opportunities created by World War II. Although it was still uncommon to do so, some women could and did choose careers over marriage, opted to remain single, and chose to work, socialize, and even form intimate relationships with other women.[58] In "closeted gay communities," such women built strong and supportive lesbian networks and an infrastructure, including a few black women, for their later emergence in all areas of American life. Although gay women were "coming out of the closet" in the forties, lesbianism was still considered "perverted." Kinsey's report documented that one in four American women reported sexual attraction to other women. Between 3 and 12 percent of single women were lesbian (sexual), and those who lived a lesbian lifestyle reported comfort with this sexual orientation.[59]

Responses to lesbianism in the homophobic black community during the forties alternated between general acceptance of differences in lifestyles among blacks and hostile rejection of "freaks" who were destroying the traditional black value system. The condemnation of lesbianism is rooted in the popular belief that homosexuality has white origins and is "a white thing" for "freaky" white people. If homosexuality was ever accepted, it was in the entertainment world. Biographers have written about Ma Rainey's homosexuality, Bessie Smith's bisexuality, and Billie Holiday's attraction to and affairs with other Hollywood women. Stories are now being told of other famous black women who were gay, including Lorraine Hansberry, Alberta Hunter, and Zora Neale Hurston. Black feminist critics suggest many points of origin and different lesbian images in the forties. Audre Lorde, for example, talks of lesbianism (a woman-identified women's tradition) in her autobiography, *Zami: A New Spelling of My Name.* Lorde tells how she has transported her West Indian background and traditions to her life in Harlem. As a black lesbian poet in the forties and fifties, Lorde wrote of the Grenadian belief that women can "work together as friends and lovers."[60] Her accounts are of a strong contrast to the "mannish" dyke stereotypes commonly projected onto gay women. Lorde writes about the invisibility of lesbians and the low level of community tolerance they could expect: "Most black lesbians were closeted, correctly recognizing the black community's lack of interest in our position, as well as the many more immediate threats to our survival as black people, to be black and female, to be black, female and gay. To be black, female, gay and out of the closet in a white environment . . . was considered by many black lesbians to be simply suicidal."[61]

Although little documentation is available on the lives of black lesbians in the forties, much can be inferred from their negative portrayal in male-centered, white, and Afro-American literature of that period. Ann Shockley believes that researchers in Afro-American women's history will continue to uncover new cultural information as the buried lives of "hidden women" are excavated.

In virtually every area and stratum of society, the forties were a watershed for American culture. This period of transformation also encompassed the black community and black women. The war decade, according to Jacqueline Jones, comprised "the seedtime years for the modern civil rights and women's liberation movements. Both movements grew out of the promises of social change that the wartime economy made but peacetime society failed to deliver. And, because black women were caught in a tangle of racial and sexual inequality, they stood much to gain from this dual challenge to the nation's caste system."[62] These observations reinforce Susan Hartmann's conclusions on the relationship between war, economic growth, and social change. In *The Home Front and Beyond*, Hartmann argues that "the withdrawal of men from customary positions at work and home, women's employment in traditional men's jobs and women's entry into educational, civic, cultural and recreational activities, the shortage of men in political affairs; the entry of women as workers into civil rights and labor rights advocacy—all these movements caused a permanent refashioning of gender and racial roles which was to mark the latter half of the twentieth century."[63] As "women's issues" became national, racial issues became international. The lives of ordinary and extraordinary black women were cast into new, larger, and more intimate social and political forms. These shifts and new developments would never allow us to return to "home-sweet-home" notions of American life.

I myself wanted to grow up to be just like Grandma or Mommy. But I also wanted to be different and better. And I tried. I took my homegrown dreams and stretched them wide around the cup from which the American dream is poured— right down to the bitter grounds.

From a historical vantage point, we can perceive a new horizon. It is from people who have experienced the "ordinary"—the usual, the unremarkable, the commonplace—that we have the most to learn. The stories told by Marilyn, Sara, Elaine, and Gwen provide a "thick description" of black women's lives on that postwar horizon.[64] What follows are the "living structures"—stories in their own words—of how they survived their dreams and nightmares. Audre Lorde asserts that stories really have "no new ideas," but "are only new ways of making them felt.''[65] *To which I add: women's own stories can give the rest of us examples of great courage and perseverance as well as new perspectives on habits of survival that may—or may not—work well for us.*

CHAPTER 2

MARILYN

Driving to Iowa City this time to see Marilyn made me very nervous. She was my aunt. I had known her all my life, but I was never going to know her like I was going to know her now. She had warned me, "You really want to know all that shit?" And now, recalling that challenge, I found myself perspiring. Her moving to Iowa and seeming to settle down did not change the fact that I had known her as a somewhat wild religious fanatic, and now she had put her religion down, changed her name, and was reading radical feminist literature. I had been the radical of the family, but as I entered Hawkeye Drive, headed for her apartment complex, walked through her door, and found myself looking at a forty-seven-year-old woman with an African wrap on her head, a flowing caftan, slippers, and a ring in her nose, backed up by sil-houettes of African women's bodies on the wall, I knew she was not in Iowa just to get a degree, and she might now be more of an activist than I was. I knew I saw before me the real guerrilla that America had to reckon with.

She started telling me about what marriage was like in the fifties. This first revelation was followed by a litany of abortive

*quests for identity, betrayals by false social expectations, use-
less self-denials, and spurious successes. Through it all, writing sustained her, and in the end, writing saved her.*

I HAD no idea that I was going to get married that day. It was
not something I wanted to do. My father and his father got
together, and because we were under age, took us down to the
court. I remember going downtown in my school clothes. I
was wearing white buck shoes and my school jacket. I was
seventeen. The judge said, "Well, since you're here, we might
as well marry you." So they got us married. Trapped. I felt
trapped. September 24, 1956. There was no preparation for
the marriage. I just got married, and I had no idea what was
going to happen next.

> *Marriage in the fifties was considered the natural progres-
> sion in the rites of passage from adolescence to adulthood. Sex
> within the confines of marriage guaranteed morality that
> would keep the girls "good." It was also a way to legitimize
> pregnancy. Young women were shunted off from or fled their
> parents' household to join another. Marilyn continued with
> the grim details of a 1950s forced marriage, unplanned preg-
> nancy, and attempted abortions.*

I went home after that, got my clothes and moved to my
in-laws'—who I had just acquired that day. I must have seen
them only three times in my life since I met Bobby in junior
high school. I just moved in one hour. I guess I had to go
because I don't ever remember being asked did I want to
marry. I don't even remember any discussion except that I
had run around a few weeks before trying to abort the baby.
I mean, I did know how to do that. And not from my mother.
Friends told me I could take some pills. I took some quinine
to get rid of the baby until my head was ringing like a bell. It
didn't work. I told my boy husband that I had taken quinine

and he got furious. Wop! And wop again. He hit me and said, "Don't you ever try to kill my children." I mean he went crazy. And I was feeling trapped.

The women—my mother and his—were not directing things. And this was real confusing to me. Women had always been the one telling "mens" what to do. To suddenly have the men take over was real confusing. And here I was with a boy husband and my mother-in-law. She took us to our bedroom, offering me one of her housecoats and some bedroom shoes. And I thought to myself, this is the end. I couldn't go to college. I was gonna have a baby. And the women wasn't doing no talkin'. I know what they thought of "mens" and marriage. And it wasn't so much from a religious point of view, because they weren't religious. The women acted like life was just to be endured because you weren't gonna get no earthly reward. They also acted like "mens" was to be endured, too. I had had one hope. I could control my mind. I could go to college. This was the way out in 1956. And since I was pregnant now, there was no way out.

Sex was very different when it's in the back of a car than when it's in a strange house and with a boy husband who was unemployed in 1956. Sex was different when Eisenhower was president and Detroit niggers were neck-to-neck poor. Sex was something you was suppose to be smart enough to know without your mama ever having to tell you about. It was assumed that I was going to be smart enough to figure boys out. I don't remember Mama ever saying anything to me about boys being dangerous, but the attitude was that nobody took men seriously. I mean that was the attitude. "Mens" was not to be taken as your friend. Not none of that Hollywood shit. Everybody knew that you would "fall in love" or you would have a man, but that was separate from what your other needs were. Your needs were met from women. I mean, men were expected to run around. They were expected to spend their money. They expected you to want their money. They was expected to be abusive. I had seen in the course of my growing up men beating women. Mr. Henry used to beat his wife outside so the neighbors would see her. I guess I thought that if you had a man you was gonna fight with him. You had a man just because, but you didn't take him on for any serious reasons. I knew about the menstrual cycle and getting pregnant, and when I started my period, at eleven, I can remember my family's response: Oh God, how inconvenient! Then I hid wearing a bra and everything from my mama.

Three weeks after I was married I remember going home and knocking on the door. My father answered. He looked at me and said to come on in. I was telling Mama how many problems I was having. Daddy interrupted and said, "You made your bed, so you gonna have to go back and lie in it." I had no other recourse. I couldn't come home. I was just like Daddy—who couldn't go home because he had made his bed in Baton Rouge, Louisiana, and he wasn't about to go home.

Marilyn's family reflects the common pattern of color, caste, and class-based marriage among blacks, especially in the fifties. An educated high-yellow mother and a "streetwise" darker father with a third-grade education amounted to a mixture of sex-role tensions between parents that, in turn, fostered sibling competition and struggles over beauty standards.

Daddy had been one of those people that when Henry Ford went to the South and said "five dollars a day," Daddy left. So he took Mr. Ford up on his word and hoboed on the train to Detroit. He had no education. I think about third or fourth grade at best. Daddy was a gambler and a storyteller. I can remember the time he told me the story about seeing his first automobile.

"I was walking home with my brother Oscar and seeing these tracks in the dust." Daddy started all of his stories with him and Oscar—"Oscar and me" or "me and my baby brother, Oscar." Anyway, "We didn't know what these tracks was, so we thought they was snake tracks. So we hid in the bushes. Shortly we saw a thing coming down the road and it didn't have no horse pullin' it. We was absolutely petrified at the noise. So me and Oscar took a bush, because we thought the track was wicked and looked like snakes, and started scuffing the road until there was no more tracks. That way them snakes would never return."

As I said, Daddy was a storyteller. And his past was his reference point. And though I was fascinated listening to his stories, I just thought that he and Oscar were full of silliness. Daddy was always cutting language short, as Mama would say, because he couldn't pronounce certain words. He had been one of those "Creo niggers" from Louisiana, who were mixed with the French blood and ways.

I hear tell of Daddy having a lot of "street kids" (a bunch of babies by different women), but I was the only legitimate child he had. He had loved the trains as a boy, and he would tell these long stories about the magic of the railroad. When we left the housing projects, we moved to a dead-end street near the railroad track. The trains would go by and shake the house and that was a big thrill to him. Mama would get sick because she just thought it was horrible. Daddy thought it was just wonderful. So it was just from his two different connections, with the railroads and Louisiana, that I got a real sense of what was important about him. Knowing where and why trains were going was what Daddy thought was important. He just kept talking about the trains, telling his stories and using his dialect—he would not stand to be corrected by Mama. That's how I learned about Louisiana and Daddy and the South and music. He loved jazz. He loved the streets. He loved Mama. Himself and me.

Mama was an educated high-yellow black woman and was used to correcting everybody. She had graduated from high school and was a teacher. She went to Hampton University Normal School in Hampton, Virginia. It was equivalent to about the first year of college. Her folks was "North Carolina niggers." Ahoskie, North Carolina, niggers. And there is a strange tale here. I think the nickname for North Carolina people is "tarheels." Mama's people was heavily connected with Indian blood and ways. They were mixed peoples. Mixed peoples stayed mixed by marrying the "bluest-veined niggers" with the Indian features, to keep the color of the high yellow. They had dark hair and high cheek bones. Straight long hair. They were the "pretty niggers." The "successful niggers." The niggers who got the education and the niggers who came to the North to tell the black blacks what to do and how to do it right.

She had come to Detroit during Depression years to get security. She had divorced her first husband, my brother's father, and was a follower of "Marcus Garvey's way of thinking": Be proud of the black man and use your skills for your race. Mama wanted a teaching job or a good job (anything other than domestic work). When she didn't see no good job for herself, she picked her a northern man—Daddy—who was twelve years older than her and had a very secure factory job that put him in the black middle class. But there was a lot of disparity in our house. First, Daddy had no education and Mama did. His ego was always the problem. He felt that he was being put down a lot of times. Daddy liked to party, wear good clothes, and looked good in a suit. He'd come home from the foundry and bathe for two hours, dress up and went out most nights. He wore the "Panama straw" of the neighborhood. It was the kind of hat Maurice Chavalier wore in the late thirties. Daddy also wore Edmond Clap shoes and silk stockings. Pomp and flash. Mama just accepted that his ways was what went with the territory of marrying this kind of man. Mama was not like this at all.

Second, there was disparity between how the family was split. I was my father's daughter and my brother was my mother's son. And there was a great difference in the way we looked. My brother looked like Mama's people and I had the yellow skin with Daddy's African-looking features. I had a sense of being ugly because of Mama's "North Carolina looks." Mama had felt like an ugly duckling herself because she was a lighter brown instead of a high yellow of almost white. It's like I could never get beyond the division. People kept telling me I looked just like my daddy. They didn't know it really hurt me because I wanted to look just like my mother. I wanted Mama to treat me just like she treated my brother. I thought that if I had only looked like my brother, things would be all right. Instead, I always had to answer these questions: "How come your brother is so fine?" "How come you don't look like him?"

And of course, my brother was also smart. He was five years older than I. He went to an all-white trade school. That was a really big deal because he was one of three blacks to get in. My mother was proud of her son. Daddy didn't pay no mind. I can remember that I used to always try to measure my grades against my brother's and I couldn't do it. There was always this business of his intelligence, and my father took offense to that.

I can remember my mother leaving my father at least on one occasion because he had been beating my brother. Daddy was very harsh to him. I was secretly happy about it. I felt like he got what he deserved because I couldn't get my mother's attention. And he could sing, too. He used to sing in the neighborhood church choir. However, my brother would bring into the house very different music. He liked "white music." Most black folks didn't listen to black entertainers like Billy Ekstine, who catered to white audiences. They listened to blues. I didn't listen to only black music. My brother and I liked Les Paul and Mary Ford.

Whenever anything electrical broke down in the house, my brother could fix it. He had a huge electrical plane and a crystal radio. He used to hang wires from the house to the trees in the front yard. We used to listen with headphones to the little crystal set. I can remember taking my friends upstairs to show them my brother's radio. I knew the other boys were jealous of him. He had a lot of problems being smart in the neighborhood. I admired him.

I was a tomboy and no one messed with me because I had an older brother. I hated dolls. I thought playing house was silly. I knew it wasn't what was expected of me. Mama expected me to use my head. I remember somebody gave me a black doll and I didn't want it. I wanted a white doll, and when I got it, I tore her blue eyes out for marbles. I wasn't interested in tea sets. I wanted to play with what my brother played with. He had an erector set and trucks, and I could tell that boys and girls were divided by the toys. I could see how they climbed trees and could pretend to be whatever they wanted. I understood what Mama meant, when she said she "wanted to be born a man." I did too. It had something to do with seeing men have more freedom and everyone expecting them to go to college. It didn't mean getting married. For the girls, they was expected to keep their eyes on the right man and live through their husband's achievement. Mama had seen and done just that in Ahoskie. Her first husband had been a tobacco farmer, and the rest of her brothers worked as sharecroppers on a white family's pickle factory.

Better job opportunities was not the only thing "white folks let us have during the war," as my Daddy used to say. We lived in a newly built, government-sponsored housing project. It was designed for those "better Negroes" (meaning those who worked). We were happy to be there. We had a "real family," by white folks standards. Daddy worked a steady job, Mama stayed home, and there were two kids. A older boy. A younger girl. By nigger standards, we was bourgeoisie. We was one of the few black families that had a new car—1936 Ford with a wheel on the back. It was a deluxe model. It was not raggedy. It was the kind of car rich white folks drove at the time. We was considered elite Negroes (acting like white folks) because Daddy had the car and Mama had the color.

I didn't have to think about white people. They were on the periphery of the ghetto. We talked about them in the context of them being storekeepers or as "the man pulling the strings." I knew they were people. I had white teachers, although I did not play with white children. My father and mother used to tell a lot of stories about white people. "They lynch niggers," my father used to say. Saying it another way, Mama talked about the NAACP and about some white man who painted his skin color black and went through the South pretending he was black. She said he later wrote a book about his experiences. She felt it was a great thing to do, exposing how Negroes couldn't drink from the white water fountains or use the white toilets. Daddy insisted that I ought to know, up front, that "the white people hate niggers." Mama quoted the papers about Emmett Till and I knew they was right.

There was a lot of privileges from "acting like white folks." Mama was always correcting me and my brother's language, so we had to speak a certain way. This meant the white teachers paid attention to me. They chose me over the other black girls. I was singled out by the teachers for the best books and games and rewards. And I wanted them. I worked even harder. This kept me in trouble with my peers. I didn't always enjoy my "high yellah" privileges.

Being elite, according to the neighbors, had a lot to do with skin color. I didn't view my color and sandy hair as no advantage. I had a lot of problems because the black-skinned girls said I thought I was "cute." I always had to figure out how to play in the games with other kids and not get beat up or not taking a bunch of shit from them.

I also went to the local public school. The other "yellow" kids went to Catholic schools. Mama and Daddy had the money but disliked that "religious stuff." Religion was something that we could pick and choose, and since the other kids were expected to go to church, I would go with them. Mama said, "It is the white man's bullshit to control the black man's mind." Daddy would go to church only so he could pick him a number and play it to make some money. He would play whatever the minister's verse was for that Sunday. His pet number was 213, and he made a lot of money gambling that number.

Gambling went along with living near Hastings Street. It was near downtown and near the biggest department stores. It was near the bus terminal (which would bring Negroes up from the South daily) and the Three Star Bar where the pimps and prostitutes hung out. Me and my girlfriends used to sneak down by the bar to see the "nasty" women (prostitutes) and laugh and imitate them. They was mostly white. We also got to know who was the faggots. There were lots of gay men.

Hastings Street had the Entertainment Show Houses; the Eastern Fruit Market; the recording studio next to Sam's Music Shop (where we could watch the musicians making records); and the Brewster Center. This was where Joe Louis used to train when he was in town. He hadn't lived in the projects but this was where we could go and see his trophies. We used to listen to the Joe Louis fights on Hastings Street. Every store and home would have their radios on. When he would win Hastings Street would be like Fifth Avenue in New York. Since we was poor people we used rolls and rolls of toilet paper for confetti and would run up and down the street. Joe Louis was a big big deal. He was our only hero.

Mama used to talk about Mary McLeod Bethune and Walter White of the NAACP because she was educated. The rest of the neighbors gossiped about black entertainers. Mama liked Pearl Bailey's and Lena Horne's singing and because they had married white men. She said "marrying white and staying black made them heroes to her."

I gained another hero in high school. Edgar Allan Poe. He was my star at Northeastern High School. Mama had insisted that we move out of the projects. By this time, my brother had married and Mama kept telling Daddy that the only way we could get ahead of "white folks" was to get some property. She wanted a house. Daddy was fifty-nine and wanted to stay with his "street buddies." During the war, he had made enough money at Ford's to buy a house, but Mama believed he had nothing to show because we still lived in the projects. So we moved into a house.

The neighborhood and new Northwestern High School had a bunch of middle-class niggers. They made me uncomfortable. I thought they talked funny. They talked like "white folks." We called them sissy. So I maneuvered to go to the Northeastern High School near the projects with my friends. I got into a trade curriculum to study tailoring. The mornings were tailoring classes and the afternoon I took electives. I was assigned a literature course that had a white gay teacher. There were several gay teachers but it wasn't a big thing then that gay people couldn't teach your children. We were grateful to have any teacher that would teach black folks. We had two black and one white gay teachers.

Mr. Riapell was white and gay and my literature teacher. He read Poe one day in class and my head spun around. I guess I heard romantic sounds. That's when I decided to be a poet. I was in the eleventh grade. Things began to clear up when I decided myself I was going to be a poet. I remember telling Mama. She didn't think it was odd. I think she connected it with teaching poetry. She didn't laugh. She knew I was a thinker. After that, high school became interesting. I dropped tailoring and took up college preparatory courses. I was in the top 5 percent of my class. I got heavy duty into literature courses and public speaking. I was vice president of my senior class. I can remember my father asking my mother when did he have to get the money for me to go to college. I got excited. I loved school. I was expected to go to Wayne State University, which was right on the other side of the projects. I wasn't expected to get pregnant. I got pregnant. Daddy was devastated. Disappointed, Mama shook her head and said, "I thought you knew better. I thought you knew to use something." I wish I knew to use something, too.

* * *

I sat on the bed with my boy husband frightened. He was trapped. I was trapped. Thinkin' aloud: This is my end.

Although the role models for blacks in the fifties were sparse, one of the more common was the assertive women who did day work. Marilyn found herself in awe of and intimidated by the women in her husband's household who held such jobs.

Living with my in-laws, I learned about the "fuck you women." Bobby's mother was a "fuck you woman." She had three of her sisters in the house with her. They was the kind of women who told a man, "Fuck you and get up and get it yourself." I had never seen these kind of women. You were expected to strategize around a man or make him think it was his idea—if you had one—but telling a man "fuck you, do it yourself" was unbelievable.

I remember Mama arguing with Daddy until he turned to fighting. Then she'd give up. But not Bobby's mother. She had the best way of saying "shit" that's ever been said in the world. No one to this day can say "shit" like she can. It was like poetry. She would say "fuck you" and "shit" to her husband and then she'd break up everything in the kitchen. I thought this was marvelous. I can remember she wanted a kitchen sink that cost eight hundred dollars. That was unheard of in the fifties. Her husband said no. She'd say "fuck you," and the next thing I knew, Sears was out putting in a new sink. I listened to these women from our small bedroom on the third floor. I would cheer them on. Right on! They were the first women I saw who worked consistently.

Mama had worked a stretch during and after the war. More for herself than for having to provide extra money for the household. Some of her happiest days were when she was working in the factory with women. She used to come home and talk about the women and how they formed a really close community. Even the white women. I had viewed white women as inferior. I thought they were "silly women," from the stories I had heard about them. Mama said the camaraderie of the women in the factory was strong because they all were glad to go to work. I can remember it was a real accomplishment to have a working mother who didn't work in white folks' houses. Bobby's mother was a cook and her sisters did day work. They worked for white folks and they came in from a full day's work and said "fuck you" whenever it suited them.

I was scared to be a "fuck you" woman. I was scared of everything. I was scared when the doctor gave me a pelvic exam. I was scared when my boy husband kept referring to the baby as his child and how happy he was that he was married. I was scared when I didn't feel like reading Edgar Allan Poe. I got scared when I was asked to cook on the second day of marriage. I knew nothing about cooking and cleaning. I knew nothing about having a baby or being a wife. I knew about literature.

Motherhood was a mixed blessing for Marilyn. A premature baby reinforced her sense of inadequacy and entrapment. A move away from her in-laws, as an army wife, began to reshape her identity. Typically, however, traditional sex-roles in her marriage replaced earlier parental domination and led to a different and equally disempowering sense of frustration.

The baby was born early. He weighed three pounds and seven ounces. He had to be put in an incubator. The doctors didn't know if he was going to live or die. I was concerned about him living, from a human point of view. But I knew I wouldn't be terribly distraught if he had died. I didn't like the whole setup. I wanted out of the marriage. I thought if he died, my father would let me come back home. I didn't have to stay married. I could go to college. My son came home from the hospital and tightened the trap. I resigned myself to this thought: This was the way my life was going to be.

My boy husband and I decided he would go into the army to get a job. They were accepting families with one child. His mother didn't like the idea. Although I enjoyed the women in the house, watching all the freedom they had to come and go, I wanted something for myself. My boy husband and the women in the house thought of me as Bobby's wife. I was not real to them. I didn't have an identity. I was the babymaker and the one that kept their lineage. So I wanted out. The thought of going somewhere, anywhere, was wonderful to me. He went to Fort McMacklin for basic training. There was no room for privates' wives on the base so we took a small apartment miles away. Bobby came home on weekends. I was a wife only on weekends. I had my own space. I had not counted on the isolation.

I had absolutely nothing to do during the week. I was not a group person. Once I got pregnant in high school, I didn't have girlfriends because their mothers didn't want them to associate with me. When I was a married woman I lost all my male friends. So I had to deal with spending a lot of time by myself. Alone, I decided after a month to move back home with my parents. This time I could come home because I was married and I had a child. I finally achieved some status. I was married and a mother and a black who had traveled. I had ridden a plane. It was not travel to come from the South to the North. I had traveled as an army wife. I got army wife's pay. My father was delighted.

Bobby was shipped out to Santa Fe, New Mexico. This was perfect. We were away from his family and mine. I fell in love with the Southwest. I had two more babies in New Mexico. The first, another son, died deformed. So here I was in a married army barrack with two kids. Bobby busy in the army in a peacetime war, and I stuck like a bunch of women left at home. I didn't mix with the women. All they talked about was baby diapers. I turned to reading. I would go to the library. I read all day. The fact that I had gotten away from Detroit and was living differently than the folks at home didn't feel so much like a trap.

I loved this setup in New Mexico. Bobby didn't. He wanted to come home. We did. And it seemed like there I was in a cell again. We moved back with the in-laws and then to a public housing project. Bobby wanted a wife that cooked, a wife that smiled when she took care of the children, and a wife that listened to everything he was doing and where he was going in his world. I was restless. I wanted to work. I saw myself doing something in the way of a career. He saw me in connection to what he was doing. I had nothing to call my own. The children belonged to him. Being his wife, I belonged to him. His career belonged to him. I wanted something that was mine. I just didn't know what it was.

The watershed of change garnered from the Civil Rights movement created a host of opportunities for education and career development for blacks. Marilyn's quest to study litera-ture, which could have been furthered by these changes, only precipitated problems at home and at school. Confronted with racial prejudice in the classroom when she did try to escape and constrained by a husband made jealous by her attempts to get an education, she lapsed again into self-abnegation.

"The white folks are paying for us to go to college." That's what my girlfriend had said, and I was off to get the money to go. I got a National Defense Student Loan. You had to pay it back, but I didn't even think of that. There was an avenue out, I thought.

I had to sell Bobby on the idea. I strategized so he would let me go to school as long as I supported him at what he was doing. We moved into the Jefferies Project, which had student housing just three blocks from Wayne State University. Daddy had just retired from the factory in 1962, so he could pick up the kids Monday, Wednesday, and Friday, while I went to school. And Bobby would pick them up at night. I hadn't prepared to be thrown into a classroom with middle-class blacks. I also didn't take into account Bobby's insecurities would come out.

I was intimidated by their age. There was a vast difference in experience. I spoke in an east side slang. These middle-class niggers were embarrassed by me every time I raised my hand to ask a question. I also did not know how to study. It finally dawned on me that I couldn't write a simple sentence. I was failing. I had not even thought of any of these possibilities. My instructor called me into his office and asked me what my major was. I said "English." He choked and calmly said, "I can't pass you. Your papers are absolutely terrible." I was devastated. Here I was again, another failure. I can remember him taking a book off the shelf, throwing it in my lap and saying, "Go home and teach yourself how to write and speak English. I'll take you next semester. And I'll let you write what you want to write. You don't have to follow the class subject but you have to write if you say you want to be a writer."

I was angry and humiliated. I had the summer off, read the book, and wrote my first paper. A long poem. It was called "The Bulldozer." It was about white people coming down in the black community and bulldozing our neighborhoods. This is what they called urban renewal. I used to watch the bulldozers and think, you're sweeping away the houses and you're sweeping away the weeds, but where are you sweeping the people? My teacher was shocked. I was still saying I wanted to be a poet, so he took me to the then poet laureate of the college and asked him to read my work. The poet asked if I was the one who had failed his colleague's class. I nodded. He told my instructor, "She writes very well." He called it intuitive writing. I laughed because I didn't know all that structure and theory. When we read Homer of the *Iliad* or *Odyssey* and shit, it didn't mean anything to me. The instructor let me write what I wanted to write after that and I did. I wrote about what I knew about and that was my life. I wrote about growing up and being black. After this school was very, very, very interesting.

Bobby reacted. He saw school as a threat to him somehow. He expected me to do everything in the house, study when he wasn't home, and, worst, accused me of having a "nigger on the side." I could never stay at school to study after that. I could never study at home, with the arguments and kids. My grades started to slip, the fighting started, and all that talk about being a poet and writer and maybe someday teaching and having a career seemed like such a distance away. I stopped the fighting because I took everything in the house and broke it like his mother. He quit beating me. But I was already beat. So the long and short of it was I quit school. Trapped again.

> *Faced with failure in school and the locked door of domestic life, Marilyn joined an organized religion. For a time she found a purpose for her talents and an avenue for self-expression. Even religion offered less solace when she discovered that it, too, supported her entrapment. Her new-found freedom was, again, challenged by her husband. The consequences this time were divorce, single parenthood, returning home to elderly parents, and a search for employment, although she had no marketable skills or experience.*

Being depressed and seeing Bobby's career moving forward and the kids growing, I turned to God. I started studying the Bible. I had the help of other members of a door-to-door ministry. They were coming by and teaching me. At first, I wasn't interested in religion but I did like their approach to the Scriptures and the business of the teaching process. Learning began to take a lot of time and filled my emptiness. I began to enjoy the Scriptures and I was becoming disillusioned about school. I began to think of school and all this talk about being a poet as fairyland. And not knowing what to do, I got pregnant. I could get Bobby off my back about going to school, I could study the Scriptures at home, and I could tell myself I was a realist.

Sometimes, I could get out of the house and attend church meetings, participate in door-to-door ministry, and talk to new people about something that was important to me. My religion had an international perspective. I expected to minister someday in Africa, and I met members from all over the world. I felt like I was involved in an international organization. It was grander than the storefront churches in the ghetto. And I felt that my church was calling black women to play an important role in the ministry. I felt we had a real heavy-duty part to play in international affairs. So the religious organization kept me traveling and I was satisfied. My third son was born, Bobby was hired by a large manufacturing company, and I was traveling a bit—and this seemed like a way out. I was satisfied. Bobby got a career and I'm doing religion. And I'm getting damned good at it. I'm teaching and I'm enjoying it. I got a vision. I've got something that belongs to me, and Bobby is tearing up my religious books now.

"Give it up or I'll leave." Bobby put it to me plain. Give it up or lose the house, security, and good sex. Be my wife and nothing else. By this time, he's become a fighter again on a regular basis. And generally the fights would come before the fuck. I was very definite as to when I wanted it and when I didn't. So we fought. Verbally and physically. He'd say I was a bitch and a whore. I was getting tired of fighting and being attacked about my religion and perplexed about trying to live up to the Bible Scriptures: Whatever the man does, a woman should accept that. You're supposed to take it. Even when he is physically beating your ass. And I don't like the fact that I'm feeling foolish. I mean that doesn't make sense to me. The *T* in trapped is filling up again. And this time, I've got three kids and a man I can't live with no more and no education and a no-making-sense religion that I enjoy that says "take it"—and I still don't have nothing that's really mine.

I choose God. Bobby leaves and tells me I'll have to crawl

back. I go home to Daddy again. I got no job. I was absolutely scared to go out and get a real job. I went down to the unemployment office in the city of Detroit. They kept asking me if I could type. I couldn't type. Then they gave me nineteen million forms to fill out and I was exhausted. I got to this desk and the receptionist asked me a simple question and I blew up. I started screaming about not having a job and having three babies to feed. I was hysterical. A tall black woman came up to me and asked me to sit down and calm down. I was mumbling underneath my breath that "this was a bunch of shit, these people ain't gonna get me no job." "I'll have a job for you in two days," she said. And she did. This was just a few months after the Detroit riot of 1967.

I had applied to the phone company three times. Before the riots, they weren't hiring Negroes, now called blacks. I got the job as one of the direct benefits of the riot. I was making $78.50 a week. I was a technician. I put in the cable so homes could get personal dial tones. They needed women to handle the equipment because of the dexterity of our hands. At first, we was hired together. Black and white women. The white women got promoted for management. We were kept on the lower echelons but we didn't complain because this was the best salary some of us had ever had. So all the black women did the physical work, up and down those cable ladders, and the white women became supervisors. Every once in a while, a hillbilly would stay amongst us. She was generally considered a "white trash" type of white anyway. The union didn't look out for her or me.

It was a small office and I was scared of being fired at any time. At least for the first year. The thought of not being able to feed my children was terrifying. I was never late or absent. In fact, I remember calling my kids and making it clear that they were not to call me on the job unless it was a real emergency. They had to take care of themselves. After awhile the job got routine. I also knew the bosses didn't know from one minute to the next what the fuck we were doing. We weren't supervised. So I made a big production about everything I was doing to appear busy. To appear like a good worker. That way I didn't have to work that hard. I could bullshit them the way they bullshitted me come evaluation time. The way I saw it, as women, we were both fucking animals trying to cover our asses.

Seven or eight years later, they made me management and sent me to a branch office. It was an all-black office with a white supervisor. I had the job of managing black people. I was a "straw boss," as my Daddy used to say. That's a boss with no power. A boss can be a function or a head. I could make no decisions. I couldn't hire or fire anybody. I couldn't set up any plans of how I wanted the job to go without checking with my boss. And I especially didn't like the fact that my supervisor could tell me how to treat black people. So I quit and went back to the cable lines with the rest of the black women. I didn't see it as a career. In fact, black women that I know didn't use that word. I felt I was part of production. I learned the job and I was supposed to do it. Not thinking about it. If someone had asked me what I wanted to do for my life, it certainly would not be working for the phone company.

I got an apartment a few doors from my aging parents. I got my own money and it seems ok. I'm active with my church and I have a way to support my kids and myself. Bobby is darting back and forth through the door saying "the marriage can resume any time you're ready to quit that religion," and I've got my eye on putting some money together and traveling. Thinking about Daddy and how he watched those trains.

Although she was meeting the challenge of being on her own, Marilyn became disillusioned with her life when the racism in her church became clear to her. Living alone and sexless, she embarked on still another quest—a disastrous search for a mate, which led to her attempted suicide.

Mexico was a good way to make a start after the divorce. I enjoyed it. Although I'm living a very tight life in terms of men because of my religion, I'm on the move. I'm taking trips now all the time. I'm enjoying ministering. Mama points out to me that I'm not saving money to do anything. She thinks I should spend more time with the kids. It was a repeat of what she had told Daddy: "Get some property and buy a house." I reacted like an animal in a cage because I don't want no house.

I'm paying sixty dollars a month and living in a condemned building but it's giving me the money to travel. Traveling is what is most important to me, not buying a house. I'm doing well at the telephone company and they keep giving me promotions. Bingo! More money to travel. I'm doing well in my church and traveling all over the world now, speaking about the "Truth." Things appear to be going well. And by now I'm beginning to see the racism in the church. I see the great disparity between how black poor people live under the tenets of religion and how white people live their lives. I see how black converts living in the inner city took shit jobs to devote more of their lives to religious work, and whites had professional jobs and took vacations. I reacted to the church views looking down on education because I wanted to translate my spiritual vision into writing. I need to translate the Bible into me and Daddy's language, and I need to move this organization, like Mama said, "to save black people."

I began to see the connections between "male rule," which puts women, who do all the work, in the very lowest level in the organization. And I admit to myself that I am in a religious organization that is sexist and segregated and I have been in it for twenty years. Then the trap begins to close in on me. In the back of my head, I'm thinking about the confines of the religion in terms of relationships. It's demanding marriage as a way of exercising sex. But I know the prospect of somebody marrying me with three kids and a strong religion is slim. So I'm feeling the pressure of being alone. I want my husband back (who by now is living with this woman). And I know I don't want to marry a man in my church. They seem like sissies to me. And the "street niggers" won't accept my church. I need a man and sex, and the religion makes me feel useless without a man. I'm feeling odd and confused because I know a sense of self doesn't come from a man. I'm getting tired again. Mama and Daddy are getting older. Mama won't go out of the house and Daddy's behavior is getting crazier and crazier. And the trap is tightening again. The only way out . . . is traveling, and I'm doing it every goddamn chance I can get. But to travel, that means I've got to work ten hours a day. And I'm tired. So I take a chance to get out.

I started going with a fellow from high school. He says "marriage" and I feel it will give me validity in the community. I'm viewing this man as a way out. He won't join my church, but he will be my husband. I'm needing to get some rest somewhere. I feel real tired. I'm exhausted. So on my way to work one morning, about six o'clock, I decided to stop at his house because he was on my mind and a woman answers the door. I was shocked. She says, "Who in the fuck are you?" I ask her, "Who in the fuck are you?" "I'm his wife!" And I swallow twenty-seven sleeping pills. I go out. I really want out. So I lay down in the middle of the street.

I end up in a psycho ward. I'm spitting up my shit. I'm groggy. I'm coming in and out of reality. I am in rage. Everybody asking me why I did it. I keep saying "fuck you" and they call Mama. But Daddy comes down to the hospital and I tell him to go get fucked. Finally, the doctor says if I don't cooperate, then they are going to chain me to the bed. I stop cussing and ranting. I get real quiet. "If you don't tell us why you did this, we're going to send you to Eloise" [the state mental hospital]. And I know he means it. And I'm trapped. So I say, "I really don't give a fuck what you do to me, but if I get out of here I'll never have reason to return again. I will never suffer this kind of defeat again."

The doctor is intensely listening to me now and taking me real seriously. "I know you saved my life and I'm not that insensitive to not say thank you. But I'm not going to be in here again." He believes me and releases me. "I wish you would consider out-patient therapy," he says. "I don't have no time to go to therapy. I gotta work. I have older parents and children and I have this and that . . . to do." And I'm thinking now, twenty years in the religion and it has failed me. My friends pick me up and were silent all the way home.

Mama says, "I hope your brother doesn't find out," and I turn and say, "Don't worry, they not gonna put this in the paper." So I decide I have to decide something. I decide, Marilyn, you tried every way that you know how to set your mind free and don't look like you're doing such a good job, so the best thing you can do from heretofore is to try to make the best of a real bad situation. And that's what I did.

> *The death of her parents, an "empty nest," and an unful-*
> *filling though secure job opened Marilyn up to a lesbian*
> *affair. More restless searching eventually led her back to*
> *school, and most importantly, to writing.*

Daddy died first and Mama two years later. I went to Spain, and the kids were leaving, one by one. One marries and the others go to college. I'm making all kinds of money at the telephone company. I do buy the house and it's all working. Somewhere I'm getting back on the track, I take a woman lover. I didn't think of it as a lesbian experience. I think of it as something to fill the "dying inside" part of me. And Gina becomes part of my life. For the first time there is somebody that was anticipating my moods and what I want first and not making a judgment on it. She spends her time nurturing me. Picking over me. She picks my movies. My clothes. My hair-styles. She becomes my therapist and she puts me back to-gether again, Humpty Dumpty style. Piece by piece. But the pieces aren't quite fitting, but she is trying. Slowly I'm coming together. I don't know what Gina is getting from this, but she is making the difference between whether I want to breathe one minute or the next. And she is wanting exclusive devotion. I feel trapped. Somehow, I'm feeling my space is being taken away again. So I ended it. Remembering the twenty-seven pills, I decided I was going to see my life through. I was going to put my head on in one direction. Period. So I missed the men in many, many ways, but the exchange was suffocation and I couldn't do either. So I started running.

I started this Toronto thing. Every six weeks. It was a place where I could feel pretty good about myself. No one knew me and no one cared. I'm thinking life is a big joke anyway. The nest at home is cleared out and in some sense I'm scared because soon there will be nobody to buy shoes for and no coats to get and everybody doing their own thing. That gives me all the time to run the streets. I'm running as far and wide as I can because I don't know: What is my thing?

College. Poetry. Writing. Came up again. So I decide to take a class. Not for a degree. I take two classes—poetry and literature. The poetry class is filled and requires that you have five poems written for entrance. By this time I have completely missed the sixties. Bits and pieces of it filtered into my life but I felt sorry that I missed a many splendored thing.

And there are black poets now with loud revolutionary voices. There are black women's poetic voices, too! Poetry to me was like singing the blues. It was about: the man leaving, the bills unpaid, the pain of being black in America and the shit that gets dumped on you 'cause you got a pussy. So I go home and write five poems. The instructor reads them and lets me in. She ask the first day, "Who is Marilyn?" I raise my hand and it starts. She would put a word on the board and tell me to get up and show the class how to write a poem. I wrote and wrote. She kept after me and now I know I'm a poet. I'm a real poet because I'm doing it. I start saving my work and I start reading it over the radio and at poetry workshops and in bars. And I'm feeling. Just feeling. Me.

Accidently, I take a class taught by Mary Helen Washington and lo and behold I learn that black women are writing books.

And that's the first time I hear about Margaret Walker, Alice Walker, Toni Cade Bambara, Toni Morrison, Gloria Naylor, Zora Neale Hurston—and I see women telling stories, using my Daddy's language and from our point of view. I can't afford her class so she lets me monitor it. I hear black women's voices and I decide that I want to be one of those black women. Writing. Really writing. So I start a novel in between the phone company and the ritual of church and trips to Toronto.

The novel was taking up my time, but the emptiness returned for the man. So I put it down. I remarried a younger man. An African who really wanted a green card. And I really wanted to play "African Queen." He was exotic and macho. We both got what we wanted and divorced. I decided to take a trip to Kenya. They welcomed me. Going to Africa was like making a connection to my mother and father. It was real important to me to talk to the women and make that international connection with them. I was surrounded by black people running everything and it felt good. I felt good.

By now I'm pushing eighteen years with the telephone company. The grandkids are born and I ain't no grandma type. I got a house I don't need, and a cushion of money, so I move into a luxury apartment in the suburbs. Southfield. That's where the "middle-class niggers" go, and I guess I'm middle class now. I've got a car. I've got all the things that would seem that people wanted. Although, I'm feeling religiously bankrupt. I don't feel comfortable calling on the "Father" any more. And by this time I'm reading about women's spirituality and I'm real confused. I feel displaced. I'm in a lot of pain. And it's a trap. So I start to write again.

"Why don't you come to Iowa?" my niece said. I didn't know where the fuck Iowa was! I had no idea it was on the other side of Chicago. I thought it was in the Southwest and I loved the Southwest. So I go to Iowa. I thought: Why the fuck not!

The long and short of it is, I apply to the University of Iowa and they want me. I can get that minority money and cheap housing. And all I know is that I don't know how I gonna go to school and work. What kinds of jobs are there in Iowa? Yet, I'm tired of working. And I want to go to school. But I don't want to leave the phone company—my pension—and have nothing. I'm confused. Scared. I don't see how these pieces of me are all gonna come together. I think my niece was full of bullshit because she ain't old and she got two degrees and she's talkin' about me leaving everything. So I go home.

My niece sends me a story she writes for a class. I am the writer in the family and she wants my approval. I am jealous. She doesn't define herself as a writer. She defines herself as a sixties radical. I sure ain't that. But I am a writer and she's doing the writing. And she keeps asking me "what do you want to do" and I say "write" and she says "come to Iowa" and I say "I ain't got no money" and she says "yes you do, you can get financial aid." That shocks the shit out of me. It means I can come to school and I don't have to work.

I recognize this ain't got nothing to do with money. I see myself as a spiritual person and I ain't got faith in me from twenty years in religion. And my niece, who was my brother's child, was showing a lot of faith in me, and she didn't even know me. So I know, I never really tested myself against myself. I never really had a chance to take a challenge without the babies' wants and the "men's" wants and the parents' wants and the bill collectors' wants. Just for me. I freak out when a poem of mine wins second place in a State of Iowa poetry contest. And I'm dreaming, every night in Detroit, of coming to school in the summer. The mailman brings a letter saying I got the money. I mean I'm really shocked. I go to work and give them my two weeks notice, pack up my shit in a U-Haul and a week later, I'm on the road to Iowa. And as I'm driving here, I'm remembering what my boss said: "We can only give you thirty days off and after that you don't have a job." And I'm thinking, well, you're gonna take another shot at this college shit at forty-six? And what makes you think you can do something at forty-six that you couldn't do at twenty-six?"

I'm in Iowa. Classes begin in three days. I'm feeling like I ain't got no money. I need a job. My niece arranges an interview for me for the position of librarian at the Women's Resource and Action Center, and I get it. So I've got a job. I've got my own space. I've got my books and I'm working with women. And it's all happening at once. I mean all of it, it's coming together. I'm scared because school might really work. I'm scared because I am writing my ministry. And, I'm really, really scared that I might really be me.

Marilyn's interpretation of her life exposes the complex dynamics of how she was oppressed within her family and society. Her story tells where, how, and why, through private rebellions, she simultaneously resisted and adapted to that oppression as a kind of "loyal opposition." Marilyn believed other women seemed to have fewer options than she did. So when she looked out in the world and realized what she could change was limited, she rationalized. If she could not change her family, community, or the world, she could change what was in her head. Acting out an internal theater of "antagonistic cooperation," she apparently went along with what she did not like.

Her story is very complicated, and lives like hers have always been close to invisible. They have been invisible to American history, white feminism, and Afro-American male-centered history. It is only with the success of black women writers, whose work "spoke" to Marilyn as it has to so many others, that such stories have begun to surface.

Marilyn had the habit of surviving through private rebellions. The failure of such private rebellions is that they develop skills that at one level seem admirable, indeed are admirable—such as cunning, patience, and the ability to rationalize unpleasant realities—but never lead to complete liberation. One adapts from within.

Marilyn adapted to the existence of an intraracial color-

caste system; she adapted to a forced marriage of the fifties; she adapted to the roles of mother and wife. And the price she paid for these habits of surviving was denial of large parts of herself. She had internalized the many external features of oppression. She denied that she was a writer; she denied that she was a leader; she denied that she wanted to be part of a worldwide revolutionary ministry.

Private rebellions—in this case masked as suppressions— never challenged the institutional features of her oppression in family or in society. More open rebellions and efforts at self-liberation would have moved her beyond a habit of survival and its corresponding adaptive skills. They would have required disengagement from not only conventional female roles but from those roles sculpted by black family life and by white society which made any kind of black family life even more difficult. Not surprisingly, this was not possible for Marilyn until later in her life—and until the times were comparatively more open. The eighties, after all, were not the fifties.

Divorce, grown children, and a job with seniority—it wasn't until Marilyn had all these things that she could consider liberation. By forty-seven, she was prepared to take these risks. She knew by then that survival was a lot, but that it was not enough.

CHAPTER 3

SARA

Sara and I met three times at a university student union. I always felt pressured because Sara had to get back to work. We met in the Union's child-care room. But I blocked out the stuffed animals, toy trucks, and huge colorful pillows on the floor. We behaved very formally. I felt as if I was being lectured to. She talked carefully, selecting her words. At times I sensed that she was on the brink of trusting and sharing her feelings along with the details of her well-structured life. But then she would catch herself, stop abruptly, and recollect her proper posture and composure.

Sara dressed in brown and grey, coordinated professional clothing, and sat with her legs crossed at the ankles, toes pointed and tucked to one side, in a dignified manner. She consciously sat with a rigid arched back, arms folded. Every now and then, she would pull at her skirt and recross her legs. I sensed she was uncomfortable talking about her feelings. She was not really going to let me know her; that was not what she was trained to do. I, on the other hand, became increasingly impatient with her unnatural control, and sometimes found myself barely able to refrain from saying, "Now, be for real."

Sara told me the story of her fifty-two years of class con-

*sciousness, social and intellectual ambitions, and career aspi-
rations, involving making the correct decisions at the correct
time with the correct people. Not surprisingly, her obtaining
the Black American Dream was always threatened by racism,
sexism, and intraracial disharmony.*

It was 1954 and the Supreme Court was making the decision
on *Brown v. The Board of Education,* the old separate-but-equal
law. I was living in a mixed neighborhood. There was a white
school just one block behind the back of my house, but I had
to walk about a mile because I was supposed to go to the
colored high school.

*The 1950s was the beginning of the challenge to U.S.
patterns of racial segregation. Sara describes the impact of
integrating southern public schools on her family, friends and
the community.*

The NAACP had a legal strategy for fighting the segregated
school system of Baltimore, Maryland. I was a test case for the
NAACP in Baltimore. I was selected because I could go out
my back door and within one block I could be in a white
school. Whites and blacks lived so close to one another, but
they used to put those white girls on buses so they didn't have
to walk in our neighborhood. Sometimes this led to fights
when the white kids would come into our community and yell
out nasty remarks. In May, the Supreme Court ruled in favor
of Brown, and I graduated from the colored high school,
never experiencing the benefits of a lovely green lawn, a football field and stadium, or brand new textbooks. The colored
high school had a fenced-in blacktop playground and left-
over books from the white schools. On the first day of class at
Simon High School, the teacher would stack eight books on
the first desk in each row and tell us to select one and pass the
rest back. If you were in the middle or in the last seat of the
row, you got the worst book because each of us would search

for the book that had the least foul language. I didn't know if I wanted to go to the white school, for school's sake, but I wanted to go because it was new.

The connecting link between the black neighborhoods and the world was the news from the *Baltimore Afro-American*. You could learn all that was happening to ordinary folks, leaders, and about community affairs by reading this newspaper. It was also a social as well as a political outlet. You could read about different people and all the different things people were doing. I was always trying to get photographed. I ran for high school sorority queen and did fundraising work so I could get my picture in the paper. Having your picture in the paper was very important. I made it as the high school queen and the same day I got married.

> *Like Marilyn, Sara confronted the influences of color caste and class. She was determined to acquire social status and upward mobility based on her belief in a parallel system of stratification in the black community. Sara's strategies for success depended upon her understanding of the political system and the power structure. Unlike Marilyn, she had access to the upper echelons of Baltimore society.*

I heard about the local NAACP and joined when I was a sophomore in high school. It was a strong group in Baltimore. Our city had been the home of its national president [Clarence Mitchell]. The black schools would do fundraising for the NAACP. That's how I got involved. The black sororities and fraternities were always having contests. We also had a political family named the Mitchells [Parren Mitchell, a member of the U.S. House of Representatives] who were involved in leading the bus boycott and assisting student groups. Some of their children were my age and we became friends. The Mitchells were people you wanted to identify with. I got to know the mother, dad, and the grandfather, who were all leaders in the NAACP. They were attractive people, with straight wavy hair and fair complexions. Juanita Mitchell used to hold sessions in the high school, teaching us the difference between the Democratic and Republican parties. She taught us why we should support the Democratic party. She and her mother gave speeches that often ended up in standing ovations. They were political and could get a lot done in the black community. The Mitchells were people you wanted to know.

In high school I learned how to be popular with the right people and the successful people. I selected friends who had successful parents. One friend of mine's father was a Ph.D. chemistry professor. I was so impressed with him. I didn't know what a Ph.D. was but I decided then to get one when I went to college. He was my mentor. Although this girl and I had different lifestyles, it was important for me to be friendly with her to be associated with her dad. It was important for me to call her my friend and that we visited each other's homes. It was important that her dad knew that I existed. I learned how important it was to be associated and known by people who could get you someplace, or who could say a good word for you. Later, when I was in college and in the chemistry department, I could say "Hi, Lana," and she would answer, "Oh, hi, Sara." To me, I was saying to her dad, I'm a friend of your daughter. That's how I got recognition.

I learned how being labeled something good was another way to keep a good image and be successful. I was the teacher's pet. I can remember the other kids hated me, but the teachers showed a lot of confidence in my ability by asking me to do favors for them. They would ask me to grade papers or go to the library or clear off their desk. I did it to be in their favor. They could see from my being a helpful person that I would keep my promises and follow through in my work. It was also important that I be progressive. I wasn't gonna be old-fashioned or a goody-two-shoes, and I wasn't gonna be a challenging fool who attacks all the time, either.

There were also the powerful people. In college I learned that Martin Luther King was a dear friend of the minister of our church. When he came to town, I always managed to be involved in our minister's campaigns. That is how I got a chance to ride on the bus from Baltimore to Washington with Martin Luther King. In 1958, he was just one of the many leaders, but when I tell people now that I knew Dr. Martin Luther King, Jr., it just blows them away.

I wanted to know influential people. I looked to the high school assembly. That was where the principal would make public affairs announcements or introduce special programs or guest speakers. Week by week, I learned about the campaigns of the NAACP for racial integration. One assembly meeting I learned about the National Guard units that were called into Clay, Kentucky, and Mansfield, Texas, to help black children through the lines of howling white mobs who were demonstrating against integration. Then someone came on stage and made an announcement about the murder of Emmett Till. The boys were silent and the girls sobbed aloud. All I could think about was how could white people be so cruel. This event stirred up a fire in me. In that moment, I decided that I was going to be an activist and do something to break down some of the racial barriers.

My family wasn't involved with the NAACP. They were not joiners and they were conservative. Conservative meaning we'd listen to the radio, read the newspapers, and watch the TV for social commentary. I never remembered my mother going to a civic meeting or getting up in public and expressing her views, but she pushed me to be the leader in the family. She gave me a lot of freedom and support to attend the meetings. There was never any resistance to my being involved because I had housework or some other responsibilities. My mother expected me to be successful, and she expected me to be a leader.

Sara described the impact of the premature death of her father, the dispersal of the children to various relatives, the

*forced employment of her mother, and the threat of having to
go on welfare.*

My father's untimely death made my mother a widow with
three small kids when she was barely twenty-four years old. He
caught pneumonia following his appendectomy. My mother
split us up and went to get a job in the city of Baltimore. My
brother was sent to North Carolina with relatives and my sister
Betty and I were left with my grandmother (my father's
mother) in rural Laurel, Maryland, where we had all been
born. Everybody in the neighborhood knew Grandma and
called her Mother Willis.

Laurel was a rural area but we didn't call it a ghetto. We
had land all around us to play and grow our own food.
Grandma was very strict because of her Fundamentalist religious views. She was very active in her church and used to take
a lot of trips to church conventions. She was also very bent on
raising us correctly. Mother Willis didn't like "womanish"
acting girls. She wanted us to act our age. We were taught to
say prayers on our knees as little girls each night before going
to bed and to say grace before every meal. She made us wear
lots of heavy clothes, long dresses, and long stockings.

Betty and I would take a bag lunch to school with bread
biscuits with jelly and ham. We never had sliced bread, and we
were ashamed because the other kids were buying their lunch.
Betty and I always stood out because of Grandma's old-fashioned ways. When Mother finally came to get us, Mother Willis
said, "No, you can't have them." I can remember this one
particular time Grandma was away at a convention and
Mother told us she was going to take us for a ride sightseeing.
She stole us away from Grandma and took us to Baltimore,
saying "these are my children."

Mother was working two jobs during the war. She was a
seamstress in Crams Pants Factory and a waitress in a greasy-
spoon food restaurant. We had almost all of our meals in the

restaurant because it didn't cost anything. And it didn't cost Mother for a babysitter when we'd sit up in the kitchen until her shift was over and do our homework after school. When Mother would have to go to work at her other job, we would promise to lock the door and stay in the house while she was at work.

I started cooking very young. I would stand on a stool to reach the stove. I especially enjoyed baking yeast breads. I was eight years old. This was also during the time of rationing and war stamps. My sister was the kind of person who used to wear her shoes out all the time. Mother used to trade sugar and coffee stamps so that she could buy my sister some shoes. She was getting two new pairs a month, and that was tough because rubber was scarce.

We were a household of three women. We lived in a one-bedroom apartment, where the living room and the bedroom were connected. We shared the work and we worked together. We had a division of labor which was based on who could get the job done. So whatever had to be done, one of us was going to have to do it. We just grew up knowing this and knowing we were all assertive and strong women. Now, Betty and I joke about how we married shy, weak men who would rather push us into the forefront because that's where we are comfortable.

Being strong women was part of my family legacy. My great-great-grandmother, Vivian Markstone, was the first family member I heard them speak about when I was growing up. She was the daughter of her mother's slave master. When the Civil War was over, she inherited a big piece of land from her father. Vivian and two others had built our family church in North Carolina. It is the Markstone Chapel Baptist Church.

Mother and Daddy were both born in Rocksborough, North Carolina. They were third cousins and their parents didn't want them to marry. After efforts to keep them apart failed, Mother Willis and her sons (including Daddy) moved to Laurel to work at the U.S. Naval Academy. My mother was sent to college in Virginia so that she would forget about my father and get into an environment where she could meet other people. Back then, the eighth grade was as high as you could get in free education. She stayed in Virginia for a short time and then she moved to Laurel and eloped with Daddy.

Growing up poor in Laurel looked different than being poor was in Baltimore. In Laurel, poor meant not having material things. All of our neighbors lived on homesteads and we all seemed poor. We were grateful to get one toy from Christmas to Christmas, and we had no money to spend. In Baltimore, there were levels of poverty. You could see differences in poor people by the differences in how they talked, what they owned, how they dressed and what church they were affiliated with. And the big difference between being poor was what people expected from you. In Baltimore poor folks talked about each other. I can remember it was Easter and we didn't have any money to buy Easter clothes. The neighbors used to feel sorry for us and talk about how we were such poor children. My mother overheard a neighbor say, "Well those kids next door won't be able to participate because they won't get an Easter outfit." That night Mother took one of her old dresses and took the seams out and made me and Betty a new outfit. When we got up to join our neighbors at church they reacted because they couldn't figure out where we got the gorgeous dresses. Being poor meant lots of incidents like this one. It meant getting newly painted second-hand bikes for Christmas and Salvation Army clothing.

Mother disapproved of welfare. She didn't like the idea of a check coming every month when she was healthy and could work. And she didn't like to beg for money. Mother felt that if she accepted welfare it was a handout and it would cost her her self-respect. Once I remember seeing the welfare worker coming into the neighborhood and deciding that I wanted to be a social worker. They acted with authority and this was very important in my eyes. They helped people who were less fortunate than others. I liked that, but I also knew people didn't trust social workers.

Deciding what I wanted to be when I grew up was not the only thing that kept me busy during my teens. I was becoming a woman. I remember the day I got my period. I noticed spots on the back of my dress. I knew what was happening. I had been taught in school what to expect and how to protect yourself from getting soiled, but I didn't know how to ask Mother for help because we had come from such a strict background. I didn't want her to think I was a "fast girl." I went into the living room and told her, and after that she monitored more closely my activities with the boys. She felt that she had to make sure that nothing happened to us that might reflect on her as a mother.

I didn't dare ask at thirteen if I could go to the movies with the school gang if there were going to be boys in the group. When I was sixteen I had to be home at 10:30 and as Mother demanded, "Don't come home alone." Once, it was 10:30 and nobody was ready to leave the party so I chose to stay. I was having a ball and I knew I would get in trouble when I got home. I decided that as long as Mother was going to slap me as soon as I got home, I would say goodbye to my date at the steps. In Baltimore, most of the houses are row houses with white marble steps. We had eight steps. I stopped my date on the first, said thanks, and ran up the stairs. Mother was waiting for me and she looked like she was going to knock me down. It was only 11 o'clock.

Her mother's remarriage secured a middle-class status for the family, but at a price. Unlike Marilyn, most black women chose marital stability over economic independence when they had children and wanted higher social mobility.

Mother worked eleven years before she married our stepfather. I was fourteen. She said she married him for security and that she gave up her job because he wanted her to stay at home. Betty and I hated the idea. We didn't understand about companionship and sex. It didn't seem right that our mother was just a housewife. She was so strong and good at budgeting money. I couldn't stand the way he dictated mother's life and intruded on ours. My sister and I resented him telling us anything or directing our lives. We didn't like the fact that he was paying the bills. He bought a house in a mixed neighborhood because he wanted to live a middle-class life and we felt like we had to fall in line because we lived in his house.

There were so many fights, especially with my sister Betty, who felt picked on. Many times I'd say to my stepfather, "Don't tell me what to do, you're not my father." He finally quit. He got smart and started to discuss things directly with my mother. Mother would then bring them to us. It was like a third-party system. She would be the one who would have to relay messages. Mother was always in the middle. When he didn't like the guys I was dating he would never speak. And the guys would say, "Why doesn't he ever say anything?" Once a guy confronted him saying, "If you disagree with anything I'm doing, why don't you tell me?" He just quietly walked away. We knew what his silence meant and just couldn't wait to get away from him. We hated him. Betty got married at eighteen and me at nineteen.

Sheltered but ambitious, Sara proceeded to move up the social ladder. She made all the appropriate choices and connections for a woman who expects to have a family and a career.

All the important people I knew went to college. I never wanted to be just a housewife. I wanted to be a working woman like the women in my family. That's one of the reasons I didn't get a permanent fellow in high school, because I wanted to get good grades so I could go to college and become a professional woman. I knew I wanted to go away to college but I didn't have my stepfather's support and Mother was not working. My high school counselor had said that because I lived in a middle-class neighborhood I was not eligible for financial aid. But I was offered a three-hundred-and-fifty-dollar scholarship to Bennett College in North Carolina.

Bennett was an all-women's college in the small town of Greenfair. Two months before school was to start, a group of us went to Bennett for open house. We were in the reception room talking and laughing when one woman asked me up to her dorm room. She had a small room with two beds. I sat down. The woman sat down on the bed beside me. Within a few seconds, the door flew open and it was one of the campus leaders and she told me to go out. Later she took me aside and told me this girl was a lesbian and that I should never stray from the group again. I felt foolish because I was so naive. I had never come in contact with a lesbian before. I knew they were negative. I was scared. I decided not to tell anyone and decided that was another reason not to go to Bennett.

I went to college in 1954. I chose Morgan State because I didn't have to pay out-of-town tuition. It was one of the best-known historically black schools, in which 80 percent of the faculty had Ph.D.'s. It was fifth on the ratings charts after Morehouse, in Atlanta, Georgia. It was also in Baltimore, which is right on the Mason-Dixon line. Most people didn't consider Maryland a southern experience. However, it wasn't a northern experience either. At the same time, it wasn't like the Deep South. I also was pleased to be at Morgan State because my girlfriend's father was chair of the chemistry department and I had now decided to be a teacher. In the black community, I knew you were most respected if you were going to be a preacher or a teacher, and I chose to be a teacher.

I got married after my freshman year in college. It was the summer Anthony got discharged out of the service. He had been the first guy I had ever kissed and I chose marriage to have sex. I saw the marriage as the best way to be socially and family-wise accepted as a sexual person. We got married because it was convenient. He was also from a single-parent household. His mother had died and his father had remarried. One of the things that impressed me about Anthony was that he believed that we both should be able to support the family if something was to happen to one of us.

Anthony was not a professional man, but he was extremely supportive of my becoming a professional. He was studying to get a trade as a television technician. Our first few years of marriage, he went to school in the day and drove a cab at night. After graduation, he worked at General Motors a few years as a technician and quit to start his own trucking business. He was successful and was able to support me while I finished college. In fact, he always provided the financial security when I wasn't working and going back to school. It was clearly understood between us that marriage was not going to stop me from finishing college or pursuing my career goals. I remember this was mother's fear when I married Anthony in college. I told her over and over again, "Nothing is going to stop me from finishing," and she said, "The babies might." I was determined that I was not going to have children until I was ready. I went to the doctor and got a diaphragm. I used birth control for three years until I graduated from college.

Marriage was a plus for me as a college student. It was different because most people were not married. I thought it was an advantage because I didn't have a social life. I could focus on my studies while most of the kids were involved in fraternity life. When I did join an extracurricular activity I made sure it was to promote my career. I believed that if you joined the right groups and got to know the important people, you could get a bigger price tag. So I was always out front. I was trying to get into a position to be able to call important people by their first names. I would go out of my way to be at the right place to meet those so-called important people. Joining the Future Teachers of America Club introduced me to a network that I knew would someday have something to offer me. I knew this was a bad strategy, but it was important to me to get the right opportunities. I learned to network with organizations and different people in different positions, and how to judge which people would promote my cause and which would not.

I enjoyed college and I had fun at Morgan State. One of my favorite things was to sit in the lounge and socialize a little with the girls before and after classes. I would watch them learning to smoke. I never did learn. I did learn about sexual harassment, but we didn't call it that then. A girlfriend of mine took a class from this history professor and she kept getting A's and I got D's. We used to study together, and sometimes we would go to his house and get extra help. A few weeks before the final I went to my advisor and told him of the situation. I knew there had to be some biases because I had copied off her paper exactly, and the grades came back with me getting a D. Finally the advisor interceded for me and arranged it so that I could take the final again. I did and got an A+ but an A− in the course. I was furious. Then the gossip around campus was that the professor wanted to go out with us and since I was a married woman he knew I would never go out with him. This kept repeatedly happening with professors.

My biology professor would call me up at home and ask me if I was studying for the exam or busy doing something else. He knew Anthony was not home and that I'd be there alone. I always told him I was studying because I didn't want to talk to him. The next day in class he would have a pop quiz. And if I talked to him for an hour or two he wouldn't give me a quiz. It got to the point where my classmates could call me up and beg me to talk to him so we wouldn't have a quiz. I resented this shit but didn't know what I could do.

After graduation in 1958, I wanted a job and a baby. But I didn't get pregnant. This was a catastrophe for me. Each month, we wanted for my period to be late. I knew I didn't want to be a married woman without having children. I was afraid of being empty, and I knew I didn't want to be married if I couldn't have children. Besides, it was expected of me when I graduated to have a baby, but my body wasn't responding. I felt like I had no control over my body. I was used to control over everything in my life. I wasn't one of those women who let people and situations pull me down. Anthony and I went to the doctor and took all kinds of tests. Everything was ok. Eventually I got pregnant in 1959, while I was working in my first job.

> *As she built her career, Sara met racial and sexual barriers. She alternately challenged or maneuvered around these limitations. Sexism within the black academic world drove her to arm herself with formidable credentials.*

I was a laboratory scientist at a state institution. This was an important job in the fifties for a black person because the majority of people did not have college degrees. I had a professional job, but I was put in the hematology department, where all we did was blood testing. My job was to draw blood from the patients and test it for sugar or other diseases. Although this was a very important part of the medical care, when I looked at the white people around me, they were doing real research. There were two other black women in the laboratory and we were relegated to do the routine shit work. It got boring. I started hating to come to work. I could see all the white boys moving up in the positions and I recognized that was the way things were set up.

After my son was born I decided not to go back to the situation. I applied for a teaching job because it would give me more time with my family. I had a daughter four years later. I got assigned to Glens Falls, a predominantly white junior high school, teaching science. It was a public school whose science department was predominately white and male. I soon realized that integrated schools were exploiting black teachers. If you were a good teacher, you were put in a predominately white institution because the courts had said you have to get some black teachers in these white schools. For the first time in my life, I realized that white students were dumb, too. Some couldn't read. This was shocking to me because I had grown up in a segregated society in which all the stories were about blacks not doing well in school. If I had a white student who had disciplinary problems, the parents would tell me the reason their child wasn't doing well was because they had never had a black teacher. One parent said her daughter had only seen a black painter come to the house and it was difficult for her to see me in an authority role.

In addition to the racist attitudes, I got all the slow classes, composed of students who didn't want to learn or who had emotional problems. These were the less challenging classes. I didn't have the choice to teach the honors class. I taught for nine years and asked for a transfer to an all-black senior high school. I wanted to be transferred to Simon Senior High, the school I had attended myself. The white school administration took its time to give me a transfer. I began to use my networks for new possibilities. My undergraduate advisor, who was on the National Science Foundation, suggested that I apply for a grant to study for a master's degree. I did and got it. I was glad because I was tired of all the garbage in the public school system.

While teaching full time, I always had someone come in and help. Sometimes it was my sister-in-law, a nurse friend, or some other relative who would help with the minor household chores and kids. When I was in graduate school my grandmother would come and stay weekdays and return to Laurel on the weekends, while I studied and Anthony was on the road. I didn't think of myself as being middle-class because I had some help. I thought of it as what was necessary in a two-career household.

I started teaching at Morgan State College, my alma mater, immediately after I received my master of science. I took a four-thousand-dollar pay cut from teaching in the public schools. But it was important for me to be a college professor regardless of the rank. I got community recognition. I would get letters that would allow me to open a line of credit and inexpensive insurance policies. I also got my picture in the newspaper. Folks would cut it out and send me a congratulations every time I was interviewed or asked to be part of some program.

I taught biology, algebra, and the other physical sciences. I knew that I was given so many different courses each semester to prepare for while the males had only one or two preps. This was unfair, but all of the department chairs and the administration were all males. The black males were against the black female instructors because they felt threatened by female competition. I was determined to make some positive changes in the area of sexual discrimination, so I joined the tenure review committee. I was given tenure with a master's degree, but I wasn't getting promoted beyond the instructor position. I couldn't even get assistant professorship status. Their excuse was that I didn't have a Ph.D. After five years, I was tired of fighting with black men and asserting my rights for advancement. I began to look into opportunities to return to school. I applied for government faculty development money in 1972 and a Ph.D. program in science education. I received a full-salary faculty development grant and selected a university in Minnesota to complete my education.

Sara had no illusions about her priorities: career, children, and husband, in that order. Where Marilyn was self-suppressing about her priorities, Sara was assertive—always trying to break through barriers, always putting herself first.

I knew that I have always given a great deal of importance to my career. Next came my kids and then my husband. I had sacrificed career for children, but never career for my husband or the children for my husband. My health was important to me, too. I didn't believe I could do it all—the perfect mother, wife, and career bit. I didn't have a tidy house most days. When I hired babysitters, I expected that they'd clean up the house. Occasionally, when the windows would get so dirty,

I'd wash them, but most times the cleaning didn't get done. Housework just wasn't a priority. There were no Perma-Press clothes then, and the ironing got done when we needed a shirt or pants. If I was planning to have company or give a party, I'd do an all-day housecleaning thing, but normally, since I was teaching, grading my papers came first. I married a chauvinistic man who believed that certain jobs were for women and certain jobs were for men. He was only willing to do a "woman's job" if it was absolutely necessary. When the dishes were piled up and they got in his way, he'd do them, but he would never get up from the table and begin cleaning the kitchen. Anthony would never prepare dinner because he was the first one to come. But Anthony learned very early that I was not going to do it all. I mean I was strong enough to say "I can only do so much" and that's what I did.

I wanted my children to attend "good schools." They went to a public model school named Mount Vista Elementary School. We carpooled with other black parents. When my son graduated, I sent him to a private military academy from the seventh to the ninth grades, which cost two hundred dollars a month. It was expensive, but I managed to afford it without too many loans. My daughter attended model schools until we came to Saint Paul and they both got what I felt was an excellent public education.

The problems in the marriage did not begin with our move to Minnesota. I'm sure in many areas things in the marriage were not pleasant for Anthony, but he never verbalized it. I can remember his sisters saying, "As soon as she finishes the degrees, she's gonna leave you," or asking my husband, "Why do you keep on paying for her to go to school?" But he never complained. I don't know if he was ever jealous of me or if he thought about me and another man. This is something I've never been comfortable about in the marriage. He never expressed jealousy. I couldn't tell if that was good or bad. I knew that there was strong concern about my whereabouts, but most times he'd go out of his way to make sure he didn't act like he was jealous.

Anthony was actually excited about moving to Saint Paul. He wanted to live in the Midwest and he wanted to start a franchise of his business here. But the franchise idea fell through. So I decided to bring the kids and finish my Ph.D. while he remained back east working for three years. A lot of my girlfriends thought I was crazy. Some friends didn't even believe I had a husband. But it was fine for me. I was glad to see him come and I was glad to see him leave. I had plenty of work to keep me busy and I didn't want to get behind.

The coping skills Sara learned in her predoctoral career served her well in her role as a graduate student. She learned self-control under unpleasant circumstances. Eventually her leadership abilities gained her a position of power. Sara's career success, however, exposed the anomalies in her marriage.

The Ph.D. program was in science education with an emphasis on biology. I came to find out that many of the professors didn't like nonmedicine majors in the core classes. One professor was teaching that Jensen stuff about blacks being racially inferior and openly treated me and the other blacks like dirt. Most of my black classmates accepted it. I decided that I would not let this man treat me like this. After one of our tests, I counted up the score and noticed that it was added wrong, reflecting a lower grade for me. It made the difference between a B and a C.

I went to his office. I tried to talk to him about my exam and he immediately got defensive. He would not let me continue to speak. He finally said, "I don't want to talk about this anymore, because if you had a half a grain of sense, you wouldn't even be in my office talking to me about misgrading your paper." I was about to burst so I left. I went to the ladies room and stayed in there crying for a half hour. I had been taught never to cry in front of white people. After I finished I went to the department chair and he suggested I write a formal complaint. I did. A few weeks later the teacher refused to call on me in class. I decided that I couldn't fight this. So I took a drop slip to him. He asked me if I was "still angry" as he signed it and I didn't say a word. I decided to change my major to environmental science.

With the change in departments, I got a lot of support. The department and professor were very open on a personal level. It was a small department and we had close ties. They were especially concerned about the numbers of minorities in the program. We would engage in many discussions about admissions and recruitment policies. They didn't see me as a timid person and gave me strong academic recommendations after graduation. These recommendations were helpful in my committee work as a volunteer with the National Science Board. I got a chance to serve and I took advantage of the learning experiences.

Soon after I graduated in 1977, I was offered a position at a university paying almost twice as much as Morgan State. The university had a lot of federal funds and had been looking for a black woman to fulfill its minority goals. I had learned a long time ago that you use what is available to get what you want to get and go where you want to go. So I took advantage of the situation. I didn't take the attitude that I was that good for the job, but I knew they were using me so why not use the system. So I accepted the job. I quickly was promoted from one higher administrative area to the next until I worked for four years and used my networking skills to meet new important people and create mentoring relationships that would take me on trips to Washington to represent the college or expose me to new career opportunities.

Anthony moved to Saint Paul and took a job as senior division manager with an auto merchandising chain store. My son entered high school and my daughter was finishing the sixth grade. We purchased a larger house, and I'm not home very much because I'm happy building my career. The marriage is functioning because we are both doing what we want, and I'm ignoring my son, who by now is wondering why his parents' marriage was not the storybook type. One day, I remember telling my son that it's been many factors of our marriage that have been making it go on. I knew we didn't have the kind of marriage where you'd hear people say "they're just so happy" or that "they were inseparable." I felt that was bullshit. I told him there had been times when love played an important part to overcoming obstacles and times when security played the role that kept us together. There had been times in which I didn't know what the purpose of marriage was in my life. I tried to explain to him how and why I got married in the fifties. I went on to say that times have not only drastically changed in the seventies, but that neither his dad or I could dare to say that it was love at first sight or that things hadn't never gotten stormy. In fact, through all these changes and years of marriage, I guess we were just fools staying together for the sake of staying. I knew this was no comfort to my son. And I wasn't sure if I had great admiration for enduring it either.

> *For all of her professional success, Sara eventually had to come to grips with the burden of black female leadership. Walking a tightrope between a marriage that was faulty at many levels and a highly visible but demanding career, she found her future in limbo with respect to her previous priorities.*

I was nominated vice president for academic affairs at a small college in upper Minnesota. I accepted immediately. I had been warned about the racism there because the community was 99 percent Lutheran and German. I was told that it was a very closed society, unless you were Caucasian. My friends told me that I would always be considered an outsider.

I took the job anyway, in the summer of 1982. Anthony did not understand why I wanted to change jobs. He felt that I made enough money. So we kept the house in Saint Paul and bought a condo near the college. I would work five days a week and then come home on weekends. Sometimes Anthony and the kids would come up, but they didn't like the idea of two households.

I worked for a woman president and I worked hard. Sometimes my days were twelve to fourteen hours. I joined a health club to reduce the stress. I was pumping iron three times a week. Six months after I was on the job, I read a headline in the paper in which an appointee on the Human Rights Committee was referring to black people as jungle bunnies and Polish people as dumb. The next day I wrote a letter to the editor. Within a few days, not only had they published it in the paper but the mayor put me on the agenda of the city council meeting. I was angry. I didn't attend the meeting, but it was televised, and folks were addressing me as a troublemaker and making speeches about outsiders coming to town and doing all sorts of things. They were openly talking about "the nigger this" and "the nigger that" and I was appalled.

I started getting telephone calls saying that I needed to keep my mouth shut or get out of town. Some calls came to my boss for her to fire me. The final straw was when the police commissioner called and told me that I ought to be careful and said that "the kinds of things you said aren't said in our town" and that maybe "you ought to get a gun."

I warned the president of the college that I had no intentions of compromising my values and asked for her support. She promised to support me. I stayed two years after that. Whenever I went to eat out, people would turn and stare. I left the job when the president resigned. I returned to Saint Paul as the recipient of the Human Rights Commission's Human Rights Award and I am reminded how two cities only ninety miles apart can see a person so differently. I was a hell raiser in one, while the other was saying thank you for doing good.

I guess I've always been a peacemaker and have been driven to help people, no matter what it takes out of me. I got it from my mother and the church. I just can't say no. Sometimes I drag in the house tired and whipped, wanting Anthony's understanding: "God damn, Anthony, can't you see I'm doing all these things for black people, and for our children's future?" He'd say, "That's your choice. Nobody is going out and making you do all of those things. And if all those things are bringing problems at home, then you need to stop doing them." He'd respond, and I'd listen and feel hurt because he never asked me "What do you want me to do?" He just thinks I run around and do things for everybody else. I know he knows it's a need and he respects me for doing it, but at the same time he would love for me to be home every night and watch TV with him.

I returned to Saint Paul, and conflict surfaced in the marriage. I had received an invitation to apply for an assistant commissioner for higher education for the State of New York and I wanted the position. I would have been the deputy commissioner responsible for all kinds of academic decisions around accreditation for more than two hundred and eighty schools in the state. This was a significant position and paid at least ten thousand dollars more than my last job as vice president. Anthony had no desire to go to New York at all. I went out for the interview. I was asked to come out for the second interview and to bring my husband. They were making a decision between two candidates—a man and me. I knew Anthony was not interested in maintaining two households. The kids were grown. My son had married and moved out two years before and my daughter was in college. They weren't really a consideration in my decision. My friends told me that between our salaries I could fly home every weekend. It had come down to the relationship between my career and my marriage.

I had pretty much decided to take the job, although Anthony didn't come for the second interview. The search committee members didn't mention anything about marital status but talked about the stress of the job and that they wouldn't hire someone who didn't have a supportive relationship with their spouse. I guess it was divine intervention or something but they decided to offer the job to the man. I didn't have to choose this time.

I don't believe my husband has ever seen me cry. We have been married thirty-two years and I know that it has a lot to do with me being a black woman. When I get angry with him, I will raise my voice or walk out, but I will not let him see me cry. I don't think tears get his or anybody's sympathy. I avoid tears because it is important for me to appear to have control over the situation. I don't want the person in power to know that I have lost control. I need support and I get it from some of my closest friends. Lately, a lot of them have been leaving Saint Paul. Support for me doesn't have to be black. One of my dearest friends, that supported me four years through the Ph.D. program, was a Caucasian woman and a lot younger than I. I could come to her and talk and cry and she could do the same to me. She has left, too, and I really miss her a lot. I also had a black male friend who recently left and went to the Northeast. We were very close. He gave me special attention and I enjoyed it like any female. He was someone I could talk to in quiet intimate situations. He filled the void, but our relationship wasn't sexual. Ninety-nine percent of the time I work with males and I am the only woman in the situation. I have to go to social events and it's always men and their spouses. I enjoy an occasional flirting comment or I'd flirt sometimes. But there has never been a void for sex in my marriage or security or for those things some people have extramarital relationships to fulfill. I don't have a desire to get out there and have an affair.

I think I am missing an escort in my life. If there is a Christmas party and the dean expects me to come because that is part of my job, I want Anthony and me to go. If he knows someone, he might go; if not, he won't. He is threatened and uncomfortable around these kinds of people. Now if his boss is having a Christmas party, he expects me to attend. And when I point out to him that he didn't attend mine, he'll comment, "Well you can go or not." I generally go because I know it will be embarrassing for him if I don't. He explains my being there because I enjoy social situations. I really don't, but I go because they are job related and it's necessary for the success of the job.

I ask Anthony if we had to live our lives over, what would you change? He says he would not change anything. I have said a hundred times, yes I would. We seem to understand things so differently and we understand where each of us is. He knows it is uncomfortable for me to go places alone, but he doesn't come. I do understand, but I don't accept the fact that he doesn't go out of his way to accommodate me more, when in fact I go out of my way to accommodate him. When I look at the pros and cons of my marriage, that's a situation I wish I could change. But it won't change, so I look at all the other good things. I don't believe that because one thing is out of place you should let everything go. I look at the total picture. I don't zero in on the negative. I look at the things that I can control.

One day I was returning from a business trip. On the flight, I sat next to a man who was reading a Minnesota newspaper. In bold letters it read, "Director Sara Steward says," and the rest was a misquote. I sat back in my seat thinking, "Oh God," while the tears just kept coming right in front of a total stranger. I felt like a total failure.

"Selective thinking" reinforced Sara's hopefulness and her drive towards self-empowerment and control over her life. Yet, ironically for Sara, success never freed her from the vicissitudes of being a black woman in America. She could never do enough to protect herself from racism.

Sara's belief that blacks are as good as whites is connected to her commitment to the struggle for racial equality. Although she is more than a survivor, she also feels like a loser at many levels. Her constant state of "being tired" from service to the people drains her physical and emotional health, causing her to question what she puts in and gets out of her highly public life and pseudotraditional marriage. Yet, by compartmentalizing her needs and expectations, she is able to perform a remarkable balancing act that prevents outsiders from detecting the flaws in her survival system.

Sara's balancing act involves planning her life minutely, so that opportunities do not slip away simply because she forgets (for once) to be at the right place at the right time. Sara's exertions to get beyond the mere habit of surviving involve knowing important, influential, and powerful people, people who can make or break someone else's career with a phone call. She relies on her religious background (providing the zealous conviction that she has a right to get ahead) and luck (using her female intuition) to get her fair share of the perks. The questions Sara's story raises have to do with the sacrifice of a fulfilling personal life for the sake of career goals and just how long one can endure the pressures of such a rigidly controlled existence.

In many ways, Sara's is the opposite of Marilyn's life— Sara consciously acts on her world, shaping it as best she can, inventively using her marriage as a safety net and springboard for success. For many black women, from the forties to the present, having a man who won't get in your way (even if he doesn't actually support you) is a better choice than being without a man at all. Sara chose to compensate for the emotional flaws in her marriage through politics.

For Sara, playing politics also became the art of political involvement, an answer to what she perceived as the call of leadership. Essential to this mode of transcending mere survival is knowing exactly the limits of racism and sexism and constantly outmaneuvering the structure that holds black women back.

CHAPTER 4

ELAINE

*I flew to Washington, D.C., to meet Elaine. She picked me up
at the Dupont Circle metro stop after she got off work. Her
daughter—my best friend, Patricia—had told me so much
about her mother that I was nervous when her car appeared.
I wanted to impress her. She wore a fashionable wide-brim hat
tilted to the side and a cashmere coat with a fur collar. Elaine
was in her mid-fifties and very sophisticated.*

*In an elaborately furnished condo, after a meal of Lean
Cuisine and spiced apple cider, we talked. Over a weekend of
conversation, we unpremeditatedly exchanged roles. Before I
knew it, Elaine was asking me questions, skillfully probing
my own personal life. "I love to get into people's minds," she
later admitted.*

*Elaine's story is of poor immigrant parents and a stable
family life; however, her parents were not emotionally or
physically demonstrative. After taking advantage of educational opportunities, she outgrew the traditional family roles
that she was encouraged to play. Education freed her from a
loveless marriage and led her to an identity crisis.*

MY father looked through the book and saw that I had
graduated with honors. He was beside himself. "You've come

a long way baby," he said, and with those words I knew I had. I had graduated from college. I was the man's pride, and his pride in me was heaven. It meant everything to me. It meant that I hadn't done it for nothing. It meant that all that hard work and stress had paid off. I had done something that other folks thought was really astronomical. And when the commentator asked all the parents of the folks who had graduated with honors to stand, there was Mama on one leg, holding up her program. Wow! I had been saying all along that I wasn't going through the graduation exercise.

Like Marilyn's, Elaine's early childhood experiences were shaped by a patriarchal family structure, a close attachment to her father, and an emotionally strained relationship with her mother.

I think that in many ways the neighbors thought we were somewhat special because our folks came from a different country. People treated my parents differently because they spoke with an accent. They had come from the British West Indies. When I was growing up, I'd hear folks talk about West Indians in a negative way, in that West Indians thought they were better than common black folks. We didn't think we are better, we are just arrogant.

My father had come to the United States in 1937 as a result of a friend who was very active in a religious sect. He encouraged my father to come to this country to work in a tin factory for a better wage. My sister Meryl was ten years old. For the first few years he worked and lived with a German family in a small town in Michigan. He was the only black there. Eventually he sent for my mother. Soon afterwards, they moved to an automotive town in Michigan. Most of the black folks were factory workers and feared the police. My father was a janitor at one of the department stores and a minister. He had felt it was his calling to administer to other people. He spent a lot of time in the jails because he felt they needed him the most.

And as long ago as I can remember, we had church service at our house every Friday and every Sunday.

My father was the only black minister in the sect. This group was really big on believing that one should be in the world, but not of the world. Once a month the white Brethren would come to our house for a prayer meeting. It was never a good feeling when they came because our family had to play a role. We had to pretend to be something that we weren't. You had to be false and be something that you weren't. Mama resented the Brethren, but she went along with it. When they would come, Mama would flop a hat on her head because they believed in wearing hats.

The Brethren was strict and didn't take to playing the piano, singing loud, or having a Christmas tree. I can remember one Christmas somebody called and said they were coming for service. My father snatched that tree out of the living room and took it outside. I said to him, "Daddy, now if God sees everything, then He already knows we got the Christmas tree, so why are we taking the tree out when the Brethren comes?" He gave me a look that told me in no uncertain terms to shut my mouth.

Daddy had lots of West Indian ways and was a charismatic person. People gravitated towards him. He was the kind of man that just generated great respect in other people. Being around him for just a minute made them feel that they could do whatever they chose to do. My father also had a good sense of humor and used to do a lot of teasing. It was a West Indian trait, a kind of talking about someone or a polite way of "playing the dozens." You had to have "snake skin" to be around Daddy's teasing. My sister Eve couldn't stand this playing. She would run in the bathroom as soon as we all got started. Daddy would do his teasing through a West Indian thing called "chupsin." It was sucking your teeth in between your talking. We would just laugh and laugh.

I always felt that my mother was a hypochondriac. I can never remember her feeling good. I don't know if it was from taking care of us five children (and the two of her best friends who had died) or from all that worrying she used to do about us growing up too fast.

Elaine explained how West Indian traditions, class, and color consciousness shaped her parents' child-rearing practices in America. Elaine also described her parents' marital commitment, although her parents lacked affection for each other, to the family. Like Marilyn and Sara, she had a light-skinned mother (who had more education than her father) and darker-skinned father, which fueled the continuing battle of the sexes.

I always felt that Mama believed she was better than my father and that she had married beneath her station. She used to talk about her side of the family as "being somebody" on the island. It wasn't just because she was light skinned but because her family had more education. Daddy's people were clerks while Mama's people had titles like Assistant Minister for Transportation.

Mama had lots of real strong beliefs. Although she had a certain amount of camaraderie with women, she was a loner. She used to believe that if you got too friendly, you'd just lose friendship. She also believed that we always had to be clean and decent looking. That meant we were constantly washing our clothes and heads. Her strongest beliefs came from her "how whites treat black folks" stories. Some of her stories took place in the West Indies and some, in America. She was always pointing out things we needed to be careful about. Mama didn't like us being flamboyant or too bold, and she especially didn't like no niggerly behavior, which meant acting the way white folks expected black folks to act. She believed they expected us to be loud and chomping on gum and talking off at the mouth. She told us that there was a difference between being black and being niggerish and that we'd better not give white folks any reason to think we was niggers.

We grew up poor, but I didn't think I was poor, because my father was so well liked by the neighbors. They liked his ministering and used to do a lot of favors for us since we didn't have a car or a phone. Our neighbor from across the street used to pick up Mama and take her to the grocery store.

Neither of my parents were physically demonstrative. I can only remember seeing them kiss once in my life. It was when Daddy was going to the hospital and Mama was saying goodbye. But I always knew my mother and father cared about me. I was the baby and my daddy's pet. Daddy didn't do any hugging or kissing, but he used to snicker because he liked the way I tested him, with what he called my "saucy ways." He didn't spank me either. Not even the time I hit my brother Weston in the head with a croquet mallet. That's why my other brother, Casey, says I had "devilish ways." Casey was a goody-two-shoes and didn't like the fact that I never got caught at anything. I was sneaky and looked innocent. I could tell a dirty joke and keep a straight face. I took this instinct from my father. We both had a good sense of humor.

In the fifties, Elaine quickly learned about a segregated society and what her "proper place" was as a black woman. Like Marilyn and Sara, she found that no matter what her skills, the educational system was not going to encourage her to develop them.

I wanted to go to school, but I didn't trust the teachers. It was Mama's stories, and the time the teacher didn't let me be Gretel in the school play, that made me distrustful. The first grade class had voted on me three times, and she chose someone else. Mama tried to explain it to me later, but all I know is that something changed in me. I knew then what it meant to be black.

I think I got the idea of wanting to be a psychiatrist from the *Weekly Reader.* I really didn't have a clear notion about mental illness. But I was fascinated about why people do the things they do and that's what I thought a psychiatrist did. Mama and Daddy never pushed us in school. They felt intimidated by it. Mama believed it was important for us to take math and English, but used to say "if it was left to the white folks, black folks wouldn't take no courses that they need to really get ahead." She wanted us all to graduate from high school and get good jobs. Mama didn't look down her nose at us working in the factory. I think Mama wanted the girls to get secretarial jobs and the boys to work for the state. None of my brothers or sisters ended up going to college. Eventually, my brothers went into the factory, two of my sisters became secretaries, and the other sister worked for the telephone company.

It was in junior high school that I realized what my parents meant when they said "you can't expect white kids to be the same after they get to be twelve and thirteen, and you got to turn to your own." My white elementary school friends stopped coming by the house and I guessed that was the price of going to what they called "an affluent school." That's when I noticed that there were black people who weren't poor. My friend Janee's parents had lots of money and lived in a big house and in a fancy neighborhood. They had a maid and used to spend every Christmas holiday in Europe. Janee had more than one pair of shoes, a Mickey Mouse watch, and she dressed in matching outfits, like white folks. Her parents shopped at Sears & Roebuck children's department while us poor people got our clothes from Montgomery Wards. I wore clean hand-me-downs and the same saddle oxford shoes until they tore up. I never carried loose change in school and I never had anything that I thought was expensive. It has always been clear to me that white folks lived like Janee. I felt I wasn't as good as Janee was.

Adolescence increased Elaine's awareness of a woman's place as defined by the conservatism of the late forties and fifties. Moreover, white beauty standards, white models of femininity, and the socialization of young girls for marriage

shaped her female identity. Rather than rebel outright, she
struggled to survive by appearing to conform to these norms—
while privately breaking rules.

I looked real gangly and skinny in junior high school. My clothes just hung on me. The other girls had breasts and hips. I had a matchstick figure with no behind. I was taller than most of the girls, with big feet. I never felt attractive except for my long hair. I was always able to do something with my hair. A lot of black girls had what Daddy called sniffbrain hair, which meant your hair was so short you can smell the brains. I wore it in braids because we had to take swimming. We could tell who had the good hair and the bad hair then. White hair was good hair and black hair was bad hair. Fixing your hair after swimming was always a major crisis for me, and that's why I was always trying to get into swimming as the last class of the day. Most times my bangs just stood straight up and the rest of the head looked a mess.

I was still a tomboy in junior high school. My daddy used to say, "You're a girl now, and girl's don't get to run with the boys." He felt I should carry myself like a lady. "Be a lady, not a goat," he'd say. That was Daddy's view from the West Indies, because they let goats run wild in the streets. He didn't want his daughter to be no goat. He didn't want my brothers carousing around the street corners either. He preached that the idle mind was the devil's workshop.

Mama had taught us not to be niggerish, but Daddy didn't want me to be a Sapphire, like on the radio show "Amos and Andy." My father didn't see no excuses for that. In fact, he didn't like excuses period. He used to drum that in my head. He'd say, "Don't tell me about what so-and-so did, tell me what did you do?" And if you weren't doing what you were supposed to be doing, you caught it. I guess that's why I had an "I'm going to walk right alongside the rule" philosophy. If there was a rule, then there was something about that rule I was gonna deviate from. I would break it even if I had to do it in private. I didn't let nobody influence me, and I always got even, one way or another.

I can remember when I had the responsibility to collect and stack up the books in my class, and one person had done something to me earlier. I would make sure that when I got to them, a few books would fall on their head. I would be good and say, "Oh, I'm sorry" or "Whoops, I didn't mean to do that," so the teacher would know I didn't do it on purpose. I got even by bending the rules. You would never catch me out of my seat when the teacher came in the room. And if I wanted to talk, I'd always get my classmates to come to my desk. I knew the rules and I knew what Mama said about white folks who make the rules: "Black folks can't be talking about being like white folks because they are sick and running everything. So don't bring any of that stuff home with you."

Knowing the rules in school made me feel like I was living two lives. I had to be socially acceptable to white folks but I wanted to hold my own. I was not a dummy but I knew they didn't expect most of us blacks to finish the ninth grade. I knew the difference between being the best and being a leader. I didn't want to stand out on either extreme. I was a leader somewhere in the middle, which gave me a lot of moving room. I didn't necessarily want to be the top person, I wanted to influence the person at the top.

Getting into high school, I can remember wearing a page-boy hairdo, reading *Ladies' Home Journal,* and *Reader's Digest.* I didn't like comic books, but most of my friends were in comic book clubs. I liked the trash reading from *True Story.* Most of my friends were boys, and everybody used to say, "You think like a man." I thought the girls were petty. They were too competitive over things that didn't make any sense to me. I didn't like attitudes such as if you are Suzy's friend you couldn't be Mayline's friend. I didn't want my friendships limited.

High school changed things at home, too. Mama became preachier. I mean she had more rules and regulations for everything. She kept nagging about keeping your dress tail down, having your head looking right, and keeping lotion on your legs. She didn't use the word *woman*, but when she called you "girl" it was in a derogatory manner. I could tell because it was mostly followed with "Go over to the mirror and look at yourself, can't you see how you're looking." Mama's biggest nightmare was for us to have a pin in our brassieres or holes in our slips or underwear. She used to say, "Don't wear holey underwear 'cause you may get hit by a bus."

Like Marilyn and Sara, Elaine wanted to go to college. But the lack of funds, the educational tracking of blacks in high school into vocational training programs, and the parental emphasis on secure and practical employment forced her into an early marriage.

Not only did I take college preparatory courses in high school but I was active in clubs that were college oriented. The local community center had after-school programs where you could participate in sports and crafts. It was there I took my very first black history course. A black college professor taught the class, and he later became a school superintendent.

One of my favorite projects was raising money to buy a jukebox for the center. We had an ice-cream social. I later became the officer who got to go to the record shop and buy the records. I remember buying songs like "Merry Christmas Baby" and songs from artists like Julius Mack, C. C. Rider, and Joe Hunter. Around the corner from the center was a little hamburger joint for blacks named Starlights. That's where my sister Eve and I would double date. Our parents would tell us to stay together, but we would go our separate ways as soon as we would hit Starlights. We used to hook back up at a certain time so that we could come home together and "keep our stories straight." On the nights we had to sneak in the house my brother Casey would be right there watching the door. And Mama would start fussing. Getting grounded wasn't as bad as hearing her fuss. She would fuss for a week and there would be a Monday version, a Tuesday version, a Wednesday version, and on and on, and I knew I'd almost rather have a beating.

In the eleventh grade I recognized that I had no money to go to college. I began to feel inadequate although I knew I wasn't a dummy. I had already started working part time as a elevator operator, but as far as I knew scholarships were nonexistent for blacks or unless they had the GI Bill, like my brother Casey. I had been raised to think that if you didn't know what to do, something must be wrong with you. I knew I didn't want to be a secretary. The only thing I was sure about is that I wanted to be a psychiatrist. I just didn't think being a psychiatrist was in the realm of possibility. I guess my algebra teacher confirmed my feelings when I asked for help on one of my problems. She told me she didn't know why I was in her class because as a black person I was going to end up in somebody's kitchen. I remember distinctly being devastated, but I didn't want her to know it, so I said, "Well if I do end up in somebody's kitchen, it won't be yours."

I was in a dilemma. I wanted to go to college but I didn't have the money. I wasn't expected by white people to succeed. I wanted to get away from home, and I knew I would not learn to be an autonomous person as long as I had two older sisters and two older brothers. I decided to get married.

Louis had been in the Marines and was a student on the GI Bill at a state university. I met him at a dance when I was fifteen. I didn't do a whole lot of dating in high school because I knew it was two kinds of girls: those who did it and those who didn't. I was one of the wallflowers who wasn't giving up nothing. Most times my brothers would scare boys off. Louis was friendly with my mother immediately, and sometimes I didn't know whether he was coming to see Mama or me. As far as my parents were concerned, Louis was mannerly, well dressed, older, and lived in a big city. To them, I had got me somebody who was going to make something of himself, so he was acceptable to my family. They didn't resist our marriage plans. Actually, I was afraid to get married.

My choices for what to do after high school were narrowing down just at the time that Malcolm X was having a profound effect on my life. I was moving far away from my parents' way of thinking about most things. I knew we were going to have to part the ways because I was moving from being a Negro to black. I had had a strict Christian upbringing, which saw us as coloreds hoping to be Negroes. Malcolm X was preaching and shaping my way of looking at white people's system and myself. My father looked upon Malcolm X as a crazy person.

Malcolm had grown up in a nearby city and his mother and Mama were friends. I had grown up with him. When he was young, he was an articulate hipster. We used to listen to him talk about New York and we were fascinated. I remember once he dropped by the house and put some marijuana cigarettes in Mama's china cabinet. We didn't find out until years later, after he was converted and would visit us. He always told that story over and over.

By the time I was in high school, Malcolm X was giving lectures at colleges across the country. He'd send us tapes of his other speeches. Malcolm was involved in the national and international movement as spokesman for the Nation of Islam, and I was becoming radicalized. I knew my father wasn't going to permit this kind of talking in his house. Malcolm was a very seductive kind of person and he interacted with my mother in a very positive way. From the time he walked in the door, my daddy would give him the suspicious eye. They didn't have too much to say to each other because Malcolm talked a lot about what Christianity had done to black folks. Malcolm believed that white folks' religion was the opiate of the mind. He said, "It was like going to a dentist. The dentist is working in your mouth and you're sitting there not knowing you're in pain, because you got your mouth shot full of novocaine." That's what the Christian religion represented to Malcolm. I hid my ideas from my parents because they saw my disagreeing with them as disrespect. I hadn't grown up having dialogues with them. It just wasn't done. So I took the socially acceptable way to break away from my family, without causing a lot of trauma. Louis had decided to quit college and return to his hometown. Shortly after my graduation from high school in 1949, we were married.

Marriage and parenting for Elaine assured her stability, but left a curious vacuum in her life. Like Marilyn, she was ignorant of birth control; a rapid succession of children locked her into a full-time mother/wife role. Her traditional marriage to Louis evolved around the children and was strained by differences over the care of them.

I wasn't ready for marriage. In fact, for the first year I spent two weeks in my husband's home and two weeks in my hometown. I quickly discovered that marriage wasn't going to give me a chance to be independent and make my own decisions. Finally, Louis decided he wasn't going to drive me back and forth to my parents' home, so I had to grow up.

I didn't know what marriage was supposed to be, and I didn't know how I was supposed to feel. I guess I loved Louis, but not in the way I thought you were supposed to love a husband. I loved him more like a brother. It took me a long time to recognize that. Often, I felt like I was sleeping with my brother. It felt incestuous. I really didn't know much about sex, but there didn't seem to be any passion between us. We were more like friends than husband and wife.

Louis was a perfect husband as far as I could see. He worked. He acted as if he cared about me. He didn't run around with other women. And he also didn't seem as if he would abuse our kids. So I thought whom I could tell, my mother, because he didn't make my toes curl up at night. I did tell my girlfriend Wendy. She said there were women out there who would kill for my husband. I kept on complaining, but I wasn't going anywhere. I knew that we were more affectionate in our marriage than my parents, and we didn't act like those I saw in the neighborhood where the marriage was over but the people still live in the same house. But I knew our marriage wasn't an "I can't live without you" marriage either.

I didn't know anything about birth control and I didn't think of it as a choice. I knew you had one baby and then another. I had two by the time I was twenty years old, and I finished with four.

The first eighteen months of marriage, Louis worked as a skycap. At night we used to count the money from the tips and put them in a jar. We were saving up for a house. Louis answered an ad to hire up with the fire department and got hired. He was the first black fireman in the town. He worked twenty-four hours and was off twenty-four hours. The twenty-four hours he was off he still worked at the airport for extra money. He did this for nine years. Finally, we moved in our own house with our two kids, Joyce and Patricia. After that, Louis used to say that he was tired of working two jobs. I would get very upset. I'd ask him, how are we going to make it? We didn't have much money. It never occurred to me that I could go out and get a job. I guess I didn't think about it because my mother hadn't worked.

Louis and I had lots of differences. His views of white folks was entirely different than mine. He had not been confronted with racism. He believed that people were just people, at least until the incident at the fire house. The cook had refused to cook for Louis because he was black. After weeks of this the captain finally said, "Louis I know it's wrong. Everybody knows its wrong." The captain solved the problem by ordering every person to have a turn cooking. He never did fire the cook. Louis was affected a bit by the incident but tended to look upon it as an isolated thing. It was entirely foreign to him to try to figure out where people were coming from. He just took people at face value. I thought this was naive. When the kids entered school and I began to indoctrinate them on how to deal with white kids, teachers, and white folks in general,

Louis told me I was brainwashing them and filling their heads full of garbage. I ignored him and told them what I wanted them to know because, as my mother used to say, "Elaine ain't got no lazy tongue."

It was not my idea that in marriage men were superior and women were inferior. We shared everything fifty-fifty. Although Louis had a job, I didn't believe I worked any less than he did. We both worked from sun up to sun down and made the decisions together. I think the fact that I wasn't head over heels in love with Louis had a lot to do with why I was level-headed in this way. We just agreed on work and money matters. We didn't agree on how to raise the kids. Louis pampered them too much, and I was determined that the kids were going to be independent. I would demand that they pick up after themselves and straighten up their rooms. As it was, I felt housework was a never-ending thing. It was not rewarding. You clean the house one minute and it's dirty the next. You wash dishes, you eat, you got dirty dishes—and you're back to washing them again. I took the attitude my father had: Do the best you know how to do and that's it. So I did the best I knew how to do.

One of the things that did cause tension was at the dinner table. Louis felt the kids shouldn't waste food and insisted that they eat every single morsel on their plates. His philosophy was, if you took it, eat it. And there were many days the kids would cry at the table. We didn't argue. I didn't believe that it was appropriate for children to see their parents disagree. If I felt he was doing something wrong, I'd discuss it with him later, never in front of the children. I wasn't about to harangue and nag him. I would make my point and be through with it. I guess I liked how we worked well together. I valued Louis. He was an organized man who could tell you where the scissors were because he believed that things belonged in their place. He worked hard and wasn't the shucking and jiving type. He was a steady fellow.

Louis and I were very active with the PTA. He was the

president and I was involved in other school-related things like neighborhood and school improvement. Our town was slowly being affected by the Civil Rights movement. It had been a city that was very white and very conservative. Most of the people were Dutch by origin and still called themselves Hollanders. They were very fixed in their thinking and membership of a Christian Reform Church. They were strict, pious, and self-righteous. Since our kids were being educated in this environment, Louis and I felt we had to pay attention to what was happening to our kids. I think the school officials were somewhat on guard and knew that they should treat our children fairly.

Elaine compensated for a lack of intellectual stimulation and career by joining clubs, reading, and watching TV serials. When her youngest child started kindergarten, she enrolled in college. Graduation, her first job, and community activism deferred her marital crisis.

We were members of a black club composed of black couples. It was called the Visionettes. We had lots of social functions. We had jitterbug dances. I loved to dance the bop. I didn't like to slow dance. That was during the time of artists like Tuxedo Junction and Bill Doggett who sang "After Hours." No matter what dance it was, the song "Afters Hours" opened and closed it. We used to say that even the deaf, dumb, blind, and crippled would get up on the dance floor. We considered it the Negro National Anthem. We put on at least four formal dances a year. My girlfriends and I would whip out our sewing machines and throw some threads together. Sometimes we would go to somebody's clearance rack and find an out-of-style formal dress. Then we'd doctor it up. We even put tissue paper in our bras because we didn't have bosoms.

The club also got together and discussed ideas. We didn't use the word "intellectuals," we just saw ourselves as discussing the issues of the day through black eyes. We used to laugh about how white folks would study anything and put labels on people to make them feel bad. We didn't believe that all black people were deprived. We read *Black Like Me, Imitation of Life,* and all of Richard Wright's, Frank Yerby's, and James Baldwin's books. Most of our conversations were about how we saw the world and the black folks' struggle. I remember some of our discussions were about the 1954 school desegregation order; the governor of Alabama, George Wallace; and the things that were happening in Little Rock, Arkansas; and the murder of Emmett Till in Mississippi. We saw ourselves as people who had to stay in step with what was happening.

When almost all the kids were in school, I began to get increasingly frustrated because I had no intellectual challenge in my life. I was very busy doing things outside the home for the kids but I didn't have any goal in mind for myself. A girlfriend told me she was going to work. And my sister, who lived in the same town, had children and had always worked. I hadn't thought about working because I had all the material things they had. Slowly, Louis and I had been able to stretch our nickels and dimes to get a washer and dryer and to remodel our kitchen. We were the last ones in the neighborhood to get a TV. I wasn't overwhelmingly envious about their working.

I was an avid reader before television. I would read what was called high-class sleaze. I would read things like the Mandingo series. I read when the kids were napping and after they went to bed. When we finally got a TV, I started to watch the soap operas. I was hooked on "Search for Tomorrow." I even named my son after one of the main characters.

Louis felt that he didn't need to go back to school. But I wished he was a person who enjoyed discussing different points of view. I liked confrontation. It was just stimulating to me to get ideas out on the table. I tried to get Louis to read the books I read. But he would have none of that. He wanted me to read to him and I wouldn't, so I just found other people for intellectual stimulation. I just didn't depend on him in this area. I guess I had never been into really expressing what my own needs were. Expressing what you needed was a foreign concept to me because you really had to be open enough to say what you needed. At best I could tell Louis what I wished he would do, but I never expressed it in terms of a need.

I remember a conversation with my friend Diana about going to college. She reminded me of how old we'd be in five years. My response to that was, "Well, how old are we going to be if we don't go?" I talked with Louis about going to college. He really didn't think I wanted to do it. Although he agreed, we didn't know where the money was going to come from. I started to save from the food money. He didn't know that at night I'd take the homogenized milk and mix it with powdered milk. I also skimmed on the meat.

I enrolled in a junior college in 1955, at twenty-eight years old and on the very day I took my baby daughter, Melissa, to kindergarten. I knew we didn't have enough money for me to ride the bus both ways. I made a decision to ride to school and walk back home. The walk was two miles. I can remember my neighbors saying this was the dumbest thing that they had ever heard, a senior citizen enrolling in college. So about a few blocks from home, I'd stop at a stoop and comb my hair, put on a little makeup and pick up my step to a cocky walk. I didn't want them to see me slouching down the street.

I enrolled in two classes, math and English. There were a few other women with children in my class. It took me a while to get over the shock of being older. I began to see advantages to being older. I knew why I was there. I wasn't interested in a social life. I was there to learn. My teachers were quite pleased to have a woman with four kids attempt to come back to college. I developed some friendships from the class but the hardest part was juggling all the things I had to do to go to school plus studying at night. It was stimulating for my mind but it was tearing my body up.

To keep the kids busy, I enrolled them in everything. They

were in museum and nature programs, the YMCA, swimming, and summer school. It was the best way to keep a routine because I knew they were occupied while I went to school. Louis watched the kids a lot but never closely enough for me. He had a kind of laissez-faire attitude and let them roam around the neighborhood. My attitude was I always wanted them in the backyard so that I would know where they were.

With Louis I knew, as Mama used to say, "what the traffic would bear" and what things about this juggling would tick him off. I knew he was going to be more upset if you left the top off the toothpaste or if the house was inordinately junky. Sexually, he was not a dominating person. He was still working twenty-four hours on and twenty-four hours off at the fire station so we didn't have to do it but every other day. It wasn't as if he was wanting something from me that I couldn't fulfill. He just wasn't an emotionally dependent person. He liked people and on his days off, he would visit folks. He'd be gone from 10:00 in the morning until 1:00 the next morning. I never questioned what he was doing because I never became overly concerned about his whereabouts.

I juggled things so I didn't have to depend upon where he was in the scheme of things. Lots of times I felt that I didn't need Louis anymore, even in bed. We would be in the bed and I would say to him, "Did you remember to do so and so and such and such?" He would just get angry and say, "Here we are in the middle of loving and you're asking me if I locked the door!" I just remember I would lay there and make my grocery list in my head. That's how involved I was in sex. When I'd get with the girls in the Visionettes Club and talk about all these feelings, I discovered that nothing was wrong with me. Some of them had experienced feelings similar to mine. I had thought that being sexually retarded was my fault. It didn't occur to me to think something was wrong with the situation or that Louis wasn't doing something right.

After I graduated from junior college in 1958, I was invited to enroll in a new elementary education program at the state university. It was an internship program that demanded that I take up residency. I would have to make a commitment for four summers. It never occurred to me to leave the children with my husband. They were very excited about going and Louis was supportive, too. He said, "You've gone this far, so go on." In the summers, the kids and I would pack up and move to the state university in the town where my parents lived. We lived in a two-bedroom university married-housing unit called Roseville Manor. I had to learn to drive. I got a lot of help from my parents, but they thought it was a bit much for me to be going to school. Again, I got the kids into programs that would keep them involved in productive activities. Louis didn't join us, but he'd drive up at least once a week.

There were lots of days I woke up and asked myself, "Girl, what have you got yourself into now?" There were a lot of days I wanted to quit. However, after two summers it just didn't make sense to waste the money and not finish. I had a scholarship, but school was becoming a financial drain on the family. It was also an emotional drain because I felt guilty. I wasn't sure what effect this was having on the kids and how they'd turn out.

School had become my overriding focus. I was getting to deal with ideas themselves, and that was stimulating to me. I wasn't getting any direct flack from my husband or parents and my friends admired me. Everything was ok.

I took my first job after I graduated in 1961. My children were teenagers and I was tired. In all those four years, neither the kids nor I had gotten sick. I didn't have time for any of us to get sick. If they would whine about a sniffle I'd say, "Yeah but we're all still going to school today." I started gaining weight. I taught the fourth grade at Victor Park Elementary school for six years straight.

These were uneventful years except for the time I challenged the principal and almost lost my job. The principal was white and the school was predominantly black. She never touched the kids. If one of the kids touched her, she'd wipe her hand. I went down to the Board of Education and lodged a complaint. It just happened that my sister and a group of other women had come to complain about the playground equipment and the officials automatically thought I had put them up to it. They said I was creating a community situation and it didn't help that that was the same day Medgar Evers had died. The principal got transferred, the equipment fixed, and I began to get interested in the affairs of higher education administration.

Like Sara, Elaine found that the completion of graduate school and the pursuit of a career continued to undermine her marriage's shaky foundations. Attempts to improve the failing relationship were futile.

More income had a positive effect on the family because the kids were nearing the end of their high school years. Louis thought of it as a time for him to relax. He did. In 1965 my oldest daughter, Joyce, graduated, and I was helping her prepare for college, when Malcolm X was assassinated. He had visited us a month before and looked horrible. He had shared with us the number of assassination attempts on his life. He kept saying that he just didn't know what was in store for him. The phone call woke me up Sunday afternoon. Malcolm had been killed. I was shocked. My sister and I decided to go to the funeral. We drove all night through a snowstorm. I was praying all the way and absolutely frightened when we got there because of all of the security. We went to his house to talk to his wife, Betty, to pay our respects. I was uncomfortable the whole trip, but it was something that I just felt I had to do.

A few years later, I heard about a program at another nearby university in guidance and counseling on so-called ghetto and disadvantaged kids. I told Louis and he took off a whole day to drive me to the campus. He was very adventurous that day and I got a feeling he was living vicariously through me because he had not finished college. Anyway I was accepted and promised a scholarship and expected to be back in Kalamazoo in five days. And to top it off and cover my other expenses, they told me they had a vacancy for a fourth grade teacher in the public school. So my daughters and I hiked on up to the university. Joyce transfers and we enter school that semester. My middle daughter, Patricia, was a senior in high school, and my son stayed home in order to play football. My youngest child was in the ninth grade and I am forty years old.

Two years later, I graduated. Two kids were in college, and now I was very aware that my marriage was in serious trouble. My head was no more in it. It had gotten to the place where Louis and I were like two people sitting in a room, one speaking French and one speaking German. Every once in awhile we could pick upon the same thread of a word, but it's becoming clear to me that things are getting worse. I wasn't thinking about leaving, but my marriage gave me back a bad reflection of myself. I realized that I'm gonna have to "fish or cut bait" because I had filled my life with education as best as I could. I decided to go home and work on my marriage even after the college offered me a job. I was going to concentrate on spending the time with Louis. I guess for the last five or six years I had felt selfish having everybody's life revolve around mine. I don't know what I was thinking. Maybe I thought I could come back and work some magic or at least be sure I was doing whatever I needed to do to make a clearer decision.

When I returned home, I began to get heavily involved with a Model Cities program. I guess I did try to raise the issue of our marriage to Louis, but he would just look at me and say, "You read too many magazines." The city had instituted its program for public school integration. The black kids had gotten on the bus to ride clear cross town to a high school which was predominantly Polish. Everybody believed that black and Polish people never got along. There was a riot. The black kids were attacked with chains and by antinigger crowds. A lot of us were afraid for our children.

A friend of mine and I organized a boycott and closed down the school for four days. We organized at the churches to tutor our kids. I got accused of being a rabble-rouser. We were on TV every day of the week until the uncle tom director of the program sold out to a call from then President Gerald Ford. He was a Ford flunkie and we think he was told to get the niggers in line. President Ford had graduated from the high school. Once things had settled down, my son, who had finished his high school requirements, quit school and enrolled in a junior college.

I got elected to the Model Cities program's board and my time was absorbed as never before. I enjoyed it, but subconsciously I realized Louis and I were further apart. Finally, I ask him again to talk and he says, "Why do we have to talk? We don't spend any time together!" That really hit me and I thought of my parents. I didn't want to grow old with someone I didn't communicate with. I recognized that I needed an entirely different emotional situation than my parents. My mama had died before Malcolm was assassinated and Daddy died in 1972. It wasn't until they died that I knew I could ever leave Louis. I knew that the marriage was holding me back. Everything came to a head when all the kids were gone. Louis asked me to spend the summer with him away from home.

I am faced with a summer with my husband whom I have nothing in common with, and I almost die. We would try to have conversations, but he could not see I was not the same person. And he used to pride himself on being exactly the same person he was when he graduated from high school. I prayed to the Almighty to get me through this summer. One night Louis reached for me in the bed and I say I can't do this or it's going to drive me crazy. I told him that I had lived this lie as long as I can live it. The next day I tell him that I want out of the marriage, that I have a job waiting for me in another city and that I'm leaving on the weekend. On the ride away, I break down to a tune on the radio by Gladys Knight and the Pips called "Neither One of Us Wants to Be the First to Say Goodbye." The words hit hard. It wasn't until Thanksgiving weekend in my new home that we actually told the kids. At dinner Louis told the kids I wanted a divorce. Everyone was crying but we managed to get through the dishes and they all went back home. The following Saturday, Louis called me and said something had happened and he just had to come up and talk. When he arrived, he said, "I was mopping the floor and started to cry. I hadn't cried in years. My first thought was to go out and to buy a gun and kill you and then myself. Then I realized that wasn't the answer, but that is how I felt." Louis shared with me that he had been abandoned by his mother because he had been born out of wedlock, then adopted, and said, "First my mother leaves me and now you." He asked me what he should do to change and I said nothing. I knew I could not go back. This was the first time in thirty-one years of marriage that I had known what I needed and said it. I tried to explain it to him. "Louis, it's like when you go out to shovel snow and you've got the whole yard to do. Someone comes out and offers to help you with the last two shovels and you say hell, I needed you at the very beginning." He didn't understand what I was saying. He tells folks even now, "I don't know why Elaine left me."

The divorce was final and I was most concerned about my two youngest children. My son developed a relationship with a woman he was seeing and got married a few months later. A year later he came to visit me while I'm attending a legislative reception. I invite him to come along because I can tell he has something on his mind. In the middle of the dinner my son said, "There is something I need to say to you. I know that you don't think I know why you left Daddy. You know I didn't like it, but I want you to know why. I reacted for only selfish reasons because I needed you at home. One of the reasons I got married was because I couldn't go back to that house if you weren't there, and I just thought you needed to know this." My youngest child, Melissa, still can't see me as a woman, only as a mother.

Much like Sara's, Elaine's divorce was followed by a bur-
geoning career and all the problems of being a black, single,
middle-aged career woman in the late seventies and eighties.
Her life-long emotional detachment and unclear emotional
needs surfaced when she searched for companionship. Unlike
Marilyn, who had married a younger man for convenience,
Elaine chose to remain alone.

I took a job with a national corporation as a consultant in
minority affairs. I worked in that job for five years. I was
forty-seven when the corporation promoted me to an office in
the South to coordinate women's concerns for the company.
Moving south and being single was the first time in my life I
ever felt shut out of the social system. My friends and I started
a singles club, but it didn't improve the dating scene.

Then came the move to another, larger, more progressive
southern city. I had yet another position with more responsibility. This new job required more traveling and it was difficult
to establish a relationship with anyone. I experimented with
dating a man my children's age. It was fun. But the relationship was headed nowhere. Sooner or later the guy reminded
me of my ex-husband and I recognized that I hadn't dealt
with a man who was my emotional equal. Then I dated a disc
jockey but I didn't see anything permanent with him. He had
grown up in the streets. I had never dated a street-wise person
before. I was sure he wasn't somebody I wanted to be with the
rest of my life. I just couldn't get an emotionally rewarding
relationship going for myself.

Once again I accepted another job and promotion out
East. I took the job for the wrong reasons. I felt obligated. It
was devastating. I didn't want to be in the job and supervised
people who did. It was a mess. I quickly gained thirty pounds
because I couldn't deal with it and I felt inadequate. I didn't
feel like I could do the job. And then I met Charles. He was
from my home state. His wife of over twenty years had recently
died and we had a very good exchange. It had been a long

time since I had felt emotionally connected with anyone. In between the dating cross-country and other things, I think Charles couldn't make up his mind about me. I knew he was seeing other women, but when I stopped by for a visit and a woman answered the door, I just turned myself around and went back home and acted like nothing had happened. Yet inside, I knew the connection I had let myself make was something that profoundly affected me. It came up in a conversation with an old fellow I used to date. He told me, "I am going to get married. I don't know if it's this week or next year, but I am not going to spend the rest of my life by myself. I see too many old people by themselves without any family. People are nice to you, but you can't fill up your life with a job." My friend had just put something on my mind.

My daughter Patricia called Charles when she knew I was coming to town. A few years had passed since we dated and I didn't think anything of it. He called me and said that his sister had just died and he was on his way to the funeral. He asked me to call him later in the week and I did. Charles and I talked and talked and talked and talked. He kept asking me when we were going to get back together. I thought to myself, "I didn't need anybody who had hurt me as bad as he did. I can do bad by myself." But I kept exposing myself. He invited me for the weekend. He said, "What have you got to lose?" "Nothing," I said, "because there sure ain't anyone else." We met in a neutral state and it was like we'd never been apart. We talked and talked and talked. Charles told me he wanted to be married and he wanted to marry me. He said, "I'm tired of being out there in the streets and running around with women. There are only two things I want to live for and one was to be closer to God and the other was to make you happy." I was scared half to death at the depth and the range of feeling that Charles had. And I knew he was the first man I had really ever trusted my emotions with. It was a wonderful and terrible feeling all at the same time. I told him I needed some time to think. I knowing all along I'm not going to put myself back in the same spot with him and risk my total self again. Some months passed and he was pressuring me to marry him. The relationship was getting better and better. I'm learning how to peel off the different layers of me. But I feel timid. Charles buys me a ring. And I've got to make a decision. I make it listening to an old girlfriend who went back a thousand years. She says, "If the man I'm dating said all that he wants to do is make a commitment and get closer to God, I wouldn't hesitate for a minute." We got married when I was fifty-two years old.

Elaine described how love challenged her fear of intimacy.

We both had our kids at the wedding. It was icing on the cake. I was finally letting something come in and not having everything go out. I could feel myself. Now I guess I've got to take the next step. Charles and I have been married and living apart for two years.

Moving beyond survival is especially problematic when a woman is locked into a martyr role and deprived of enough time to be herself. As a member of a traditional black working-class family, Elaine was always arranging and rearranging the lives of her family to get the job of surviving done. Placing her own emotional needs on hold, she stole moments for herself between being a wife and a homemaker. She read books to keep herself occupied and got involved in her children's education because she longed for meaningful work and intellectual stimulation. She was living vicariously; taking care of the kids and home was done with factorylike efficiency. Elaine acted like a "foreman" in a woman's apron and was emotionally detached from the job. Getting out the quota, getting out the meals, coordinating the kids, and playing at sex with an emotionally absent but "good" providing husband and father became the substance of her life. She turned to school as an outlet, and it saved her life and ended her marriage.

Elaine ended the domination of parental authority and marital roles over her life when her parents died and her children grew up and left home. Her mid-life crisis pulled her in the direction of a new definition of herself and new career choices. Breaking out of the "sacred cow" mothering role, she has been able to fulfill a personal agenda that includes fighting social justice and intimacy. Now married to an emotional and intellectual equal, Elaine has gone beyond the habit of survival to a new order of priorities. She can make her needs and wants important in the scheme of her life.

CHAPTER 5

GWEN

I heard my name announced by the President. "And now, Dr. Scott, our Minority Scholar at Penn State-Harrisburg, will make a few remarks." I walked to the podium slowly because I was not sure what I wanted to say. My mind was preoccupied with thoughts of Gwen's presence. She was standing in the back of the room in a lime green and white print dress with white pumps and hose, a large pearl-studded brooch on her left lapel, with Diana Ross–like makeup, permed hair, red lips, and a neck held high in dignity. Since we had arrived at the reception I had been watching her work the crowd. She was announcing to folks who she was, chatting with her best voice and smile about the plane ride from Detroit. We both knew she was here for the interview.

Was she the same lady I had picked up twenty minutes before . . . wearing a King Kong–size baggy man's shirt, straight-legged jersey black pants, and high-topped dirty white Reeboks, who looked like an overweight teenager? Yes. That was her too!

"I want to thank President . . ." I began to hear myself speak and I noticed her in the corner of the room. "And finally" (I was now saying, in my best anglicized college

professor voice), "a minority presence at a predominantly white institution means . . ."—but my thoughts were again on the questions I would ask Gwen, who was now a religious fanatic, by some folks' standards. She had traded her American-made "hustling skills" for the predictable life of serving the Lord.

We started interviewing immediately when we got home. I listened to a feminist story of Dr. Jekyll and Mr. Hyde, ghetto style—the good girl/bad girl dichotomy that came from being taught the "act, dress, and look right pattern" beyond everything else. Gwen filled out my contemporary feminist cavities with anecdotes about three generations of alcoholism, incest, and abandoned children; with seemingly insurmountable battles against internalized sexism, male-centeredness, and with the social and emotional price she paid for rejecting marriage (as an institution and promise for the black women of her generation). Her survival story is about a prescription (etched out of the feminization of poverty) for going from the middle child and racial obscurity to family, community, and national recognition. And if choices reflect values, Gwen's story is about the void not filled by giving unconditionally to everyone.

I WAS potty-trained like our dog. Housebroken is what they called it then. My two sisters, Louise and Justine, and I slept in the same bed. I was about five and still wetting in it at night. My mother, Roberta, didn't like that 'cause she thought I was too old. One morning she pulled back the covers and of course they were soaking wet. She put my nose in the pee and spanked me. I don't remember if I ever wet the bed again, but I do remember learning early in my childhood that I wasn't supposed to do anything that would embarrass my mother. But embarrassing her wasn't the only thing I was to remember. 'Cause when I was six, my mother sent me and my sister to get a dozen eggs. Every time we stopped, Louise would break one of the eggs. By the time we got home we had one egg left. "What happened to the eggs?" my mother screamed.

And before I could even speak, my sister said, "Gwen broke them," and my mother spanked me good about that. I could never understand why she thought I broke the eggs. She didn't listen to me either. So I just figured what my Uncle Reggie had said was true: "You can't kill a cat, because they have nine lives." And I surely tried. I was really cruel. I put our cat in the trunk, stomped on him, choked him, put him under the stove, and threw him off the roof of a two-story building. And that old cat just walked away. And so did I. I just walked away and lived the way I wanted to, and I didn't care if anybody listened to me. I convinced myself that I was strong as a cat with nine lives.

> *Family favoritism, birth ranking, sister rivalry, and the use of harsh physical and psychological punishments set Gwen's emotional agenda and outlook on life. Like Marilyn, Sara, and Elaine, Gwen's role model was her strong working-class mother, who was subservient only to her husband.*

I was born in Pittsburgh, Pennsylvania, in 1935 and I was one of three girls. I am the middle child. I vaguely remember the cobblestone streets, street cars, and hills before we left Pittsburgh to come to Detroit in 1941. I do remember Louise and I knowing our younger sister was different than us. Louise and I used to do unkind and bizarre things to her. We wanted her to act like us. Justine just couldn't keep up. We learned later that our mother had been told by the doctors that "Justine would never mature beyond twelve years old."

I think we had come to Detroit because my parents wanted better job opportunities. At least, that is what was said to us. But I remember everyone my father worked for, he'd end up playing around with their wives. When we arrived in Detroit, my mother worked in a hat shop and eventually opened up her own on Hastings Street, which was the black strip near downtown. I had a lot of pride about going to my mother's shop. It was lovely. Daddy, on the other hand, was hustling on the streets for odd jobs until he began to manage her hat shop and was spending her money as fast as she would make it. My father always had a "scheme" or wanted to "get over" on somebody and be a big shot in the community. He knew how to make money, but it was borderline illegal. My parents basically had similar ideas to succeed, but my father's notion was by hook or crook and my mother's notion was to socialize her way to the top.

My father kept losing everything he got because he wouldn't pay his bills. Eventually he started working in a bowling alley and he sold my mother's shop out from under her. It was at the bowling alley he ended up shooting this Mexican man (whose wife he had been messing with). My father was arrested. I remember bits and pieces of the trial and how my mother had instructed us to act. She told us how to look, dress, and what to say when we saw him in court. We were supposed to run up and hug him until we were asked to sit down by the white judge. Daddy got a murder sentence in 1942. Twenty years. This was devastating to my mother, who saw herself trying to move into some kind of status within the community by owning her own business.

My sisters and I didn't understand the trial stuff. We just thought our daddy was handsome and women loved him. Including our mother. Our father's infidelity wasn't nothing you talked about. We just knew he wasn't home when he was supposed to and that my mother and father would have these stormy, drag-out fights. I don't know if he'd hit my mother, but once I can remember her ending up with a black eye. Back then they used to buy worms or leeches to draw the blood out. My mother put this on her eye and lay on the living room couch half the day. When I asked her about it, she'd say, "Oh no, he was never cruel to me. I fell and hit my eye against the dresser." I didn't believe her because what she said didn't fit with what I knew about my father.

Like Marilyn, Gwen accepted a double standard for males, wife abuse, and sexism. For these two women, complying with such behaviors was a way of life, just as compliance with the white man's ways was necessary for black women who dreamed of assimilating into a racially segregated American society. In either case, black women in the forties used their marriages as vehicles for social mobility whenever they could.

My father's name was Earnest Bakerfield, Jr. He was born in Uniontown, Pennsylvania, and was one of the oldest in a large family when his parents died when he was twelve. All the children were orphaned and sent to be taken care of by other people in the community. My father's younger brother, Uncle Reggie (who lived with us all my life and after I divorced my husband), was raised by middle-class blacks and grew up liking opera and classical music and things like that. My father, on the other hand, raised himself. He drank. Gambled. Liked to party all night and he used to say he lived by the laws of the streets. Survival of the fittest. I guess I knew this was true 'cause I'd heard my Uncle Reggie say, "Your father grew up hating people. He used to sit up in the hills of Pittsburgh as a very young man and just shoot randomly at people."

I knew Earnest Bakerfield, Jr., loved beautiful cars. We always had one. It had something to do with his manhood and being successful. He used to prance around and say in a scary hipsterlike voice, "I am a man and nobody ain't gonna take anything that is mine." He just felt he would be less than a man if he couldn't protect what belonged to him. My mother divorced him while he was in prison. When I was a teenager and he got out, I saw he was cruel to women. He used women to take care of him. But he had never been cruel to me and my sisters. He wouldn't even let my mother spank us when he was around. He only spanked me twice in my life, and he'd use only the tips of his fingers.

My mother's father, we called him Granddaddy, bought a house on Theodore Street in a Polish community and my mother, us girls, and Uncle Reggie (my father's brother) moved together when I was eight. My first memory of living in this white community was of a girl next door with long blond hair. I wanted long hair all my life. My Uncle George (my granddaddy's brother) used to tease me and say my hair was as long as his fingernail. I used to cry about this and put hats on my head with long ties that looked like long braids. We were the only black family on this side of the railroad tracks which divided blacks and whites and the downtown Detroit area from Black Bottom, where the blacks lived. Black Bottom had the Brewster Projects [a government housing unit] and the Brewster Center [where black entertainers rehearsed]. My sisters and I attended Garfield Elementary School, which was all black. We were teased and called "uppity eastern niggers" because we were from Pittsburgh. We got beat up because the kids said we talked funny and thought we thought we were cute. Once a boy chased me home and I ran into this lady's house. I was terrified. I stayed there until 6:00 and when I got home my mother really did me in. I got whipped for not standing up and fighting back and not going home and not calling her. The next day I went back to school and when this boy jumped me I had no choice but to turn around and fight him. I whipped him good. I felt pretty confident and started acting out in school after that. I had a reputation of being rebellious. I'd put my foot on the desk ahead of me and refused to do my work.

When we transferred to all-white Ferry Elementary School, things changed. I just went along with the program. I became good friends with this white girl. We lunched and studied and played together for about a year, when she invited me to her birthday party. I was excited. The next day I went back to school and she was crying at lunch. I asked her what was the matter and she told me that I wasn't going to be able to come to her birthday party. That was the first signal that something wasn't right because of my race.

Black women in the forties acted out a feminist version of Booker T. Washington's "climb from their bootstraps." Like Sara and Elaine, Gwen was trained to be a lady. This black version of the Victorian lady was an imitation of upper-middle-class white lifestyle and values.

I guess as long as I can remember I didn't tell my mother much. I knew I adored and admired her. She was very beautiful. She had long black hair and small feet. Once my mother bought me a pair of Easter shoes that were really too small. I told her, "Oh, no they don't hurt." I wore them the whole day with my toes cramped up 'cause I had big feet. My mother was very upset and took them back. She stayed upset with me, I guess.

My mother was a perfectionist. She wanted everything in order and everything to be perfect. She was fanatical about house cleaning. When we got older she'd make us get on our hands and knees and scrub the floor and she'd say, "Don't forget the baseboards." I hated to do housework. I hated that everything had to be so ritualistic. Dinner just had to be just so or else. And she was the same way about dressing. She was a seamstress and loved fashions. My mother was one of the gorgeous women in the community who dressed immaculately. She used a "rat" it was called in the forties, which was made from rubber. It was like an elongated bun that you'd wind your hair over so it would stand out, like Joan Crawford. My mother was gorgeous. She acted just like her mother, a light-skinned, uppity-class black who was born in Virginia and lived in New York. But my mother was dark-skinned like her father.

She was an only child and born in Pittsburgh. Her full name was Roberta Clara Jean. My mother had two middle names. Her father, who was from humble Ohio origins, was a famous and wealthy black musician of the time. He played the piano and saxophone. He traveled with Ethel Waters, Lena Horne, and other bands in the twenties and thirties, when fashionable men wore spats over their shoes and were called "dapper men." For a short time in the thirties, he owned a black minor-league baseball team and a famous Detroit black nightclub-restaurant called Tom's Cabin on Eight-Mile Road. He and his brother, George, were what they called "legitimate businessmen" and played music at the nightclub. My Uncle George was also a "ruffian" and served as the bouncer when things got out of hand. Everybody knew that no white police would come in a black community.

My grandparents had a short marriage because of class differences. My mother, Roberta, lived with her mother until her father kidnapped her to live with his people while he was on the road. My mother had been pampered and sheltered because of her father's status in the community and because he was an entertainer. Her lifestyle was a status symbol. She had gone to white schools in the teens and twenties and lived the lifestyle of the wealthy black in Pittsburgh. And she wanted that lifestyle for us. My mother's perfectionism was her way of passing on to us the attitude and importance of who you were, knowing your own status, and what you were suppose to have, know, walk, and talk like, which was a whole series of things that made you a "lady." My mother had been a part of the elite black and she expected nothing less from us, no matter where we lived or what we ended up having. My grandfather lost his money and businesses during the Great Depression. That's when he went to work in a factory and bought the house in Pole Town. This was the same year my father went to jail. I recognized much later that my sisters and I were so sheltered we didn't even know our grandfather was so famous. I guess it was an embarrassment because he had lost everything.

I went to Grizer Intermediate School, which they called junior high schools in the forties. I was not an all-A student like my sister Louise, and I wasn't hidden away in special schools for the "slow people" like my sister Justine. I was average, and my parents had their favorites. My father doted on Justine and my mother adored my older sister, Louise, who could do no wrong. It seemed on every holiday when my mother went shopping there was always a difference in what she bought for one as opposed to the other. Louise got the nicest and then I got second best. I guess I recognized the difference but I didn't know where it came from. I just know that after my father went to jail all my mother's energy was more directed toward Louise. I felt that there was really nobody who cared about me. So in school, I just acted out. I wasn't expected to do that well. But this one time, I made up my mind to do some good school work. I turned in my writing assignments and the teacher said they were so good that she didn't believe I did them. I was furious. I didn't tell my mother because it was a waste of time to be anything less than perfect. And she wouldn't believe me anyway. I was already having problems with authority figures so I just did enough to get by. I didn't want to flunk out or my mother would come after me. But I felt I lived a double life: the life as a kid at home (in my mother's image) and as a rebellious hoodlum in school. I intimidated the other kids and irritated the teachers steadily. Once, I openly farted in class and dared anyone to say anything. Nobody, nobody messed with me. I didn't see myself as a bully, but I didn't take any guff from anybody. From whites. From students. From my teachers. Only my mother.

> *The strains of living in an extended family were compounded for Gwen by alcoholism in the family and by relatives' attempts to create and reinforce positive self-esteem—difficult to do for black children in the forties. Similar to the other women who grew up biculturally, Gwen was influenced by her black church and the predominantly white media.*

I grew up living with my grandfather [the musician and weekend drunk]; his girlfriend, Leila, an alcoholic [who became his common-law wife]; Uncle Reggie, the classical music lover, artist, inventor, Civil War historian [who installed sanitary napkin dispensers in businesses and public schools for a living]; and my mother, Roberta, who worked as a waitress. She went to school and was the pillar of the church. Granddaddy paid all the bills, bought and cooked all the food. My Uncle Reggie took care of us while my mother worked at night. Then I was a tomboy and put on boxing gloves and jumped off barns and garages.

On weekends my sisters and I spent our time at the movies and at church. We went to the Warfield and Castle movie houses on Russel Street. Back then were "chapter movies" or cliff hangers in which every week there was a new ending. They'd begin about every twenty weeks. My favorite actor was Bob Steele. I loved all the other cowboys of the forties—Roy Rogers, Tim Holt, and Randolph Scott. I also liked Buck Rogers and the mystery movies of Charlie Chan, and the hard-nosed, strong women, like Betty Grable, Betty Hutton, Joan Crawford, and Bette Davis, because of the way they dressed. My mother and Aunt Juanita (an adopted family friend) made and wore clothes like them with sparkles, rhinestones, and sequins. For ten cents we saw a double feature, a chapter picture, a cartoon, a preview, and a newsreel. The news was mostly about the war and Japan after the bomb.

After church, me and my sisters, and Aunt Juanita's kids (who became our adopted cousins) would pack our lunch of egg-and-mayonnaise or sugar-and-butter sandwiches and go to the movies. This was the highlight of our week. In fact, if I had done something wrong early on that week I take the whipping. So I wouldn't have to miss the movies. The other neighborhood kids went to the Forest Club for roller skating, but our mother wouldn't let us go. She thought there were too many ruffians. In fact, my mother kept us from doing a lot of things the other children in the neighborhood did. And we ended up feeling different. We were isolated because we couldn't hang out at night, or go to the famous Paradise Club in Black Bottom like the other kids. It wasn't until I was fifteen that I went with my mother to see Billie Holiday, Cab Calloway, and Duke Ellington.

Other than movies we did a lot of reading at the public library. I read mystery books about the Bobbsey Twins; cartoons like *Phantom, Lulu, Dagwood and Blondie, Little Orphan Annie,* and *Li'l Abner;* or took trips to the Detroit Institute of Arts and had classes at the YWCA in cosmetology, modeling, and dance. My mother insisted that we have a social class and position. We got a clear message not to play with the other kids when my mother would say, "Did you see what they had on?" or "They don't bathe" or "Their clothes aren't clean." I knew distinctly that there was something wrong. Looks were paramount to my mother, and if the person didn't look good, if they came from a too-big family or if they didn't have anything, we just basically stayed away from them. I guess this is how I saw differences between who was poor and who was not. I looked at how they dressed and what they had in their houses. We were the first to have a refrigerator while everyone else had ice boxes. We were the first in the neighborhood to have a gas furnace when others had potbelly coal stoves. I believed we were well off—at least, that is what my mother told us.

> *Gwen's self-confidence grew mainly from her church life. There she gained recognition for her talents and acquired, temporarily, a positive social standing in the community. Like Marilyn and Sara, Gwen's mother transferred her dreams of "making it" to her children.*

Church was also where we lived most of the weekends. The House of Jordan. We were taught about healing, the "laying on of hands," and the faith of God to perform miracles. By the time I was about twelve years old I was having religious premonitions. Our church had a large congregation and many special church activities. We would do plays about the Creation and dramatized the books of the Bible. I used to sing in the choir. I loved to sing. Louise and I joined the La Grainian youth choir when we were in our teens. It was directed by Loren Grant who was affiliated with the nationally famous Nolan School of Music. We sang not only gospels but semiclassical music. The choir would sing and dance at the Music Hall and churches all over the City of Detroit. Louise and I even tried out for the "Ted Mack Amateur Hour" on TV in 1951. We didn't win, but it was fun.

Church was also the place where we had it rough because it was very, very important to my mother that we looked right. I remember once when my mother had to work midnights and we stayed with Aunt Juanita. Sunday morning Juanita took us to church while my mother slept late. When my mother got there and saw us, she drug us out. She was very upset. Screaming, she just tore our dresses off of us in the car. I thought it was totally nuts. I knew it had something to do with the way we were dressed. She placed a high value on how we looked to others and who had seen us. She had fears that we would be held back if we looked bad.

> *Trying to date and "keep your respect and dignity" was difficult for black and divorced women in the forties. Sara's and Gwen's mothers attempted to counteract the myth of the promiscuous unmarried woman. The search for and capture of Mr. Right was no cure—although, of course, many black women tried it.*

Roberta, my mother, worked in a bar called The Three Sixes in Black Bottom. It was next door to the only black hotel in downtown Detroit called the Gotham Hotel. The Three Sixes had big-time black entertainment, like Billy Ekstine and all the great musicians of the forties. My mother was opposed to doing what they called then "mazen" work or day work. "Mazen" work was work in which you had long odd hours and on weekends. A lot of black folks did this work but hated it. I had heard some people in the community talk about how horrible that work was because you'd have to take a lot of crap from white people. The most highly respected jobs then were nurses, doctors, secretaries and, of course, teachers. My mother had quit school and married at fifteen and chose to work where she could regulate her hours, go to school during the daytime, and use her beauty to increase her income. She got good tips and hoped to find a "good, decent, respectable man" with some money. Once she didn't have enough money to register for classes and a wealthy customer in the bar gave it to her. This was in 1947, and she took accounting classes to get a business degree.

My mother had many suitors, or "friends," as they were called in the forties. Men were always there. They used to say there was something about my mother that was different than other women, not just her physical beauty. They thought of her as the dark-skinned Lena Horne, and she carried herself, they'd said, "with an air of confidence." And because they wanted to marry her, these men were nice to us. We called them our uncles. Somewhere in 1950, my mother met Mr. Randy who had a nice grade of hair [straight] and was light-skinned with freckles. The folks in the community would say she "captured" him because he owned a cleaners on Saint Aubin Street. Back then, blacks had to serve each other. There were jobs they could and couldn't get. We had our own funeral homes, stores, restaurants, dentists, doctors, and tailors. Blacks weren't extended credit in the downtown department stores. We moved in with Mr. Randy and his mother on Winder Street. I didn't like him very much and things didn't get better between us as things went along. He was more abusive to my mother than my real father, and my mother's and my relationship got a lot worse.

My mother had this attitude that every man in her life had a kind of first place. This meant that my sisters and I had to always put our energy into pleasing and elevating the men in her life. I guess I thought it was her responsibility to cater to him, but I didn't think it was our responsibility. We had to wash his clothes, clean his room while my mother worked. And if he liked certain food, that's what we'd eat, whether we liked it or not. Mr. Randy used to like scrambled brains. It would make me gag, but I had to clean my plate. Or the way my mother left the best piece of the meat to him. It was just that way. The best was always for a man, and I got the impression that I wasn't worthy to have the best piece. Besides, Mr. Randy drank, too.

We had left my grandfather's house because of my step-grandmother's drinking and extreme violence. After she cut my grandfather, my mother used to tell me to hide the knives before she'd come home from the bar. I was cleaning their room when she went into a fit and started striking her hands and scratching on her arms. She told me to get these bugs off her. I didn't know or understand what she meant. I was terrified. I kept saying there were no bugs. "Oh yes there are," she screamed. I knew her behavior had something to do with alcohol so I jumped over the chair and ran out of the house. I was gone for hours. I told my mother about this when she got home from work and all she said was that she was confused.

I guess my mother eventually felt this wasn't a good place for us to be any longer. She wanted a higher level of society. My mother didn't like the fact that the neighborhood had turned all black and was getting bad. My grandfather had always been involved in "playing the numbers," but my mother wanted us away from the degree of drinking, gambling, and "house parties" going on daily across the street. I remember my grandfather had a few house parties and made a lot of money selling food and booze. You could make a couple of hundred dollars in one night. But he stopped when he stopped drinking.

So my mother took Mr. Randy up on his offer. He lived in an exclusively white neighborhood and was willing to fix up the attic into three bedrooms for me and my two sisters. My mother was still working, though. She had finished school, quit the bar, and worked as a tax accountant for the federal government. She was making good money, but it seemed to me that most of it went into fixing up Mr. Randy's house.

In the forties, with the absence of any positive black beauty standards and the pain of the color caste in the black community, Gwen had to accept her place in the beauty hierarchy. Like Marilyn (who was high-yellow), Sara (who wanted long hair), and Elaine (who was skinny), she struggled to define what it meant to be a woman.

High school made a change in me for several reasons. I began to change the way I saw things and myself. I didn't think much of teachers and I only wanted to be a nurse once because my sister Louise wanted to be a doctor. Since I couldn't be the best, in a sense, I'd take the next best, I thought. I knew I wanted to be looked up to in the community and the only real cool person I knew was my mother. I wanted to get married and have three children like her. I also liked my pastor's wife because she was a seamstress and designed clothes for fashion shows at the Waldorf Astoria in New York. Somewhere in the back of my mind I thought I wanted to be an entertainer like Nat King Cole. People in the community looked up to him. He was famous and handsome. He was ugly, too. He had what folks called ugly features. He was real dark, had a wide nose and wore slick hair. That's what they called "kunked hair" or a "do." The men would put some kind of grease in their hair and tie it down in a head rag. I never liked it. I liked Cole's music and the fact that he was kind of soft and masculine but he wasn't very handsome. And that is when I began to accept certain things as being ugly and certain things as looking good.

I began to see myself through my own community eyes and realized that I wasn't so cute. I had short hair, skinny legs, and big feet, and that wasn't acceptable. I knew I was never gonna be light-skinned so I decided to work with what I had. I kept up with the pace in fashions. My mother thought I was ok, or at least she had me think I was ok. When my Uncle George got home from World War II, he used to tease me until I cried about the way I looked. He didn't tease my other sisters. He used to say, "You can't do nothing with that nigger." I would try to put on lipstick to look better, but he'd wipe it off in front of my friends. I got angrier and angrier. I couldn't change my looks. I couldn't get all A's and I wasn't gonna be cute. I remember distinctly saying to myself, "When I marry somebody, I ain't gonna marry nobody black and ugly. I will marry someone light-skinned with beautiful hair so that I can have beautiful children."

Deciding to have beautiful children fit well into my mother's idea of being a socialite. She believed in looking right, dressing right, and having a successful marriage. This was the key. To "marry well, marry comfortable, and if you're cool, smart, and attractive enough, there is no reason why you couldn't attract an upper-class black male," she'd say. My mother's aim had been to get me groomed to marry well, and I believed it. I could marry the man with the physical qualities that I wanted because I had been groomed to do so. My mother was also gung-ho on education and expected us to go to college. She believed "education was an insurance" that you can marry well, along with proper grooming and social upbringing that would put you in a certain standard within your community. She expected me to marry into the black elite.

The only thing I knew was that I had great taste in clothes. I will never forget the time I bought a peasant blouse and skirt. They were full of lace. The blouse was sleeveless, let down on my shoulders and was tight on the bustline. That is when I first felt some kind of female in myself, a womanness. I'm not sure what the feeling was but it was nice and I could use it. I was sexy and the boys found that attractive.

I remember flashing on the last fight I had with a school-mate. She had beat my butt good. I had decided that very day to change. I was going to be a lady. So I had began to wear more feminine kinds of clothes and stop bucking the system. I gave up always having the last word, started doing better in school, and boys were really attracted to these new changes. In fact, one boy I can remember was mad about me. His name was Ray Boggs and I liked him a lot, but he was from a large, poor family and had a cracked tooth in the front of his mouth. He had been the Golden Glove Boxer and was sought after by many girls.

I was beginning to enjoy boys' affection, touching, and becoming aware of a little bit of good feelings I got from them. This feeling was different than what my mother had told us about "keeping your dress down and your panties up" or "don't have no bastard children." She had given us books about sex, male anatomy, and intercourse, but I got clear messages from her: "Don't have no sex." And even when I saw her with boyfriend after boyfriend, I knew something was going on. Sex was for adults.

> *Adapting to contradictory standards of womanness (being a "lady" versus being "sexy"), Gwen faced new problems, attention from the "boys," which coincided with attention from inappropriate persons. Like all of the women I interviewed, Gwen feared that being "too womanish" was unladylike.*

Louise, Justine, and I were always careful how we dressed around Mr. Randy. We stayed mostly in the attic to stay out of his way. Louise and I went to different high schools and left the house at different times in the morning. One time when my mother had already gone to work I came out of the bathroom and Mr. Randy was standing in my bedroom door. There was no other way out of the room and I was terrified. He approached me. We tossed and tussled. He was trying to molest me. He wasn't trying to put his penis in me but to have oral sex on me. I didn't know what was going on because I knew about sex in the "normal" sense. I struggled and screamed. His mother was home, but she was hard of hearing. There was nobody to rescue me. Finally, he just quit because I was yelling so loud. He left. I hurried up and got my clothes on and got out of there.

I went to the bus stop, shaking like a baby. I didn't know what to do and I didn't know where to go. I didn't know nothing. He drove up to the bus stop and asked me to get in. I told him no. I was so afraid. I didn't know if I should or was suppose to get into the car. I was terrified. When I got home from school I told my sister what had happened. She said, "Well, it happened to me, too." And I was shocked. She was two years older than me and nobody had told me. Not her. Not my mother. I didn't ask her what happened when he tried. She just told me to tell our mother.

This incident with my stepfather just blew me totally away. So when I told my mother about the incident and all she said was that she would talk to him and have him come apologize, I was confused. I know there was no point in depending on my mother. She didn't see it as an issue to keep us away from him. She didn't think it was an issue for us to move out of the situation. And I knew that if she didn't move when it happened to my precious sister, I knew she wasn't going to do nothing because it happened to me. My mother was only concerned about keeping her status in the community. She wanted to cover it up. I had seen my mother talk on the telephone and change her voice to act "proper." Louise and I had caught her several times saying, "Oh, why don't you come up and see me some timmmmme" instead of "sometime." She cared about clothes, the way the house looked, and protecting her position. So I made a decision to protect myself. I decided that I was going to have to leave or kill Mr. Randy. I decided to get out of the house. That is when I started to have sex. I got pregnant. I got married. I got out.

Nor surprisingly, Gwen's quick marriage to the first avail-
able light-skinned man did not fulfill her expectations. "Mar-
rying right" in the forties, as Marilyn and Elaine did, might
have been a cover-up for unwanted pregnancies, but it did not
provide black women much control over their lives and bodies.

I met Leonard Chapman when I was fourteen and singing
and dancing with the LaGrainian Choir. This was the time I
was playing sports, in the drama club, and very popular in
school. He was bright, cute, and very shy. Leo, I called him,
was the picture of what I wanted a man to look like. He was
very light-skinned, tall, with straight brown hair. People
teased us because we were the youngest members of the choir.
We liked each other, but I was too young to date. A lot of girls
liked him at Northwestern High School. He used to call double dating "keeping each other's company." Louise and her
date and me and Leo used to go to the movies.

Leo graduated from Henry Ford High School at sixteen
and had been going to Ford Trade School for two years to
become an electrician. He was already working in a local
foundry and making good money. When I told him I was
pregnant we got our parents together. We sat on the back
porch steps discussing what we were going to do while our
mothers talked in the living room. They decided there was
nothing we could do but get married. That was fine with me
because I wanted out. My mother was kind of glad I had made
a good choice and said, "At least he ain't a bum, so to speak."
She had in mind that Leo would probably go to college, and
after the baby, I would graduate from high school. I didn't
have any concept at all of what marriage meant.

Leo and I had a small wedding in my mother's house in
September of 1952. He was seventeen and I was sixteen. I was
"showin' good," they said. I was a teeny bit embarrassed. As
we got to the end of the ceremony I started laughing hysteri-
cally when the pastor said, "Leo, now you can kiss the bride."
I was glad it was over. I was tired from all of my mother's

ritualistic wedding preparations to impress people. Actually, I hated it.

We rented a room in the house of some family friends of ours. They worked long hours and were hardly home. I had no idea of working. I had never worked before. I had to become a housewife. I had to fix dinner, wash, and clean, and I found it boring to be home all day. Everybody I knew, including Leo, was in school. I had nobody to talk to. I just felt isolated. Louise would visit me from college, but not often.

Then Leo began to change. He wasn't as nice as he had been. He'd work. I'd stay in the room. I felt restricted. Besides, I was sick all the time from the pregnancy. I got fat real fast. I had pain in my back and sex was difficult. Leo and I began to deal with sex in different positions because of the weight. I was very disoriented and dissatisfied. I wasn't in school. I wasn't in the choir, and I didn't have any friends. I noticed I was being treated more like an adult.

My mother began to talk more about the pregnancy and the coming baby. She took me to get a gynecologist. He was a white doctor, and that was unusual in the early fifties. After the first exam, I got excited about being a mother. I didn't have expectations about labor, but I was looking forward to this baby being nice and light-skinned and having "good hair." I didn't feel like an adult before, because my mother took me to the doctor's appointment and my husband paid all the bills. I wasn't used to being responsible. So I began to go to the movies by myself a couple of nights a week in order to feel independent.

> *Multiple pregnancies, child abuse, living the "secret" of family violence, and her loosened ties with the church brought Gwen to the realization that divorce and great self-confidence were essential to her survival. Unlike Marilyn, who joined the church for personal security, Gwen rejected it in order to gain greater personal freedom.*

Sharon was born in February. She was real light-skinned, almost pink. She was also premature. I had to leave her in the hospital a month. I went back to see her almost every day, and each time she was darker and darker. The day I picked her up she was almost black. I was flabbergasted. This blew away my theory on color. But I loved this little baby. Leo didn't, and that was rough.

He resented her and he let me know it. I couldn't understand it. We began to fight. Big fights. I mean, physical fights, because he wanted to do things to hurt this baby. I couldn't handle his attitude of meanness. He'd scream at Sharon because she was crying and put hot stuff on her fingers to keep her from sucking her thumb. When Leo took to spanking a three-month-old, I just jumped on him. I began to dislike him a lot. The more he hurt her, the more we fought. I'd ask Leo why, and he could never give me an explanation that I could understand. He'd say he was sorry and would never do it again, but this got repetitious.

I was pregnant again almost immediately and fighting daily over my daughter. I had vowed after my mother's bad marriages that I was never going to take abuse. And here I was, watching my husband abuse his daughter. I couldn't accept it. That is when I knew I had to protect this little daughter of mine. I didn't love her just because she was so close to me, but because someone was trying to hurt her. I lost the second child. Her name was Mary and she died thirty-six hours after her birth. My mother-in-law had said "it was really better that this baby be dead than have a father like him." I guess I agreed with her.

By the time I was nineteen I had been pregnant for a third time, and my son, Herbert, was born in 1955. Mentally, I was a mess by then. The constant battles over Sharon had stopped once Leo had a son he could focus on. We had moved twice and finally bought a house. Leo was a full-fledged electrician and had a part-time TV-fixing business in the basement. I still hadn't had a job. In fact, I felt my job was baby making and

Leo and I wasn't even compatible genetically at that. Every child we had, had a birth defect. Sharon was premature and underweight. Mary had only one lung and died. Herbert was born with club feet, and my youngest son, Rayford (born five years later), was born breech with some blood problems.

As a parent, I was obsessive. I washed the children three times daily and changed their clothes just as much. I was fanatical. I remember once taking Sharon to the doctor because the little hair she did have by three years old began to fall out. "How many times a week do you wash her hair?" he asked. I replied, "Two or three times a day." He laughed and told me to wash her hair only as much as I washed my own.

Parenting my son, Herbert, was also strained. Leo made a real distinction between the way he treated the two children. He showered my son with affection and ignored Sharon. He separated my children from each other. This was very hard on me. I felt like Herbert was taken away from me and I resented it. But I developed very little attachment to Herbert and as he grew up I began to watch him manipulate his father against his sister. I remember once Sharon had done a school project and wanted to show Leo when he came home from work. Herbert got jealous and tore it up. Sharon got very upset. Leo just yelled, "You shouldn't have set it down for Herbert to tear up" and proceeded to blame and whip her for doing so. I was furious. This drove a permanent wedge between me and Herbert. I became even more determined to protect my daughter and myself because this small boy was in control of these fights. I didn't recognize that Herbert was struggling for the same attention from me. I made a decision that if Leo hurt me or Sharon one more time I was gonna leave him.

In 1960, Rayford was born. I didn't want this child. I didn't know how to get rid of it. I didn't want the marriage by then. I was beginning to see that if I was going to get out I was going to have to have a way to provide for this family. I began to set goals for myself outside of a religious context. This same year my mentally retarded sister got pregnant by the pastor of our church. He was still married. Here I was thinking that I had been doing all the right things that the Bible said about marriage and this incident devastated me. So I walked away from the church and God. I encouraged my children not to join any church but to explore all religious ideas because of that experience. I was twenty-three years old and to outsiders like my sister (who had acquired a "good" marriage by then) things looked well for me. I had a house, working husband, new furniture, and three well-fed children. That was external. No one knew what was really happening inside this marriage. This had been the way my family was always looking at the external things. It took my sister Justine's affair with Mr. Randy for my mother to leave that marriage, and later, her having a child with the pastor of our church, which made us all open our eyes to how she had been seeking love outside of the family. Justine hated my mother for keeping her hidden all her life and for her being born retarded. She hated all of us. I felt guilty.

I began to think of divorce when Leo began to give me a hard time about me returning to school in 1961. He refused to give me the money for classes or sanitary napkins. He berated me, saying I was an "ignorant black bitch." Most time I shopped wisely for food and had something left over to buy personal things and small gifts for the children. I left him a couple of times but always returned. Once I left Leo and had to register Sharon at the school in that neighborhood. She stayed with my dear friend, Helen, for a semester. I would visit her on weekends. Leo never did.

My son began to show signs of stress from our marital battles, and when another baby was born into the family, he became an epileptic. He was losing his relationship with his father, who was also beginning to have some serious outside activities. He was having an affair with one woman who actually moved upstairs from us. She was very attractive. At this time I could care less because it meant he wasn't violent to me. I acted like the whole thing wasn't going on. When I told him

I was pregnant, Leo confronted me that it couldn't possibly be his. That really wiped me out. It hurt a great deal. So I reinforced my decision about divorce, thinking seriously about who I was gonna save. It seemed better to save three people (me, Sharon, and Rayford) than to stay for the sake of Herbert. I had not had an opportunity to hold and to love this kid. I knew that we hadn't developed the kind of mother-son relationship that would make him a strong, healthy young man in an emotional sense. I could see it when he was young. Herbert was difficult to potty train and turned inwards. He could read books at three, and because he wasn't his father's idea of a super-jock son, Leo soon out-and-out rejected him. When Sharon began to act out in school for attention and Leo would demoralize her over poor citizenship (she was otherwise an A student), I made up my mind to leave.

The lawyer had said take everything I could, but I didn't. We had two cars and brand new furniture. Leo had taught me to drive because I was always tracking the kids from here to there. I hadn't been in school and I wasn't happy. The last time he hit me when I didn't iron his shirt correctly I landed underneath the dining room table. Two things crossed my mind. One was a plot to kill him. And the other was to pack and leave. I left. The children and I put everything in pillow cases, packed them in the car, and moved. We lived in a cheap three-room basement apartment near the coal furnace. After I moved, I told my mother, who was not willing to give me any money for a divorce (she said she didn't believe in divorce), but she arranged to give me twenty-five dollars a week if I would cook dinner and wash for her and her new husband. That was my mother's way. Instead of helping me, I always had to earn help.

I thought only two weeks about the decision to divorce. At that time there was no no-fault divorce. You could only get out because of adultery or physical cruelty. I knew it took people years and years. All this time, I was trying to stay away from Leo, who was now acting very crazy over my leaving. I was afraid he'd kill me. My Uncle Reggie (who had lived with us as a child and himself had got a divorce) moved in with me in the basement apartment. He helped pay some of the bills and protected us.

I eventually had to get a court order to keep Leo away. When he found out where we lived, he kidnapped the kids. But I made it clear that I was never going back, so he brought them back. This went on a couple of times. The police didn't respond because they said it wasn't kidnapping if they were his children. I remember once my mother saying when she left my stepfather that "if I'm going to live in hell on earth, I might as well be in hell," so I took a stand not to return.

The pressure during this time was great and I began to gain a lot of weight. I had always been a small woman in a size eight. I climbed to a fourteen. This was very hard on me. Leo was harassing me, and the kids were crying for me to go back to their daddy. Finally, he dragged me back to the house where we lived and threatened to kill me with an iron pipe. I told him to go right ahead because I wasn't coming back. I told him I hated him because he didn't let me go back to school and brutalized my daughter. He said, "I'll ask you one more time," and I said, "Leo, if you feel like you have to kill me, then kill me." He stood there in shock. I walked out and it was over.

I ignored my attorney's advice to take him to the cleaners. He said I would regret this because the courts didn't really enforce black men to pay child support. I accepted what I already had. I had my children and I was out. Leo stopped protesting the divorce, gave us back the house, and married someone else two weeks later.

Like Marilyn, Gwen's adjustment to divorce, during the Civil Rights movement, shaped her social consciousness as a black woman and expanded on her economic opportunities.

I got the divorce in 1961. I returned to night school at Northern High School and received my diploma in 1963. I had dropped back to my normal weight of 117 pounds. While in night school, I went to the Urban League to search for a job and became interested in community politics. Early on in the marriage, I had met this woman named Eliza who was married to a white man. They had been members of the Communist party. In fact, the FBI tried to bribe us with gifts if we would spy on them because Leo and her husband worked in the plant together. She had a daughter about Sharon's age and they became and are still friends today. I liked this woman. Eliza had a lot of strength. I mean she was aggressive and assertive and I admired her. I wasn't direct and I had a habit of making decisions and not sharing them with anyone.

Eliza and I used to talk about politics and the world. She had been involved in organizing a boycott to get the TV show "The Little Rascals" off the air. After the divorce, I began to study about black people with CORE. I saw that outside of my four walls there were some real problems with my people and in this country. Martin Luther King, Jr., was beginning to come on the scene, and I was watching black people being hurt in the south by the Ku Klux Klan (KKK). I recognized that I had a responsibility as a person, as a black person, to stand up for what I believed was right. I could now see this clearly in the case of how my children were treated in school by white teachers.

Sharon got better after the divorce, but Herbert's epileptic seizures got worse. I took him to a clinic and after the test they could find no idiopathic reasons for the seizures. The doctors prescribed medicine like dyline and phenobarb and suggested he be sent to orthopedic school for the handicapped. After one visit, I took my son home and told him he was not going to that school. We went into the bathroom and I said, "You are never going to take another one of these pills." I flushed the whole bottle down the toilet. "I am not going to have you stigmatized or treated any different than anyone else. If you do something wrong, I'm kicking your butt. I expect your school work to be done, or I'm going to kick your butt. Do you understand?" My son never had another seizure. I had figured it out that he was going to have to learn to function outside of his father or get his butt beat. I wasn't going to feel sorry for him and I wasn't going to take him back to a doctor.

My first job was at Federal's department store for $1.25 an hour. I got it through my Urban League contacts. I had put on my nicest dress and went downtown to get a job. I was slim and cute and it was like the other times I saw myself in this light. I began to see that I could function without my children's father. Although I didn't have an education, I had learned to speak up from Eliza and I had the ability to think. I realized I was independent and that I wasn't so bad looking. In fact, I was quite attractive. When I told them I had never worked in my life they were surprised. I assured them that I could learn to do almost anything and they knew I had three kids to feed. That is how I ended up the second black employee Federal's had ever hired.

I worked day shifts because I was still going to school at night. I got off work at 5:00, took the bus home, fed the kids, and would be at school by 7:00 in the evening. I used to share with this woman in the community childcare. She was a single parent with two kids and we were divorced women. It was hard to be with no husbands because the other women didn't want us around too much because they thought we'd have affairs with their husbands. What these women feared was true in the sense that their husbands were attracted to me. Many of them did favors for me because they thought I was a special person. It wasn't sexual. I had made a decision that taking care of my children was first and that no one was going to take advantage of them ever. I also decided that I was never gonna take no crap from any man. That meant no live-in boyfriends. I didn't want a man around every day and I wasn't gonna get married.

So I used the male friends in the neighborhood and learned what I could from them. They taught me about community activities and I discovered I was a leader.

People looked to me a lot of times for direction. I found that I could verbalize what I wanted to say and very directly. People gravitated towards me for that. The new me was developing right along with the Civil Rights movement. I was feeling the need for there to be changes for women and our roles in society. I didn't want to live the same kind of lifestyle that my mother had lived, which was dominated and controlled by men. I was getting a sense of how I was supposed to have the American dream. That is when I got black pride, too. I got an Afro.

I knew I wasn't going to stay at Federal's all my life. After about three months, I cut down my hours because they put me on afternoons, and I couldn't be away from night school. As it was I was having clashes with my mother over her idea of raising my children and mine. She believed I should try to get their father to help. But I knew that their father didn't care about them. He wasn't paying child support. I felt that no amount of nagging Leo was going to make him change. He hurt the children over and over again by breaking promises. Finally, I stepped in and told the kids that "I promise you if you need something, then I will get it. I won't be able to get what you want, but I will guarantee you, I'll get what you need." Sometimes to carry this out we'd had to go without gas or lights, but never for a long time. Once the gas people came to turn the gas off. I crept to the door and answered in a child's voice that my mother wasn't home. I just wasn't going to let them in to cut us off.

In the sixties, President Johnson's War on Poverty Programs opened up a lot of new employment opportunities for black women. Many benefited by going to school and entering the semiprofessional world. But many of them also privately used the politics of dating as a way to help supplement their incomes and enjoy sexual freedom outside the constraints of marriage. Unlike Sara and Elaine, who remained married, Marilyn and Gwen acquired new freedom and power through their single status.

In 1962, I was called to participate in an experimental nursing program. It was established because of the Federal Manpower Training Act and designed to train head of households so they could become functioning workers. I really didn't want to be a nurse. I remembered my son had seizures so I exaggerated on the application to get in the program. I was just good at talking and lying. It was an opportunity to get an education, to make money to raise my family, and a way I didn't have to spend four or five years in college. I was one of forty-one in the program. It took one year and we got our weekly expenses paid. They taught us theory, we did practicums, and we had two extensive field placements. The nursing placements were designed to teach you to take crap and follow directions to the letter. I felt it was abusive in a sense because if a patient called you a "nigger" they were teaching us to take it. I realized nursing was a thankless job, even though the patients' lives are in your hands.

When I made this decision to go back to school, I set the kids around the table and talked about it. I told them that this was something I wanted to do and that things were gonna have to change. My daughter was gonna have to run the house (she was ten at the time) and everybody was gonna have to rely on themselves. It was very frightening to them. My youngest son, Rayford, stayed with my ex-mother-in-law during the week and I picked him up on the weekends. The year was rough but I passed everything with a 70 percent grade. I knew that in a number of ways I could manipulate the rules or people to suit me and I did. So I think my teachers let me get away with a lot.

I took first a job as a licensed practical nurse at a private hospital. It was a Catholic hospital that specialized in treatment of the elderly. My main area was medical surgical nursing, which meant patient care after surgery. At Mount Carmel there was a lot of racism because your nursing team leaders were white and your supervisors were white and the nuns were white. They all saw you as a paraprofessional, which meant they didn't see you as a "real nurse." They were always challenging your abilities as a black nurse. When I spoke up to defend myself, I was considered aggressive and told I had a personality problem. To them, I was good enough to hold a dying patient's hand while the white RN's [registered nurses] would be screaming for help but I did poor on my performance evaluations because they didn't like my attitude when I didn't let patients shit on me.

I remember once a doctor had given a white patient the ok to give herself a bath. Well, she decided that she wanted me to give her a bath. I reminded her of the doctor's orders. She got very angry. I told her that I had other patients. She started to get herself worked up by breathing real hard, as if she was gonna have a heart attack, so I looked at the woman and said, "If you die, then I'm gonna kill you. And as I can see it, there ain't nothing wrong with you that you can't take care of yourself." She reported me to my supervisor.

I started seriously dating when I finished nursing school in 1964. I was like a sheep being thrown to the wolves so to speak because men were attracted to me. I hadn't dated since I was sixteen. I had to quickly learn at twenty-six what to do. My friend Marsha schooled me. I admired the way she could handle men. She'd say, "Honey, there's no point in going out with them if they can't do nothing for you. If he can't help you or give you any money, he's useless." And that is exactly what I tried to do. But it didn't work out so well. I started dating this friend's brother and I used him. I manipulated him to paint my house and I didn't even like him. Afterwards, when he started talking about sleeping with me and marriage, I told him no. He went totally nuts. He got violent and began to harass me with razors and guns on my way to work. He was right, I used him like a whore. I realized that all my life I had listened to other people about what I needed to do and this time it went real wrong. I decided that I was never gonna ask anybody for something again. If they offered me something, then they would have to have a reason for doing it. I didn't want anybody to expect anything back from me. I adopted a whole different attitude about how to approach men, because I wasn't going to be possessed.

After that, I became very selective about who I dated. I dated men who had to have very high values and agree with my rules. I insisted that they don't tell me or my kids what to do and don't ever come over to my house without being invited. These rules were important because I wanted to learn as much as I could about them but I didn't want anyone to get too close or have any expectations of me. I knew from the beginning I wouldn't date white men. A friend of mine had been dating some big executive of a major department store and he had given her a house, car, money, furs, and whatever. He'd come over on Saturday and asked her to put on a sexy nightgown, but he never asked her for sex. This went on for about six months until one day he brought a Great Dane dog to her house and forced her to have sex with it at gunpoint. So I was leery about anybody setting me up in a household situation and especially white men. I guess I believed that all they wanted from the black women is sex. Instead, I dated a broad spectrum of black and African men, from a psychiatrist on Long Island to a vice president of a recording company to doctors—the gamut of businessmen and just "street-wise" men. The latter taught me a lot.

I developed a simple theory about men: I was to keep control of the relationship by finding out what they needed and feed the need. I recognized that this way I could get anything I wanted from these men without asking. So when men with money chased me and offered me cars and furs, I would refuse them. This was the challenge they needed, and they'd fall at my feet. Some men just needed organization or to feel good about themselves, and I'd support them this way—and the next thing I'd know there wasn't anything they wouldn't do for me. I'd feed their need and I could get them to eat out of my hands. I was in control and I was feeling stronger. Who I slept with, where I went, and who I saw was none of their business. I was always very direct about this, and this floored most men.

If I was gonna have sex with any man, I did it on different grounds. Not in my house. I figured that because I had decided to remain single didn't mean that I had planned not to have sex. And not every man I was having sex with was going to be involved with my children. Especially the married men. One I dated thought I was wild because I used to call his house, ask his wife to put him on the phone, and then go by his house and pick him up. I was arrogant. Then, I was thinking that I was so attractive that nobody could turn me down and that I could do anything I wanted. I didn't care about their feelings—only about me and my kids. And, if the man didn't like it, I'd break the relationship off in a minute. I enjoyed that kind of power and control over men.

My two best women friends were single, strong, and professional women who had as much on the ball as me. If anything happened to them or their children, I was there for them, and vice versa. We were all confident, but they were always having tremendous difficulty in their personal lives because they wanted someone they could lean on—and I didn't. Men were paramount to them. My view was that men were primarily for my pleasure and for me to use or manipulate in the ways that I wanted. I didn't need them to prove my value as a person or prove I was a good sex partner. It was different for them. I guess I felt godlike. I thought I was at a place where no one could penetrate me. I was popular with men, I dabbled with Democratic politics and I had my kids. My two friends feared loneliness. My life was full. I just didn't care enough about a man to get hurt by one.

Like Marilyn, Gwen considered a career change because single parenthood and low wages forced her to. "Superwomanism" burnt her out. Like many women in this juggling mode, she began to have to acknowledge her limitations.

By 1965, I had noticed a real discrepancy in the salary of nurses and housekeepers. My salary wasn't adequate for my family's needs. I went to the nursing station and asked to be transferred to the housekeeping unit because they made more money. They had a union, we didn't. I was refused because they felt if I was a nurse then I had more status. I began to think about other ways of making more money. Singing was the only other thing I could do well.

I met Vicky at the hospital and she, my sister Louise (who had been a schoolteacher for years), and I formed a singing group called the Monets. Eventually, we auditioned for a new recording company in Detroit around the same time Motown had hit the scene big with the Supremes. That is when the three of us recognized that a lot of money could be made in rock and roll. We did not sing stomp-down, dragged-out soul tunes, but we had a special flair because we weren't teenagers. We were women in our thirties. Mature women who wouldn't be taken advantage of. No one asked us about our personal background, so we kept it and our age a secret.

Our first gig was at the famous Detroit Twenty Grand, as a warm-up group for Chuck Jackson and Richard Pryor. A recruiter for a major recording company, named Vernon Anderson, happened to see us perform one night and invited us to New York for an audition. We were shocked and lucky. Besides, there was something very special about this man. I guess it was an instantaneous thing. He would be the one person I was ever in love with in my life.

Love was an emotion that I didn't know how to handle because I had never been in love before. I could emotionally communicate with him. We shared everything. We talked about marriage and living together, but I wasn't willing to uproot my family and move to New York. The long and short of it is that we carried on a long distance of it for seven years during my singing career. I kept this relationship going even when I was opting to marry another fellow. It was the most emotionally draining experience I'd ever had with anyone.

The audition wasn't a success in that the recording company didn't offer us a singing contract because they said we weren't rock and roll enough. But we got an offer from Phillip Sloan Associates and within months we were doing regular paying gigs at night and on weekends. By this time, I had moved into another house with my Uncle Reggie so that I could leave the kids when I had to sing. I was nursing during the day and rehearsing or singing in the evenings. Sometimes my schedule was so tight, I'd get dressed and had to be at the club at 9:00 P.M. and work until 2:00 A.M. We'd go somewhere and have breakfast and before I knew it I had to be at my nursing job by 6:00 A.M. This went on for the first few years of my singing career. Then we got a big break to do a summer show for six weeks at a resort in Northern Michigan. We would have a chance to work with a producer who was Moms Mabley's son. She was a famous black comedian who had been around the world and on the "Ed Sullivan Show." We were a singing act and dubbed as dancing showgirls. We sang popular tunes from Stevie Wonder, the Supremes, and Aretha Franklin. I couldn't bring Sharon and Herbert, but Louise and I brought our youngest sons. The older children would give away our ages.

So I went to my nursing supervisor and told them I'd have to go. I had always been up-front with them about my singing career. They said that they couldn't freeze the job but could terminate me and rehire me at a lower pay. I really appreciated it under the circumstances. The pay for the gig was really low, and most times I had to work as a waitress or in the kitchen to make enough money to send home to the children. This show got us our next big gigs over the next few years and we eventually ended up at the Eden Roc Hotel in Miami

Beach, Florida. This time we met and worked with all kinds of famous people, like Billy Ekstine, Mohammad Ali, Doc Sevrinson, Miles Davis, Arthur Prysock, Sammy Davis, Jr., Jackie Gleason, the Fifth Dimension, and Carol Channing. Ms. Channing was so impressed with us she wanted to know if she could contract us for her show.

During this time, my mother managed the group and Vicky got pregnant. We replaced her with a girl we found called Keller Lee. She was a "street sister" who would curse like a sailor. But she was a good entertainer and did develop the discipline needed to be in the group. We didn't know it until much later that she used drugs off and on and carried a gun up her vagina most times. Keller was totally uninhibited and looked exactly like my sister Louise. She also added soul to our singing repertoire. Up to that time we were primarily supper club singers. The show was such a hit in Miami that we were asked to take it to Europe. The group began to have problems at this point. Louise's husband began to demand that she make a choice between him or singing, and Keller was going off on the drug deep end.

I was also having problems in my own life. Not only did I continue to date Vernon Anderson but there were two other main men in my life. I dated a high-powered man with a strong personality who was the manager of a well-known singing group, who traveled a lot—and Danny. I had known Danny before I was married and I think he was in love with me then. He had divorced, too. We started dating when my singing career was starting, and he was very helpful, both financially and emotionally, to me and the kids. In fact, he was the only man I ever let get involved or have something to say about my children. He was a well-to-do pharmacist, and although I was not in love with him, I felt he took good care of me and was a gentleman. He was just like an old shoe that fit. He made it clear that he needed to have someone to do something for and asked me could I be that someone. I was very frank to share with him that there were two other men in my life and he overlooked it. But over the years, I was drawing closer to Danny because he had a relationship with my children. They adored him. And eventually we decided to get married.

Also, by this time, my daughter was on her way to college. She had visited me in Miami, and the movie stars began to flirt with her. She was young, beautiful, and high-energy. We had told them she was the Monets' younger sister. I just didn't like the way they were coming on to her and got very irritated about the whole thing. Sharon went on to college, but I had begun to wonder if I could handle the new demands success in this business was gonna require of me.

Thoughts crept into my mind about the degenerate sides of show business and the terrible abuse of women. There was not only the drug and homosexual scenes, which Louise and I just ignored, but the politics. Once we did a gig for the Democratic Convention and were invited to a star-studded affair in an affluent Detroit suburb, with champagne flowing everywhere and spiraling staircases in every room. It was the most beautiful home I had ever seen in my life. We were offered a lot of money if we would entertain the Republican party members during the Nixon election. We told them we were not Republicans and they told us we could vote any way we wanted as long as we performed. We refused. I felt it was the principle of the thing. I was beginning to notice the real powers behind this industry were people who wanted to own and control you in order to make you stars. I can remember one man saying he'll do whatever if only we'd sleep with the owners of the company. We weren't willing to do that. Just plain and simple. So the group decided that selling ourselves wasn't worth the money.

The wear and tear of the years of rehearsals and parties, airplanes and new shows, and being with these three men was hard to juggle and began to wear me down. It was taking me more and more away from nursing and from the children. I wasn't sure if my old full-time nursing position was even going to be there for me if I returned. I began to feel that this lifestyle wasn't fun anymore. I remember one time in Miami when all three guys visited in the same week. Vernon came Tuesday and stayed until Thursday morning, Danny came on Friday and stayed until Sunday afternoon, and my other guy flew in that night and stayed until Monday. I was physically tired. I had slept with three different men at three different places for a whole week. I was so tired. I remember telling my sister, "I never want to see another dick as long as I live." I had been singing half the night and battered the other half. It was just too much sex. I had been famous for juggling stuff like this in the past because I didn't want to give them up. I tried to be there for the kids, the two careers—and my health was going all the time. The other nurses felt sorry for me. Sometimes they'd cover for me and I'd sleep my lunch hour in the bathroom toilets with my feet up.

The late sixties brought politics into the homes of many black families. Unlike the other women, Gwen had her hands full struggling with politically radical children and her declining self-confidence as a self-made woman.

The final straw that broke my back came when I began to have problems with the kids. Sharon was in college and involved in black nationalist politics. She was only seventeen and organizing with the Black Panther party. They were patrolling in our community against thieves and white police brutality. I didn't know any way I could help, but I let her use the phone to make the necessary calls to support her cause. I will never forget, the bill was $360 worth of long-distance calls. I never made a big issue over it because that was a commitment I had to make to her.

Herbert was following in her footsteps in high school but in the Communist mode. He started protesting against the government spending for U.S. missiles. He led a schoolwide walkout and was on local TV and being kicked out of school a few days before graduation. He went to Cass Technical High for the brightest young people in Detroit. By the time he was fourteen, he was a student leader and devout Communist. He was one of only a handful of blacks that kept getting arrested by the police. I thought his ideas were a bit more bizarre than my daughter's. I believed he should do what he thought was right and that maybe he needed these groups because I had failed him as a mother. Anyway, I ended up challenging the principal of the school, getting a lawyer, and organizing other parents so our children could get back into the graduation ceremony. I also had to threaten the white Communists who kept putting my son, a young, tall black boy, in the forefront of their political activities. And once again, I was having clashes with my mother, who thought my kids ought not to be doing this protest stuff.

The children had developed some strong personalities and had ideas of their own, and I wasn't holding up to supporting their battles or my own. I began to have pains in my joints and back. I kept going to the doctors to get these things cleared up and they were telling me my career as a nurse was over. And all along the singing group was falling apart. Louise gave in to the pressure and returned to her husband and family and quit the group. Keller disappeared. My mother didn't feel she could continue to manage the group if my sister wasn't involved. I didn't want to continue singing alone, so I came home, frustrated.

Danny and I had finally split over some affair he'd had while I was in Miami, and my children were all most all grown up. I was thirty-eight and I had one more child to parent. Rayford had failed the fourth grade twice and now I felt as he approached high school he needed me. He didn't seem to have the academic ability his sister and brother had, and he wasn't into political stuff. They kept telling me my son wasn't capable of certain things. I didn't like the fact that they said he can't function. I confronted everybody about labeling him and I told Rayford that I only expected that he do the best he could. He did. He ended up All-State and All-American, co-captain of the school basketball team. I looked up and found myself as big as a house.

Gaining a lot of weight only made my health problems and self-confidence worse. I didn't have any fears about growing old, but I was terrified at losing my confidence as a woman. I had always had back problems. Now I had female problems. Fibroid tumors. This led to a number of surgeries and total hysterectomy because they were near to the cancerous stage. They accidentally took out my ovaries and all the hormones that women need to keep them from gaining weight. The doctors prescribed synthetic hormones, but I gained more weight and I was having pain when I had sex. This put me in a panic and I joined a fasting program like the kind Oprah Winfrey did. I lost eighty pounds quickly, but began to put it back on.

Before the surgery I had had continuous problems of extended periods and my body's rejection of birth control methods. I had already had two or three abortions, and no sooner than I had one, I was pregnant again. I didn't go to the back alley, even though abortions were not legal. I had doctor-approved D & C's [dilation and curettage] and paid the price. I was getting concerned about what I was gonna tell my daughter about not doing these things and how to live and not to show up at home with babies.

Although I knew a lot of men, I didn't have anyone close by to share this with because most of them lived out of town. My women friends had all settled into marriages that were threatened by me, a single woman. After twenty years of dating, I wasn't interested in dating a lot of men. I just wanted one person that was sound and stable. I started dating a lawyer who had so many family problems that he couldn't give me what I needed. And this was the first time I recognized that I was not in control. That someday I would be alone and wouldn't have anything to fill this void. I figured there must be something more than this in life. But I never spoke it out to anyone that I was looking for something. I just worked at a diet center, took classes, and when my real father killed another man, I took over the business of getting him off.

So my health got worse under all this pressure. The final blow was when this orthopedic surgeon who was treating my curved spine told me that I was in this shape because of "all the rough screwing" I was doing. This was the only professional explanation for the loss of muscle tone in my vagina and the numerous surgeries to repair it. Not to mention the kidney and colon problems that stemmed from my endless dieting to remain slim while I was singing. It was so bad that I got hooked on laxatives in order to have a bowel movement. I got very indignant and asked him how did he know. But he really frightened me because he went on to say that "by the time you're fifty, you're going to be totally crippled." He told me to give up nursing and wrote me an order for medical leave from work. I was blown away. I knew I loved men and I loved sex, but by the same token, I guess when I look back at my history, there really never was any great fulfillment in the sex act itself. It was the chase.

In 1973 I decided to go back to college. The Detroit 1967 Riot had opened the admissions policy for people like me. I took classes at a community college. This time I was doing well in school. I was finding I was making A's and B's and making a lot of new friendships. But I was still struggling with my overeating, my doctors, and my being alone. Personal appearance became such an issue that I was now afraid to date. I was playing a hiding game. I didn't know this big fat person I had become.

I focused on school and got involved in my younger son's high school sports career. My daughter graduated from college a year later and left home. Herbert got continuously arrested because of his political activities, refused to go to college (because he wanted to organize workers in the plant), and got married, all in the same year. Sharon got married in 1977 and I was a grandmother in 1978.

A whole lot of new feelings came after my grandchildren were born. And a lot of conflicts with my mother about her and my role in their lives. I know I wanted to impact my grandchildren in the special way grandparents can. But I was deep in my own changes. I was finally alone when Rayford graduated from high school in 1982. I had some idea of wanting to get married, but when an old friend called me up one day and begged me to marry him, it scared me to death. I couldn't imagine how anyone could want to be involved with someone who weighed 190 pounds. I ran from him. I was so scared—and I guess there was really heavy searching going on inside of me. I didn't know what to live up to. My daughter sensed I was going through something but I tried to act like it was no big thing.

I decided to give up the house and move downtown into an apartment when Rayford went off to college. Me and a neighbor who were in the same situation, with grown children, moved together. The cost of living was steadily going up so our arrangement was saving me money. I worked as a nurse therapist in a mental health clinic near Belle Isle Park. My job title was nurse therapist.

My work with the mentally ill was challenging and frightening. I saw far too many young black people and middle-aged black women in the system. I recognized that the single mother stuff and children raising themselves were real factors in the psychosocial histories I had to take on my patients. This scared me because a few years earlier my older son, Herbert, had had an emotional breakdown. He had got the schooling and material things, but it wasn't the answer to his problems or mine. Since there was racism and paternalism in the attitudes of mental health workers, I felt, as a black professional I had to give more. I did, and still there was loneliness. There was no one in the house to care for and it was very hard when suddenly you spend twenty years with children and now they are gone. I couldn't stand the quietness. I'd lay there with the silence at night and couldn't wait until tomorrow would hurry up and come so I could at least get back to work. I was sad. I was empty. I didn't have no one to hug. I didn't have anyone I could turn to.

All of these women experienced voids throughout their lives. For Gwen, failed attempts to fill the voids led her into workaholism and depression. Like many women of her generation in the eighties, she was searching for "spiritual food" and thought she would find it through helping others.

My roommate was an evangelist and what she called "saved." I didn't know what it meant. It has something to do with always going to church. I didn't go to church, but I was searching for something. I had tried everything, from politics to spiritual dieting clubs, spas, counseling, and none of these really gave me anything. She watched this black TV minister who preached about the "full gospel." I began to enjoy it. Ideas began to click in the back of my head. I opened up to the idea of going to church with her. Sunday after Sunday we went. Eventually, I just went by myself. I particularly liked this one church with a black female pastor. She taught about the difference between man's doctrines and what God's "word" [the Bible] really says. I could sense by these teachings that something in my spirit was moved. I joined sleep-overs and study groups in which we prayed all night. I enjoyed being ministered to. This is what I learned was the purpose of the church. But I wasn't born again at this point. I only recognized that God was moving me and moving me and preparing me for something different.

In 1983, I got laid off. I got unemployment compensation checks and took the opportunity to travel with my mother. We borrowed a car and went from coast to coast. My daughter and grandchildren had moved out of state. My sons were on both coasts. I wasn't dating and I was in a depressed state. I just couldn't figure things out. I had all the things that society says would make you happy but I wasn't.

Somewhere in there, I returned to my mother's church. I met this young minister who was a bishop of the church and talked to him for just a minute, and when he spoke, there was something different about what he was saying. He said God had called him there to build this church and to bring it back to the "fullness of the word." This impressed me. His ideas scared the church membership and my mother at the time. My memories of my mother's church had been about its rituals and how they had gotten away from practicing the "full gospel." I stored his ideas in my mind and went to California in 1984 to visit my son.

The trip was unplanned and I decided to look up a woman I had gone to high school with. I hadn't seen her for years. Beverly had a peace and calmness in her that I hadn't ever seen. I asked her what it was and she said "Honey, I got saved." I said, "Oh, my god!" She asked me, "Jones" (she called me my last name all my life), "Are you saved?" "I really don't know, I truly don't know," I said. "If you don't know, you're not." Beverly asked me if I wanted to be saved and I said yes. And she led me to Christ. She started to read me some Scriptures and it was like being born again. I had accepted the Lord as my Savior and allowed Christ to live in me. I decided to live my life through the "word."

I knew I looked the same, and even though I was still overweight, I was different. I sensed a whole change in me. I came back to Detroit hungry for the "word" and wanting to stay in the "word." I began to have dreams where visions were shown to me. I didn't know what this meant. The bishop I had met earlier had set up another branch of my mother's church and I started to study with him. I learned how to pray, learned religious philosophy, used God's power of "laying on hands," and began "speaking in tongues." I finally understand God's promise to his people through his "word." I knew that healing belonged to us today, that miracles still do take place, and that he still speaks to us through his servants which are his chosen vessels. That God uses people and was using me. I was being called into the ministry.

My new religion was a surprise to my children and mother. They didn't understand what was going on. I was moving so fast "in the word" that it caused a division between me and my family. I was walking my Christian walk and they were still walking in the law of land. There was a lot of hostility. But I prayed and prayed. God answered them. I was sent to Africa. The Lord spoke to me and another sister named June to go. The money was given to us by a born-again man from India named Rashmesh Bundig. He had said God told him to pay for the tickets. Praise God! I was getting in my spirit that the Lord was beginning to use me to do supernatural healing. I healed the son of one of the leaders of the African country. And I did it in the Lord's name. This was the summer of 1986.

When I returned home, my mother had taken sick. I learned this from my Aunt Rita because my mother was angry with my relationship with the church. I knew she was about to die unless something happened. She was going to die from her stubbornness and bitterness. The Lord speaking to me inside, told me to get to the hospital. He ordered me to give her a message. I did and it was a blessing. I prayed after the doctors left her to die. They had no clue to her illness and her heart had even stopped beating twice. God had told me to tell her that in three days he would raise her up. I saw, as clear as I am looking at you, a figure lift and float from my mother's head. I anointed her body with oil and she finally surrendered and went before the Lord. She asked him to forgive her for what she had done to hurt a lot of people, including me. She told me later that God told her he would add fifteen years to her life. At that point, I knew God was real. I knew why He created me. I had ability only through him. I began to thank God for my children and all the things he kept from happening to me. I thank Him for just returning me to my humble self.

I don't have back problems, arthritis, or any physical problems because God has delivered me from this destruction over my body. And so Jesus Christ is the center of my life. He is my all in all. I don't do anything without first praying about it. Even coming here for this interview, I had to take it before the Father. I had to pray about it and see if he desired me to do it. I am so very glad he wanted me to come, because I wanted to come. Now when I look back at my life, I'm not saying it was bad, I'm saying that it's much better. I think the experiences of the past brought me to the place where I am now. God doesn't want me to be a doormat. I have a lot of work to do as long as Satan uses racism as a tool to divide the people of Christ. I believe this division is gonna continue until Jesus Christ returns and gathers up his people. He's gonna set goals on this earth and he's gonna change it. I believe that is what is gonna happen.

The habit of "dressing, acting, and looking right" for a woman is compounded when the woman is black and poor. Gwen learned early in childhood that her "female guile" was an "admission ticket" for getting the right social position and the right man. And she used it. Using what "God gave her" (a body and mind) in exchange for pieces of the privileges men get, Gwen went as far as dependency could take her. She became an extension of her husband's American Dream, and when that turned into a nightmare she had to leave and make a way out of no way.

Gwen's story is that of a black, working, single parent in a "struggle mode." She decided that she could do whatever a man could do. The outcome was the fine-tuning of her hustling skills. She became an expert in getting things done her way. Managing her own and her children's survival put her in the role of educator, manipulator of her environment and resources, political leader, and dominator of men. Gwen believed in a "no limits" philosophy for herself and her children, to the point of being deluded that she was totally self-sufficient.

The bottom dropped out of her professional "rags to riches" story when growing children, failing health, and fading looks accompanied the end of her singing career. Gwen discovered that in rejecting the conventional approved-of female role altogether, she had cut herself off from a source of companionship greater than her goals for survival. She was faced with a void and loneliness that material things or men could not fulfill. As an aging "war hero," she reunited with that source of strength that she had had in childhood. Now she tells her "war stories" and teaches her philosophy to Sunday School children. Emancipation from just surviving has come to mean the use of her "internal spirit" to reunite all of God's children, and her church has become a rest home for retired warriors. The question remains, however, whether this isn't just another "habit," but an easier one to bear.

CHAPTER 6

A BLACK WOMAN'S
CHORUS LINE

THE interviews were finished. I took them to the transcriber and told her to guard them with her life. She laughed and said she would. One month passed and the nightmares of being yelled at and chased by these women had stopped. I settled down to the comforts of my new house in peaceful Grinnell. I hugged my kids extra tight every night and told them new bedtime stories. "Jameka and Monté," I would say, "do you know what I used to do when I was your age?" They'd look at me with absolute admiration as I told my battle stories. Sometimes I would cry in the middle of the story. I shared my pain and fears that the habit of surviving had been passed on to me. They would cry, too. They would pat me on the back and tell me how much they loved me as I would finish the story sniffling and wiping my nose. The sheer and absolute comfort of having someone to tell these stories to was enough to start the healing. I began to understand why it had been so powerful and transformational for each of these women to have me listen to their stories. They all acted as if they had shed a tremendous burden.

Then it struck me that if I too had the habit of surviving, what had I already taught my daughters, aged ten and eight?

The thought made my stomach knot. Tears filled my eyes. Then I decided to take a risk and ask. I asked them to tell me the survival tactics they had learned. I had warned them not to depend on men or white people, they said, and had urged them to hold on to their heritage, and to grow up and do something for black people. All I could think about was how young they were and how different their lives were from mine or my mother's. Yet I was still passing on the armor and battle plans. By the time they are grown, they, too, will be worn out. Sometimes I feel as if I am already worn out at thirty-five.

*I*t was 11:50 A.M. when we pulled up at the Women's Resource and Action Center. Saturday morning. The campus was bare. I had picked up Elaine at the airport the night before. I fumbled through my purse to find the key to the center. Elaine and I entered and went upstairs. Shortly afterwards, I heard Marilyn mumbling and coming up the stairs. Elaine and I were already sitting in the back room that is used for therapy sessions. There were three couches arranged in a half rectangle under the dim light. The walls were beige, the carpet was brown. The room was furnished with a beanbag chair and one end table, with an almond-colored bedroom clock, Styrofoam cups, and a plain table lamp. The windows were covered with clear, short curtains. The shades, three-quarters of the way down, accentuated the room's smallness.

The women courteously introduced themselves to one another and made themselves comfortable while I fiddled with the tape recorder in the middle of the floor. It was all I could manage, in my nervousness. As if doing the steps to a routine, they sat and crossed their legs and arms back and forth. At noon, I introduced myself again and thanked them for coming. I was annoyed that Sara was late. She had made her own arrangements to be there. Finally, she entered the room, apologized a few times, and sat down, crossing her legs and arms. The picture was complete, the movements almost choreographed.

"Let me say something," I began. "In our earlier interviews, each one of you told me about your mother. Now, what I want you to do today is to talk about your mother, not just as your mother, but as a black woman. Take away all the personal and try to ask yourself, Who was this woman?" We sat in silence for about a minute. Sara began, and the conversation drifted from parental grandmothers to smoking and drinking habits to belief in Christ. Marilyn, apparently reacting to Sara's authoritative, controlled tone, bragged about the ways she would pretend she was crazy to "keep people from fucking with" her. After twenty minutes of this talk, I interrupted.

"Each one, look at your mother. Step back and look at her—a woman over there in that chair. Whatever her name was. And ask yourself who was that person *as a woman?*" This time Elaine started. The conversation wandered from domestic work to manipulating store clerks to the younger generation's sexual mores. Forty minutes passed.

"Let me just say something," I interrupted again, "because you know I'm sitting here in my mid-thirties listening to this stuff and I have all these feelings about what you are talking about. I keep asking you, who was your mother *as a woman,* and all you are telling me is what she did, and now you're all talking about sex. What I'm trying to ask is who was this woman?" There was a long silence.

"It is hard to see her as a woman," Elaine finally snapped.

*T*he habits of survival and denial are serious. Each of these women had openly shared her intimate life with me. But when I got them all together to talk to one another, they were not able to let down their guard and talk with each other as they had talked with me. They could not detach themselves enough from their defenses and ploys to see or talk about their mothers as women. Instead, they told of the glory of their own survival and covered up the pain. I felt myself sink, listening to their black superwomanism. The muscles in my shoulders tensed up, and I asked myself whether it would ever be safe for black women to talk about the full range of their lives.

Sometime later, I talked the situation over with my own mother.

"Hello, Mama, how you been doing?"

"Fine. How is your new book?"

"Not well."

"Why not?"

"Well . . ." and I spent two hours whining and complaining to my own mother about these women. And then I asked her, "Mama, tell me about your mother." She laughed and began to tell me her own story. Four hundred transcribed pages later, my mother's became one of the stories in this book.

It would be unfortunate if the high visibility of women like Maya Angelou, Shirley Chisholm, Angela Davis, Coretta Scott King, Toni Morrison, and Alice Walker, among others, were juxtaposed with the struggles of poor women in the ghettos, as if this contrast encapsulated all the ambiguities related to black women's modern political and economic status. Instead, it would be more fruitful to note the ways in which these women fit well into a larger historical pattern: how the eloquence of their own lives served to reflect those of their unsung grandmothers and sisters; and how they, like other black women of achievement throughout American history, often blended paid and unpaid work in the fields of education, politics, and literature. Moreover, in the stories they wrote about themselves, or about other women, they echoed rhythms characteristic of the experiences of so many black working women: stark, episodic confrontations with prejudice, followed by a reconsecration of the spirit with the help of friends and kin, and a rededication to a cause, or to a life.[1]

The preceding chapters reveal in intimate details not only the variations of the habit of surviving, but also the traps lying in wait for black women. These four distinct biographies, like fiction, memoirs, and poetry by black women writers, document the history of black women in America as the history of survivors. Collectively and individually, these are histories of adaptation to economic exploitation and racial and sexual oppression throughout the life cycle. Such habits, and even what might be called traditions, result from "having nothing to fall back on: not maleness, not whiteness, not ladyhood, not anything. And out of the profound desolation of [her] reality she may very well have invented herself."[2]

In their stories, Marilyn, Sara, Elaine, and Gwen tell how they invented themselves, and the high personal price that each one paid. Their stories are about a legacy passed on from one generation to the next, a prescription to be strong, and an adaptability to and struggle against oppression, both of which operate like a second nature. Their second natures became the core of their self-identities and at times replaced or co-opted an ability or desire to fulfill individual needs.

Their lives reveal the ways black women are socialized into these habits, and how these habits in turn operate on four levels—society, the black community, family, and self—always interacting with the dominant American culture. These women's stories show how habits of survival are like routine dance steps. Black women, dancing together like a chorus line, perform their ritual steps on all four levels. The choreography merits a closer look.

SOCIETAL DANCE

The habit of surviving surfaces in the workplace, in schools, and in the black and women's liberation movements. Each woman I interviewed used her habits as tools in order to meet head on the poverty and double discrimination she encountered.

In the workplace, the habit of surviving necessitates the

abandonment of feminism. Sara described her struggle as a black vice president of a small, predominantly white college in Minnesota. She detailed the lack of respect and recognition she received and how she had been tokenized. Knowing her colleagues saw her as a black token, which was already bad enough, her tactic was to hide her feminism to prevent making matters even worse. She said, "The men on the board don't even think of putting a woman on the committee. So I find myself thinking, wow! But instead of blurting out, I wait, hold back, for the right time, because I am working with these men."

Sara held back her feminist challenges, not because she thought she was not capable of communicating, but because she had been socialized to restrain herself. Black women are socialized to survive by not reacting overtly against racism and sexism. Sara said, "If I were a white man who was my age [50] and who had done what I have done, I'd be ready to go to the White House." Black women internalize societal limitations.

This picture of internalized limitations is compounded by black women's limited employment opportunities. Elaine, for example, believes that she has to be "twice as good to get half as much." Elaine describes the complex situations that arise in the workplace when black men feel threatened, when white women "spend their time trying to pick [Elaine's] brains," and when white men devalue her worth. She described one painful experience of not being hired, which illustrated the complexity of the situation: "One of the responses that came back to me about their hiring a black man instead of me was they did not want this personnel director's wife to have to deal with the fact that I was a very attractive black woman who would be traveling with her husband all over the country." Elaine accepted this rejection as part of the territory that comes with being born black and a woman. Instead of being shocked by the situation and challenging it, she expected it and accepted it—a routine step in the dance. "You have to be aware of what you will have to give up," she says, "and most times be willing to pay a higher price than you wanted to pay."

Marilyn added another perspective on the habit of hiding feminism: "I don't think I hide it, but I don't take every challenge either. Especially around older women, because they think it means I don't like men and that I've got some special loyalty to white women." Contrary to the others, Gwen hid her feminism behind the myth that "black women are already liberated" and the stereotype of the "crazy sister": "I got liberated because I stopped being like other women. I just carried myself like I didn't take no stuff. When the bosses did make jokes about me, I'd have to quickly step in and straighten him out in my own little way. I had to let him know immediately that I meant business."

Unfortunately, racism in the women's movement, as well as sexism in the black community, has further reinforced the habit of hiding feminism. To challenge sexism in the work-place is even more difficult for black women than for white women. A black woman who chooses to speak up threatens bosses and white co-workers, and alienates black men as racial allies. The risk can easily lead to unemployment and is thus too great to take.

Existing problems are, perhaps, made worse by this habit of hiding feminism in the workplace. Believing that white women can be more oppressive than white or black men, most black women give up on a potentially strong alliance and limit or give up completely the fight against sexual discrimination. Mentoring relationships between white women, who have managed to advance their careers, and black women rarely happen. Thus black women tacitly profess that keeping a job is more important than making a point. That the point might matter and eventually lead to greater employment opportunities is completely forgotten. Marilyn said, "I can't stand the way white folks deal with you as a woman one day and then as a black person the next day. I guess I felt it was more impor-tant to get my rights as a black than as a woman, and I need to not have to separate myself into two."

Just as they hide feminism in the workplace, black women put up with racism in academic settings. Black women seek education in order to better themselves and their families for survival purposes. From childhood they hear the threat that if they don't get an education, they'll "end up cleaning some white person's kitchen." But black women enter the educational realm only to encounter the full force of academic racism, which treats blacks in general as cultural deviants and black women, specifically, as invisible. Tracing these challenges, Gwen recounts the reasons she returned to school: "The sixties race riots opened all the doors of admission to college, and that seemed like the time to do something else. But I didn't know what I wanted to do. My attitudes about school had come from when I was a kid. I always did ok, but I never gave it [school] my best."

All of the women I interviewed were raised to seek and did pursue a better education than their mothers had received. Early on, they recognized that higher education was the doorway to privilege. Each used her college diploma to go after better job opportunities and to enhance her self-esteem. While all of these women used school to escape the economic limitations of poverty, Marilyn and Elaine also used it to fill intellectual voids in their lives. Sara and Gwen used school to acquire greater financial independence and social standing. During the educational process, Marilyn, Sara, and Elaine met with direct discrimination, even when they entered college as mature women. Returning to school tested not only their conventional views on upward mobility but also their survival skills.

Marilyn said, "I have taken the women's studies classes and been told in a condescending tone that I can't take racism so seriously. I just learned to keep my mouth shut if I don't want to teach the class." Black women acquire the habit of ignoring racism in academic settings in order to avoid jeopardizing their grades, antagonizing their professors and classmates, and being labeled troublemakers.

Obviously, serious consequences result from this habit of ignoring institutionalized academic racism while soliciting positive feedback for intellectual work and recommendations for future careers. Many black women have begun to question their own honesty and have deep feelings of self-doubt about how this denial destroys their racial identity and their personal integrity. However, they also rationalize this behavior as "how you get over on white people." Even with the increase of black women in the academy, as students and as professors, many black women have responded to racism in educational settings by attempting to remain as invisible as possible. This is literally and figuratively another way of "passing."

The habit of surviving in the black liberation movement meant something quite different. It meant emulating blacks who had been accepted into the American mainstream. Thus, black women, like black men in this area, internalized a paradoxical message: to challenge the system and to seek acceptance within the system. These women's lives were affected by the national heroes of the 1940s and 1950s. Marilyn was influenced by Joe Louis; Sara by Martin Luther King, Jr.; Elaine by Malcolm X; and Gwen by Nat King Cole. These famous men, who served as national role models for young black people and were symbols of dignity to black parents, sought entry into the American mainstream. Ironically, these models were all male, and, of course, such cross-gender identification takes its own toll. Black women who have modeled themselves after black or white men find themselves unable to see and understand sexism as an institutional phenomenon. They tend to view themselves as unique and to use emotional detachment to distance themselves from femaleness and from feminist collective political power. This detachment also prevents them from seeing how sexism limits and even cripples men in the workplace, in family life, and in intimate relations.

Victories in the 1960s, such as the Civil Rights Act and affirmative action legislation, helped women's aspirations for acceptance into the mainstream. Sara said, "We blacks have always focused on integrating into the mainstream. I don't know if it is negative or positive." No blueprint exists for black women entering the mainstream. For Gwen, mainstreaming as a black woman meant "not having to live the kind of lifestyle my mother had lived—looking for, begging for, dependence on a man." Some black women move ahead with academic credentials. Some are propelled by affirmative action programs. Others advance because their talents and ambitions are recognized by a powerful mentor. These so-called advancements, however, challenge Afro-American traditions. Black women (with rare exceptions, such as Barbara Jordan) are expected to reject the privileges of the affirmative action movement and to take a backseat to men's advancement. This is the tradition of "hydraulic advancement" of black male-female relationships; it requires black women to internalize the belief that they must be martyrs for the movement. According to the "hydraulic principle," black men can rise only to the degree that black women are held down.[3]

The vast majority of black women leaders have been limited to activities designed to uplift the community, and their main followers have been other black women and youth. This is "background leadership," a style of work in which black women are trapped into doing all the work and getting no public recognition. One consequence of background leadership is burnout, which blurs the boundaries between personal life and organizational life. Particularly during the Civil Rights movement, black women were treated as if they belonged to the people around them, and many of them felt as though they did. Black women who succumb to these symbolic roles do not actually lead, they sacrifice themselves.[4]

In this sort of "leadership role," black women are expected to put career and community service at the top of their agenda and, as well, to have unlimited internal resources to cope with any problems that might conceivably confront the group. Consequently, people around them are likely to be insensitive to their needs for psychological support, for reassurance, for some relief from the heavy demands on their time and energy. Sara recalled: "When I told my husband that I was tired he asked me, 'Why don't you stop going to meetings? Why don't you stay home and watch TV with me?' " However, when black women have rejected symbolic leadership, people have begun to reject them. Ella Baker's work in the Southern Christian Leadership Conference (SCLC), Kathleen Cleaver's work in the Black Panther party, and Angela Davis's work in political organizing in San Diego in 1967 were criticized by male members as attempts to do a man's job and to take over the organizations. Fear of letting the movement down led black women to become even more involved in saving the people. Davis said of men's attacks on her work that "the irony of their complaint was that much of what I was doing had fallen to me by default."[5]

Black women faced different problems and used different tactics in the women's movement. They perceived racism in the white women's movement, and that shaped another habit of survival—black women's consciousness of themselves *as women* and their notions of sisterhood. Elaine explains her antifeminist mentality: "I don't have white-skin privileges, and it's very important that we don't forget what our foremothers went through to survive. White women ignore that." Gwen, challenging the idea that her female consciousness came from a women's movement, says: "I never liked the traditional woman's role. To rebel against the way things were, I'd burn up my husband's shirts until he finally decided to put them in a laundry."

By ignoring or spurning the women's movement, black women avoid what they believe to be the "nonproductive battle" with white women over whether the movement can and should include their interests. Black women believe, quite simply, that it does not. Marilyn and Elaine cite their efforts to help white feminists transcend their racist socialization. Black women know that white women have benefitted, and continue to benefit, from black female oppression. Elaine explained how black women have come to assume that white women do not really care about them: "I can see that white women are victims, but they are also oppressors. I don't have enough faith and trust in them to believe they are really interested in changing things. I just think they want to change places with their men." Marilyn added, "They are too busy 'celebrating womanhood' and overlooking differences."

Black women's indifference to the women's movement also has its origins in and has been encouraged by the voices of many black feminists. They warn that not only is the women's movement racist, it is primarily a struggle against male domination rather than a movement for social justice.[6]

The problem with ignoring the white women's movement is that black women define their own feminism primarily in terms of a reaction against white women or white women's education. When black women use white women's racism as an excuse and elevate their own strengths and the idea of a "true" legacy of simultaneous struggle against both racial and sexual oppression to mythic status, they can become mired in negativity. At their worst, these arguments descend to the level of a fight about which movement is most "pure"—a holier-than-thou struggle. They can lead women to abandon the cause of feminism altogether. Black women's "feminist bashing" and questioning of their own shift from "margin to center" in the women's movement have raised many philosophical and strategical questions about what a "politically correct feminist movement" is.[7] Black women have moved into the nineties severely divided over these critical issues.

Finally, the societal dance involves black women's constant battle against an assault by the dominant white media and social scientists. Black women develop the habit of doubting their femininity, their very identity as women. During the forties, black female adolescents experienced a crisis of identity because of the double bind of being both black and female—a double bind with ramifications both inside and outside of the black community. Being caught in cultural cross fire in both worlds convinced them that, being female, they should not be in any way like a male, and they should ascribe to white beauty standards. The clash of black and white values makes them seem to be double failures in a black community that values female strength and is divided about black beauty standards. Although this dilemma has improved somewhat since the sixties, most young black women still feel a tremendous ambivalence as they approach their teens.[8] Marilyn remembers how and where this particular dance began for her: "I got an entirely different picture of who I was supposed to be than what I learned at home. At ten, I knew I was beautiful and that being black was ok, but everything outside of home said something entirely different." Elaine puts it another way while remembering what she learned at home about not acting "niggerly": "I had learned that if you were white you were right; if you were light, you were all right; if you were yellow, you were mellow; if you were brown, stick around; and if you were black, step back." Gwen remembers her "be-a-lady training" as compensation for the limited femininity of black women: "I first realized I was a girl when my mother began to demand that I act like a lady. Then I knew I was a certain kind of girl [black] because I didn't have long hair."

As some black women move into the professional and corporate culture, they find themselves isolated from other blacks and women and asked either to submerge or use their femininity to get ahead. One way or another, they are uncomfortable being women. The paradox of acting ladylike and being aggressive and businesslike is compounded for black women by the stereotype of the domineering, loudmouthed, manipulating Sapphire—to which they might be insultingly compared. Black women are often accused of being "Sapphires" when they defend themselves. This dilemma reminded Elaine of still another stereotype she had learned as a child, in regard to black women's attractiveness: "I was just supposed to carry myself in such a way that no white man could assume that he could have his way with me." That is, if you were noticed, there was always the danger of being treated exclusively as a sexual object. Black women have long been believed to be "more highly sexed" than white women—and the myth persists in a somewhat limited form.

The workplace, school, rights movements, and white media stereotypes have forced black women to develop and, finally, hone their habits for surviving. The wonder is that education can take place, careers advance, and some positive sense of self develop when so much energy must be consumed by guardedness and defense strategies. To compound the black woman's dilemma, all these oppressions and the habits that develop in reaction to them operate multidimensionally and interchangeably with institutions within the black community.

BLACK COMMUNITY DANCE

The institutions in the black community primarily function to protect the black family from the assault of white racism. The imposition of white control and white values defines the limits in which and by which the black community can function.[9] The black family and church have been two exceptions to this societal dominance. From them, black women have been ascribed roles in the black community as nurturers and protectors. Their roles as the makers and bearers of culture are designed to ensure the survival of the race and community. Their roles are also designed to operate within the traditions of black male privilege, heterosexism, religion, and political activism. The habits that surface at the level of the black community become the dance of a special stereotype—the "tuff black sister." Marilyn explained, "Everybody expects us to make a way out of nothing. They know we are strong enough to take care of ourselves and because we are self-sufficient, they don't think we need men." Throughout the generations these "sisters" have made a way from no way out of the "self-help" tradition in the black community. Ida B. Wells organized against lynching in the twenties; Mary McLeod Bethune organized against black illiteracy and unemployment in the forties; Ella Baker organized against segregation in the sixties; and Clementine Barfield organized against "crack" and teenage homicide in the eighties and nineties. In all cases, black women have drawn on their socially composed "independence" to create movements. And, oddly enough, as we have seen, few black women see female social activists within the black community as leaders or role models.

The three kinds of black women's independence—economic, sexual, and psychological—originate in the socialization of black women in the family and church. Political socialization of black women results in a habit of survival which takes the form of black women expecting to be leaders—but not too much so—who will "give something back to the community."[10] Sara's habit of surviving falls into the tradition of blending the political dreams of Booker T. Washington and W. E. B. Du Bois and the educational strategies of Frances Harper and Mary McLeod Bethune. Her mother expected her to take a leadership role. Her mother taught her to be prepared to live among white people without becoming a white person. Her mother expected her to be a professional woman whose career would enable her to make a greater contribution to her family and to enhance the well-being of black people. As mothers, black women have felt less ambivalent about working precisely because they have viewed their wage-earner role—like their maternal and community services roles—as normal and even desirable.

The habit of "leadership" carries pronounced internal and external hardships for black women. A black woman is constantly torn between generational expectations and demands of her race and sex.[11] This dilemma is historically linked to the role of the black mammy. Mammies carried out many functions that allowed slavery to operate on a formal and informal level. Gwen described this tradition in contemporary terms. She suggested that the community expects black women to be superwomen at home, and to bridge the gap between our community and white people at work and in the movement. Gwen expressed her fears of not carrying on the traditions of total self-reliance: "If I don't take care of my kids, who will?"

Informal expectations of black women in formal leadership roles (which are contradictory) hit black women with a double whammy. For example, in all-white groups, black women are expected to make white people comfortable with their racism by mediating group tension. In all-black groups, they are expected to make excuses for, ignore, or cajole black men who are sexist. In all-women groups, black women are expected to ensure that the political agenda includes all women's issues and to act out the slave role of "mammy" by protecting racists, sexists, and ethnocentrists from their own realities. Black women do these things at their own emotional expense. These kinds of informal expectations are compounded in the black community, especially in the black church. The black church has been a strong support system for black people's survival in America. It has also functioned to offset the isolation blacks feel in the hegemony of white culture. It has served as a refuge, a source of positive self-affirmation, and a place for political development and practice.[12] Black women expect that they will be rewarded for their roles in church and community service and hope that they can rely on unlimited support from God. Moreover, the church provides not only an emotional resource but also an avenue for spiritual release. The black church has had a primarily political role ever since slavery and on through the Civil Rights movement. In the black community's ongoing resistance against the white racist system, the black church has been the chief socializing agent for creating political leadership.

The black church is also the center of social interaction. As such, it provides benefits that are reflected in the lives of black women as individuals and as family members. Church membership provides children and adults with peer groups. The organizations and activities of the church give black people opportunities for leadership and for the exhibition and development of competencies that are not fostered by the broader society. A woman who is a domestic worker may also be the president of the missionary society. Gwen reminisces about experiencing the church as a forum where her mother could transfer her dream to her children: "My mother wanted to go into show business. But she was scared to do it by herself. She loved the performing arts and we were always around it. So my mother put our talents into the church. She directed plays and fashion shows, and my sisters and I danced and sang with the choir."

But at the same time, black women are socialized by the church to accept a subordinate role to men and to commit themselves to lifelong service to other people. Here, again, is the double bind that black women confront all their lives. Sara and Elaine were both raised with strong religious backgrounds. Sara's mother was active in the church and Elaine's father was a minister. Sara, whose life is full of political obligations to help the people, comments on one side of the socialization picture: "Religion keeps me grounded. I have a strong belief in prayer. When I make my decisions, I do things, I think they are being directed [by God]."

Marilyn notes that joining the church gave her a role outside of being a mother and wife. She describes her experiences of twenty years of religion: "It was in the church that I had a real purpose. I had a mission to be part of an international movement." But she has redefined her spiritualism since she left the traditional church: "I couldn't handle the bullshit intellectual contradictions of the church. They wouldn't let me have a voice in the church. Now my writing gives me a real sense of satisfaction because it is connected with something spiritual and service to my people."

Gwen, on the other hand, rejoins the church after twenty

years and totally relinquishes herself to her new religion and way of life. "I live by the full gospel and I believe in God's promises to his people through his word, the Bible. He's given me the tool to live right here on earth, if I live Christ's way. And I do."

FAMILY DANCE

The family dance involves the steps black women take in terms of marital roles, child-rearing practices, and family networks. All of the women interviewed in this book entered marriage unprepared for their roles as wives. The way each one handled becoming a wife was shaped by the specific habits of surviving that she had learned. Accustomed to private rebellions and self-denial, Marilyn spoke about being "trapped" by the traditional definition of her marital role and the personal repercussions of overtly rebelling against that definition. Often beaten by her husband, she felt unfeminine because she never wanted to have children. After her divorce, she was forced to take care of herself and her family. She entered the work world unskilled and aware that her marital roles had limited her: "I think raising children alone is an impossible situation when you are black. I think you are stuffed into a job. And stuffed in a community where you have very little choice of getting out." Poverty, loneliness, and double discrimination on the job radicalized Marilyn's interpersonal relationships. She was able to choose sex without love, marriage with a younger man, and a lesbian relationship. Gwen offers another alternative to traditional marital roles: "I like my 'big brother' relationships—lovers who become friends. They make it clear that they have no intention of leaving their wives and I make it clear that I don't want to get married again."

Traditional marital roles, though defined by gender, also reflect black families' adaptations to the politics and economics of the fifties. Heightened racial, gender, and class consciousness contributed to the strains on traditional roles. Sara's habits of surviving were attempts to escape these strains through knowing and using important people and attempting to be in control of her own life at all times. She has, in fact, given up traditional female roles and assumed a "male" attitude toward her career. Sara adapted her marital arrangements to fit her goal of climbing the social ladder: "I set a goal that by the time I was fifty I would be president of a black institution. I don't want to think that the fact that I am a married black woman will interfere with staying on target of these goals."

Sara demonstrated how some black women's adaptations can reshape the traditional gender roles and relationships in marriage in such a way as "to have it all"—a husband, family, and career. For example, Sara was an equal partner in the decision making in her marriage. Womanhood, for her, was inextricably bound to her own personal economic and social goals. After twenty-seven years of marriage, children, and grandchildren, Sara comments on her priorities: "If I received an offer to become president of a college now and the goal was still strong enough, I'd make a career change even if the marriage didn't mesh. It would mean I'd have to move beyond the marriage."

Motherhood and marriage can be viewed as habits of survival for black women because black women's patterns of survival have become inseparable from their roles as mothers. As Jacqueline Jones states, "The lesson of the black mother is in each of us."[13] Since slavery, when formal marriages between slaves were forbidden, marriage has been the institution for Afro-American survival. Slave marital arrangements were political weapons against a racist society. Knowing this, slave owners set out to destroy this potential power base by splitting up black families. Regardless of class, black women are doubly socialized to maintain the illusion that motherhood is both mandatory and a privileged duty.

Marriage in the 1950s was also a convenient rite of passage that made sex acceptable or concealed unplanned pregnancies. It fit the habit of remaining a good girl, for young black women. Marrying the best man you could get was the habit formed from living in a racist society that denied blacks entry into college or white collar jobs.

Getting married in the fifties was for black women also a rite of passage to achieve independence and autonomy in patriarchal and demanding extended black families. The women I interviewed wanted freedom from their family's control. Gwen recalls, "I just wanted to be out of that house. But I surely didn't have any real concept of what 'out' meant." Finally, marriage as a habit of survival was a route to acquiring higher status and identity inside and outside the black community. A husband's job or career was vicarious social status for women. "My parents liked him and I guess that was ok. Besides, he had GI benefits and that was an advantage over other men." Girls became "wives" and "mothers"; they attained status roles with names, roles that have always been exalted in the black community.

Although there is no generic black parent-child relationship in the black community, child-rearing practices as habits of survival represent the variety of skills black women acquire as mothers in which they "put their sassiness to good use in defense of their families."[14] Some black women value their role as mother more than their role as wife. Gwen recalls: "I didn't care about our fighting or his extramarital affairs. It was just fine with me as long as he left me and my daughter alone. . . . I wanted my children to know I was involved in the world. I did the Girl Scouts, youth groups in the community and Parent-Teacher Association meetings. I was teaching my children to be leaders." Black women develop culturally based "child-rearing postures, maternal aspirations, and ideas of maternal fulfillment: which serve as the foundations for their motherhood."[15] The idea that black women share completely in the "nameless aching dissatisfaction"[16] that some middle-class white women suffer is appalling to most black women, and particularly to these four women. These women, although they would not relinquish care of their children, did not have the option of devoting themselves exclusively to child-rearing and homemaking. Furthermore, because they accepted the cultural expectation that they *should* work as well as the satisfaction that working gave them, they did not share white women's guilt and anxiety over leaving their children while they worked. Sara said, "I see all black mothers as working women, because we work for our families or someone else."

As mothers, their tasks are to interpret racism for their children and to protect their children against it. Their child-rearing goals focus on building their children's moral character and future position in society as well as teaching models of femininity and masculinity that will allow them to excel socially. The four women I interviewed aspired to provide their children with some of the accoutrements of a black middle-class lifestyle.

From the narratives, a general feature of Afro-American childrearing practice emerges: the adaptation to racism and oppression. Black children learn to adapt to white racism and economic oppression. Black parents teach their children to be prepared to deal with the basic conflict between the dominant white culture and their own culture in order to function in a white and black world.[17] The black family mediates between these two views. This mediation represents a dual socialization pattern required for black children. Gwen and Elaine were adamant about teaching their children about white racism. Gwen taught her children that they were "as good as white people." Elaine taught her children to be distrustful of white people's motives and to avoid racist treatment. They were both concerned about their children having educational opportunities that they had not had, partly in order to be better able to cope with the white world around them.

Most black women subscribe to the American way of life.

Regardless of racism and sexism, they want a piece of the American pie and they internalize dual methods to get it: those from the dominant society and those from the traditions of Afro-American family and community life. Not surprisingly, these methods are sometimes conflicting and contradictory.

For example, the child-rearing strategies of many Afro-American women who work as domestics differ from parent-child relationships in the black family in general. Unlike women in many other occupations, the domestic worker is brought into a close and intimate sphere of human interaction with her employer's family. Black women who work in such situations often use the lens of white families and employers in setting goals for their children. Many times they adopt white child-rearing practices, seeking to help their children advance beyond their own occupational achievements. Gwen remembers her mother's ways: "Everything just had to be so ritualistic . . . whether it was breakfast, lunch, or dinner. I could never remember which side of the plate the fork went on. I hated it."

Using her employer's child or lifestyle as a model, a black domestic worker might imitate the employer's educational, material, and social requirements. Working was a means of attaining her goals; it provided her with the money she needed to be an independent person, and it exposed her and her children to "good" things—values and a style of life that she considered important. Moreover, she would use information from her employer as a guide for confronting problems outside of her own personal experience.

Traditionally, black women have always fostered a positive self-concept, a strong achievement orientation, and a strong motivation for their children. For example, Elaine's child-rearing posture was to be a firm and affectionate parent. She taught her children to watch out for white folks and especially white teachers. Her maternal aspirations, the plans she had for her children's future, as distinct from the plans she had for her own future, suggest that Elaine was adamant in insisting her children be treated fairly in a predominantly white school system. Elaine also praises herself for teaching her children to be independent.

By contrast, Gwen's child-rearing posture was paradoxically both permissive and overprotective. She taught her children to imitate white people and to follow the rules. Gwen's maternal aspirations took her as far as hustling men for money in order to acquire for her children material things that symbolized middle-class success. She based her maternal fulfillment on her children's achievements in school.

Similar to individual parental roles, family networks provide essential information and institutions for the black community. Generally, within Afro-American traditions, black women maintain extended family roles. They adapt child-rearing practices for group survival and carry out the tasks of joint breadwinning and providing emotional support for the family. They provide and exchange childcare and participate in socially responsible activities in the black community.

Marilyn recalls how she got her "fourth son": "He was always hanging around me and my kids. He was a good boy who needed me, so I took him in." Gwen adds, "Granddaddy would buy all the food, my mother went to school and worked, and my Uncle Reggie was always there to play games with us." This system is one of the strongest patterns in the black community. It is supported by and composed of a network of relatives, friends, neighbors, and boyfriends.

This social network helps protect the family's integrity from assault by external forces. Black people of every economic class rely on their kin for help, but participation in the "kin-help insurance policy" has been the only means of survival for poor black people.[18] It has become a viable pattern in our culture and it operates at all economic levels. Although these extended family relationships can be helpful, maintaining them puts a social, as well as psychological, burden on black women. It is they who have the obligation to help poorer members of the family, to care for aging parents, and to take in needy children.

The lives of the four women I interviewed were all shaped by extended family relationships. Through the extended family, they maximized their incomes as poor women. Sara and Gwen both grew up with extended family members, and relied on them for survival. Sara describes the helpfulness of her father's family while her mother sought work in another town. Through transitions in her life, Gwen also counts the numerous times she established collective households with her uncle or female friends. Sara's story details the black tradition of being sent to live with her grandmother. Her father's premature death split her family.

An exploration of how black women are socialized into marital roles, child-rearing practices, and family networks suggests family origins for some of the habits black women create to survive. These habits have become synonymous with the attribute of strength. Moreover, these habits operate in the context of and are supported by the four central institutions that socialize women in the black community: religion, politics, economics and education. Naturally, patterns of domestic life are connected both to styles of child-rearing and uses of family networks. The four women's narratives reveal the contradictions and tensions within these connections.

DANCE OF IDENTITY

The black woman's identity is derived from her accepted roles and statuses within her family, community, and society. Black women have to create their own positive identity in American culture. As poverty and double discrimination limit choices in the larger environment, black women's inner conflicts are likely to be expressed in "self-directed" or "other-directed" hostility, or both. In order for an "individual to feel a positive sense of self, she must come to believe that both she and the society in which she lives place value on her being."[19] Gwen illustrated the pain caused by growing up in a male-centered Afro-American culture: "My mother organized the household's life around elevating my stepfather. This was just very tight for me." Male-centeredness also interfered with female adult relationships. Gwen continues: "It boiled down to the fact that my best friend began to separate herself from me because I wasn't moving into things where we could find husbands." And, "When I finally left my husband, I had to stop putting my feelings into things and look at things as they really were. I had to face the fact that it was a cold world and I was going to have to become like it in order to survive." Gwen's identity was directly affected by the hostility of the society around her. She felt she had to change herself in order to survive. Sara, by contrast, limited her feelings and maintained emotional distance. She managed her alienation: "I don't talk about feelings. To me a person is egotistical when we always focus on their feelings."

The struggle for financial security aggravates the imbalance in black women's lives, and hence in their identities. Thus, I heard, "Not having enough money to live so I can be independent is my biggest fear because I know that this society don't really care about me. As it is, I can't seem to carve out enough time for myself to take care of me." By contrast, Sara, as a professional working wife, always worked, and always had someone else to help with child care and housekeeping. She has, however, paid the personal costs of superwomanism. "I'm compulsively busy. I haven't ever learned how to just relax. When I had the opportunity to stay home for three months I said, 'there's no way.' " Sara's experience as the "black and female talented tenth" has justified community work as a lifestyle for an identity.

Black women have been driven by the aspirations instilled by their families and lured by the widening opportunities of desegregating America. Civil Rights and women's rights movements have opened doors and led to new, and sometimes difficult, personal choices, as well as to identity crises. As a lesbian, Marilyn was forced to face her community differently. "I know niggers find it threatening. I define myself outside of the mother and wife role and I'm not looking for a man. There is real comfort in being a lesbian but none in being seen as antimale. I've got three sons."

Loneliness, myths, and stereotypes about straight and lesbian black women in turn reinforce fears that reinforce the black women's identity crisis, like "a chorus line dance." Gwen comments that "it is really tough out here alone. When I turn to my old coping mechanisms, I end up with tremendous physical and emotional breakdowns and when I think of rushing out and getting married, I ask myself—who to?"

In other words, Gwen recognizes how one's identity must include a relationship. Elaine explained how she copes with the myths and stereotypes associated with being a black woman: "Sometimes I feel like I want to hurry up and finish whatever Miss Ann's [a symbol of the system for black women] got me doing and throw them out the window. I want to go home and sit down and just drink myself some tea."

Black women want to create roles and lifestyles for themselves outside of the warrior mode. Marilyn's reflections on these pressures led her to an attempted suicide:

> I think what kept me grounded was the knowledge that when my children were small, they had to eat. Why, I still have these dreams, I dream about animals with no fur on their backs and who are always hungry. I translate these dreams to be about my children and aging parents. Somebody had to take care of all of these people. I think surviving grounds you. . . . But surviving don't keep you from thinking about what the fuck your thing is that really makes you happy. I know my own mother was happy in the backyard fiddling in the dirt with her tulips. She was totally absorbed in what she was doing. It was her way to be an artist in the little time she had each day for herself.

Marilyn's identification of her mother's need for artistic expression simplifies the yearning each of these women talk about in mid-life. The crises in black women's identities surface as they break the silence of survival to question their suffering and triumphs on the societal, community, family, and personal levels.

CHAPTER 7

MY DANCE

NOW I will try to turn the camera on me. I tell myself that one of the reasons I wrote this book was to find out where and how I fit into the chorus line. But, to be honest, I was not always sure I did. Was I beyond these women, was I better, was I liberated and they not? Have I resisted seeing that I made some of the same choices they made? In making other black women the objects of my scrutiny, have I concealed from myself the fact that I am using them, as society has used them? Do I feel guilty from having learned what they could teach me and for getting the prize they were promised?

Until I finished writing my story, I was unwilling to admit that these women and I were mirrors to each other. I was struggling to tell my story to myself, facing the reality that I, too, would be in print, face to face with my own vulnerable history. I had to acknowledge that I shared with Marilyn, Sara, Elaine, and Gwen some of the same negative habits of survival. I, too, evade, fantasize, project, delude, deny, and avoid trouble. I also transcend, empower, love, and confront injustice. Ultimately I survive.

My story is a story of a black woman who survived by learning to be political—always at every moment, political. Born in the fifties and raised in the sixties, my physical, ideological, and social world was being reshaped by a spiraling number of interlocking social movements that changed society and expanded my hopes and possibilities far beyond my childhood dreams. The seemingly unlimited social opportunities available to me in the seventies—that were not available to Marilyn, Sara, Elaine, and Gwen—propel me beyond the restraints of these women's lives. My story is about black womanhood in an era that offered more freedom to struggle against limited sex-roles, to put off or reject marriage and motherhood, and to benefit from the breakdown of racial barriers and conservative political norms. I could travel, live alone, love, and date whomever I wanted, could work in traditionally male professions, and could immerse myself in myriad cultural and political lifestyles.

My story, then, my habit of surviving, centers around my unshakable belief that I was totally self-reliant and free of restraint. Knowing myself to be "po-li-ti-cal," I legitimized my beliefs and behaviors, no matter how silly, self-destructive, or hurtful they were, with the claim that I would never be trapped by the past because I knew how to manufacture my own freedom. My story is about being "liberated from" some things and about the painful trials and discovery of what I needed to be "liberated to." My habit of surviving was such that it never occurred to me that I might be arrogant before my time.

Unlike the childhoods of the women raised in the forties, sixties children's lives were tempered by the difficulties that accompanied the new freedoms of racial integration. For many young black working-class girls, public turmoil exacerbated domestic breakdown, divorce, and undue family responsibilities. In each of our experiences with busing or housing integration, our early and painful discovery of racism was balanced by our educational and community heroes.

In my childhood innocence, I thought busing meant that I was simply going to a new school. I was only nine years old in 1962. I remember the day our teachers gave pink slips to those of us who were transferring to the new school. I took mine home with pride to my mother. She quickly signed it and I returned it to my teacher. I remember Mama and my grandmother talking about the better education I was going to get. When the fall arrived, Mama had already taken me to get some new school clothes and new school supplies. I was going to be in the fourth grade.

When I got to the bus stop for the first day of school, my girlfriends Ida and Denise and I, and the other kids, were met with cameras. Wow, I thought, a TV camera! The reporter asked us a lot of questions about what we expected from our new school. I smiled at the camera and said that I looked forward to the new swimming pool and younger teachers. We marched onto the bus with no clue of what we were going to receive on the other end. Crack. Bang. And then I realized that busing was about more than a new school.

Angry white faces saying very dirty words met us at the gate. I heard the police sirens when they began to rock the bus and some of the kids began to cry in unison. I hid under my seat, afraid of being hit by rocks. Ida and Denise were crying real loud. I reached over and hugged them tight, wondering how my mother could have thought this was going to be a better education. I was afraid, but I wasn't showing it. Mama had said after she divorced Daddy that showing fear just made things worse. So I thought of ways of keeping quiet until the police came and took charge of the situation. Busing only lasted about nine days in Detroit. We returned to our old school. But the fear of not being able to be safe has lasted a lifetime. I have always been preoccupied with how I was going to make things happen.

We moved back into the house when the divorce was final. I remember Mama having only five dollars in her pocket and the worry on her face when we went to the grocery store. I told my brothers not to ask for anything special. We had already eaten corn flakes every night for dinner for the first two weeks. Things did get better after Mama got a job. But that is when things got worse for me. Mama put me in charge of the house and my brothers when she was gone, and she was always gone working. She gave me orders like "get everybody ready for school in the morning," "make sure everybody gets home ok," and "cook dinner and clean the house before I get home." And she expected me to have it done or I'd get in big trouble. I used to have to knock my brothers upside the head to help me with the housework. I hated these responsibilities. Mama used to say I was her "big helper," but I felt like a slave.

I was always tired, and Miss Buchanan, my homeroom teacher, didn't accept my excuses when I told her I had to do my housework before my homework. I felt all closed in except for the fact that I got to stay up and watch TV one hour later than my brothers. So I thought it was worth it.

I graduated from sixth grade an honor student. In fact, I was the graduation speaker. I remember the poem: "Tomorrow, tomorrow say what shall you bring, golden good fortune that is fit for a king. A song of such joy that the whole world will ring. . . . Tomorrow, tomorrow say what shall you bring." But junior high school was fairly routine except for swimming in eighth period, which left me with my hair wild all over my head, and when Mr. Reems came to the school.

Mr. Reems was the first young, black, male teacher I ever had. I had a crush on him, and so did all the other girls in my class. It wasn't just his looks, but what he said. He was exciting and talked about civics in terms of black folks. I used to wonder what the white kids felt when he started talking about how white people had done us wrong. He helped me understand the incident with my friend Debbie. Debbie had invited me to her birthday party and when I got to her house, her mother slammed the door in my face, after calling me a nigger. Mr. Reems called it ignorance and racism. That was the first time I ever heard that word racism used in a way as to mean it wasn't black folks' fault. I decided to be a teacher because of Mr. Reems. I wanted to take all his classes, but he quit a year later because he decided to go to law school. Then I wanted to be a lawyer. A civil rights lawyer.

We moved to public housing when I graduated from junior high school in 1966. We were the first of several black families to integrate it. I was afraid. I had never really attended a predominantly white school or lived in a white neighborhood. It was a beautiful house even though it was called a housing project. I was embarrassed to tell my old friends where I lived. I used to say I lived near the Southfield Freeway, which meant you lived near white people and attended a good school. My life was filled with Motown records, going to the beauty parlor on Saturdays to get my hair permed, and writing about sexual fantasies in my diary. In school, my interests were biology and history.

I took college preparatory classes in high school. I was the only black to do so. The other black kids had special education classes. I didn't know why. I felt very isolated. One of my high school teachers never called on me or acknowledged I was even there. I just kept quiet. Until the 1967 riot. I remember that summer vividly. The National Guardsmen put up barricades near the freeway because they didn't want blacks in Detroit to riot in the white neighborhoods. And I especially remember some of my white neighbors putting on Ku Klux Klan hoods and riding around in trucks at night yelling "kill the niggers." Mama was very upset. She made us stay in the house and away from windows.

Every night I saw black people making history in the news. I learned about the bombing in Birmingham and I saw the Southern policemen set dogs on the civil rights workers. I heard Dr. Martin Luther King, Jr.'s speeches and I was ecstatic. I was so proud of him. He reminded me of Mr. Reems. Then in 1968 he was assassinated. That was a sad day. The other twelve black students and I walked out of school. I cried and cursed all the way home. I made promises to myself that I would never take shit from white people again. Never. Mama hugged us and we cried together. She said, "I don't know what this world is coming to when they kill a peaceful man."

I decided that being peaceful was not the way to take care of yourself or to make changes. I joined my black classmates in a school protest. Overnight we got afros and we all wore black arm bands to school the next day. We all got kicked out, too. We were suspended for three days. I didn't care. I was trying desperately to transfer to a black high school. Mama wouldn't let me. She told me that I "might as well learn how to deal with white people right now because they ain't gonna go nowhere." So I kept my rage and anger in for the sake of an education my mother thought was so precious. I turned my interest to reading about radical politics, preparing for the SATs, and my sweet sixteen party.

Like Marilyn, Sara, and Elaine, I wanted an education and ascribed to middle-class beliefs and values. The political gains from the Civil Rights movement made college a choice for me while it remained only a dream for these women of the forties—a dream they could have for their children or for themselves in the sixties. In either case, many of us from the forties and sixties entered colleges academically disadvantaged, one way or another, and were drawn into leadership roles in struggles against racism and against the male chauvinism in our lives.

Nineteen sixty-nine was a year of contradictions. I went to college just a few months after my sweet sixteen party. I was a revolutionary debutante with a nine-inch Afro. I was full of militant idealism and my goal was to make the *Michigan Chronicle* black society page. I believed that a college diploma would keep me from being stepped on just because I was a black woman.

I attended a community college thirty miles from Detroit.

It was predominantly white and in a very rich suburb. I was intimidated and made jealous by the white blond hair, the blue eyes, the preppy talking, and the green grass everywhere. It was like another planet. I felt very out of place. I was afraid to speak out about this to my family or peers because they acted as if I had gained a privilege by being there. And I guess I had because all of the blacks were in a special program (created after the 1967 Detroit Riot) that recruited minorities from economically disadvantaged high schools. We were bused in and out every day. Very few of us had our own automobiles.

The first day on campus there was a big Students for a Democratic Society (SDS) rally. SDS was a white leftist organization calling for revolutionary changes in the policies of the institution and the overall society. I had heard of them in high school because a few of my white teachers (those who had not left for the suburbs) were Jewish intellectuals and SDS members. In our economics and English classes, they talked about the history of the oppression of blacks and Jews. Although I did not always agree, I had learned a great deal from my Jewish and black male mentors.

After the keynote speaker's opening remarks, the SDS moderator opened the mike and asked those of us who wanted to speak to come up and say a few words. Impulsively, I went up and attacked their dream of black and white unity for the creation of a noncapitalist society. I demanded that they go home to their own white communities and recruit some "racist rednecks" for social change and that they stay out of black politics because we could organize ourselves. I got a standing ovation. The meeting was dismissed and I was elected part of the campus leadership. I was terrified. I had only acted on a whim and now I was perceived as a full-fledged black militant.

I became known thereafter as a "serious black sister," and nobody messed with me. One unexpected benefit of my elevated status was that I was immediately relieved of sexual pressure from college men who had been pursuing me. Much younger than my peers and socially backward, I had never had a date in high school. While other college women were talking about drugs and parties, interracial dating, sex, and "the pill," I was completely out of my depth. So I read Chairman Mao's and Kwame Nkrumah's little red and black books and learned to quote revolutionary rhetoric to keep back the men while simultaneously terrorizing my white teachers and getting respect from my black peers.

Within months, the draft lottery, the Kent and Jackson State killings, and the call for black studies programs radicalized me in a new and more deeply committed way. I became involved in an antiwar organization. Here was someone who was expected by her family to become a doctor's wife, transformed into a loud, cursing, white-people-hating, black separatist. My family and conservative boyfriend, Greg, were afraid for me. Possibly, I was beginning to frighten myself.

After the first semester, my black high school A average plummeted to a C-minus average. Warned by my white counselor to cut back on the campus activities and tighten up on my grades, I refused. My merit scholarship was dependent on a B average. Torn between the grades and my new identity, I found another solution. I slept less and gave up my social life. It was not too difficult to give up Greg and his conservative politics—we could agree on nothing. Although I wanted to get married someday and have kids (and not necessarily in that order), my education was important to me and so was a career. Greg and my family at this point were mere intrusions on my freedom to find my identity as a woman and as a black. With my B average safely maintained, I transferred to Wayne State University (WSU). The two schools were symbolic of the changes in me—one an all-white campus, where blacks were isolated, this other in the heart of Detroit, where I felt politically involved and close to my people.

Now I was involved in campus and community politics. I worked with a radical black lawyer and a group that had organized to combat police brutality against blacks. In the midst of a mass protest, a small group of us recognized that Detroit needed a black mayor. The next step was the nomination of Coleman Young. I organized his East Side student campaign. In 1971, he became mayor.

On campus, I was part of the Association of Black Students, Association of Black Pre-Med Students, Students Against Apartheid, Students Against the War, and the Student-Faculty Council—and I was even a writer for the campus paper, *South End.* On the weekends, I was involved in community politics, organizing black workers at an auto plant and working with a local community organization called People's Action Group (PAG). It was within PAG that my political consciousness and leadership skills grew. It was also within PAG that I became a feminist.

In 1971, the cultural and political scene for blacks in Detroit included separatist black nationalism, "back to Africa politics," the demand for black community control, and the exposure of institutional racism in white society.

PAG was to implement some of these reforms in the community. It was within this organization that I began to struggle with black sexism, although I did not call it that at the time. In fact, I did not call it anything. Sensing something lacking or amiss in the politics I had adopted for myself, I had begun to turn to white feminist books for some answers, but I only read them at home. I even "sneaked" into a few white feminist lectures, but I never opened my mouth to speak. I feared being attacked by black men (and being seen as a white sympathizer); sexism was "a white women's issue." Surprisingly, I do remember being told by the male PAG members that we had to have a women's caucus to outline the women's position in the struggle for liberation. But it was only when we got together as black women to complain about the men's sexual politics (polygamy, sleeping around, no child support, and the idea of having babies "just for the black nation") that my involvement seemed exciting. I had always kept my distance and worn a mask among black women on these issues. For the first time I began to realize that I was a woman outside the context of being a beauty or sex object—in seventies jargon, an "African queen." Now I realized that as a woman I was a thinker and a leader. Unfortunately, the women in PAG never made public the content of our discussions. Instead we wrote a statement about black revolutionary sisterhood, borrowing from African women's heroic roles in Guinea-Bissau, Ghana, and South Africa. Nevertheless, the feeling of black sisterhood was alive in me for the first time.

The second wave of the American feminist movement was not openly embraced by most black women in the seventies. Unlike Sara and Elaine, who were married and hid their feminism at home and at the workplace (for economic and security reasons), I was unencumbered. Single, free, and armed with my new-found political beliefs, I struggled vehemently against all the guises of sexism and especially against my own male-centeredness. Though radicalized by white feminist and lesbian alliances, I was disillusioned with the limitations of black macho politics. Like Marilyn and Gwen, I turned to my African roots and to Africa in a romantic search for a united people, a "better black man," and a worldwide sisterhood I could identify with.

It was in 1972, when I was nineteen, that two important events changed my life. First, I went to Africa as an exchange student. Three months in West Africa deconstructed my romanticization of Africa, challenged my idea of Afro-American politics based on African models of liberation, and (because I saw how women were treated) ended my silence as a black feminist. I came home talking about being an American revolutionist who wanted to end racism *and* sexism. I resigned from PAG (they reacted to my new political challenges as mere emotionalism) and focused my energy on reading women's literature and history for my remaining three years at WSU. I was now an out-of-the-closet feminist and my new view threw into question my commitment to just black liberation.

Second, I went to a community lecture in which Audre Lorde spoke about her experiences as a black lesbian feminist in the Black Power movement. She made no apologies for black men's sexism or white women's racism. Her words were the music I needed to hear. I was reborn. I began to know and understand feminism in a less academic and more personal way and to grasp what being female-identified meant. I had come from generations of divorced, strong, and female-centered women who knew (as my grandmother used to say) how to "deal with crap."

And Lorde talked about homophobia, a term I had never heard, although I was not totally inexperienced. My sophomore year, my girlfriend Beth and I hitched a ride to a hippie commune in California, where one night I went to the kitchen and found two women kissing. One of the women (after noticing my gaze and shock) told me not to be afraid. Loving women, she said, was an act of rebellion against male domination. I knew what male supremacy was, so she got no argument from me. But I did not understand for years the relationships among gay issues, racism, and women's oppression. The rest of the summer, Beth and I did not bring any of our men to the commune; I read the *Well of Loneliness* and looked for lesbians in women's and my own history. I realized I had known lesbians all my life. The one that I loved was my grandmother.

The more I read about black women's history, about sisterhood and oppression, the greater became my resistance to those who called me traitor. I began to use words like "patriarchy" and "emancipation" and "double oppression" to describe black womanhood. And I was beginning to be isolated by some of my women friends for using this white women's language. I was rejected for giving up the quest for a "good middle-class black man" and for being sympathetic to lesbians. My black male mentors simply dismissed the whole issue with a simple word: "faggots."

Just before I graduated from WSU, I started living with a political brother. For some reason I thought he would be an improvement over my previous boyfriend, but he did not work, did not attend school, relied on his mother's hospitality for food and a place to stay (until we got together and then *I* took care of him), and was on welfare (which he called "hustling the white man" while in the same breath calling for "black community control"). At first, I ignored the fact that he did not have a job; even worse I felt guilty and shallow for wanting an education and wanting a career. He wanted me to have babies, so I hid my birth control from him and pretended to cry each month when my period came. Eventually he got a second "wife" and I exited from the picture. I dismissed this whole affair as a disagreement over polygamy.

I graduated from WSU in 1974 and went to West Africa for the second time. During the summer I fell in love unexpectedly. Actually, I fell in awe. I liked the way I felt with Ahmed. He was very political, I told myself, because he believed in women's emancipation in Africa and around the world. Somehow I fantasized that life as the wife of an African man would be better than life with the black American brothers who kept telling me I was "just too much" for them. I rationalized this to mean they were weak men whose confidence had been destroyed by the legacy of slavery and American racism.

I had decided to go with Ahmed to East Africa (when he finished his doctorate) when my mother, quite unexpectedly, sent me a letter saying I had received a full scholarship to graduate school. Deciding that we both should complete our degrees, Ahmed and I agreed that I would return to Africa after we both graduated. So I enrolled in a master's degree program at the University of Detroit. Within a few months my advisor, who was a Catholic priest, told me that I was a troublemaker in the classroom because of the questions I raised.

In fear that he might flunk me, I went to the chairwoman of the sociology department. She listened but felt that I was overreacting. I challenged her. She said "she was not going to lose her job over me." I was devastated.

I remember calling my mother, telling her I was going to quit school. I packed up all my belongings and waited for her to come. The next morning I called her and she chastised me for not recognizing that I was a threat to everybody in the system, black and white, men and women. I listened and I acted. I took twelve graduate hours each semester, took my exams, and wrote my master's thesis in one year. I pulled straight A's. I got my degree and I helped kick his ass. My advisor was fired the year after I left and I was hired as the youngest faculty member at a community college in Detroit. I taught sociology and I taught black people. I was proud. I was also wounded. Then came Ahmed's letter. I was devastated. He had decided to quit school and return home to join a guerrilla movement. Ahmed had told me in the beginning of the relationship that his political commitment to his people had to come first. The fantasy of being with him, in Africa, that had gotten me through graduate school was shattered.

Historically, black women have used the teaching profession to exercise their political leadership. Like Sara and Elaine, I acquired another degree to ensure my personal economic autonomy and security.

I was twenty-two and a college professor. I was very frightened. The majority of the students were women who were older and who worked. I remember once having a night class of all white police officers who were required to complete this course on race relations. Each class they would challenge the validity of the assignments. Something clicked in my head and I told them, "I have two college degrees, and if you keep up with these goddamn games, I have the power to fail all of you." I was shocked at myself. I had never been that assertive.

We ended up having the best class I had ever taught. I realized again that teaching was my calling and that this job was a contribution to my people.

The rise of the Black Power and Black Arts movements in the seventies challenged the internalized anglo beauty standards of all black women. Black women of all ages reacted to this cultural upheaval, but we did not all react alike. Sara, Elaine, Gwen, and I got Afros, but these symbols of pride did not resolve deeper black female issues of weight, skin color prejudices, and health problems due to stress. The decline of the black movement in the seventies sparked a number of disenchantments. So many of us, including Elaine, Sara, and I, were burnt out in our struggle against sexism in white and black educational systems. By the eighties, I was acting out a lot of my confusion about being female and being black and in search of new personal and political answers to the perplexity in my life. We women of the forties and sixties were searching, and our searches took us to places outside of the United States, to other marriages and lesbian relationships, to more school, and to women's support groups.

The Black Power movement had died by 1976 and a number of my friends were doing what I called "Tomming." They had gotten high-powered and high-pay work in the white corporate world and had turned their backs on or forgotten all about the black community. One of my best friends advised me to quit teaching in all-black schools and implied that I needed to grow up and give up the sixties rhetoric. I felt very confused about seventies politics. I was turned off and intimidated by some professional black women whose political goals had become to get rich men and prestigious jobs. I felt I was making a political choice by not living in a suburb or driving a Volvo. I lived in a basement apartment and bought a cheap car to get me back and forth to work. I saw my lifestyle and job as a continuation of my involvement in the movement.

Teaching at a predominantly inner-city community college was very trying. A large number of the students were very ill-prepared to do college work and some of the staff were unsupportive. I'd often have to fight just to get mimeograph paper and to have my photocopying done. Some of the students often hustled me to get out of doing the course work by using "sister love and you know how the white man is on my back" speeches. I was exhausted most of the time teaching just three days a week. I took up running to relieve some of the stress.

I was also getting depressed from the dating scene. I was dating a lot of men who were crazy about me, but I was not interested in making a commitment. Commitment terrified me. I felt I was too young to marry. I felt I was too inexperienced with life to settle down. And the idea of settling down seemed so dull. I wanted to accomplish more in the way of travel and involvements in political organizations. So I kept men at a distance because I recognized that relationships took up a lot of time. And in most cases a date meant a show, dinner, and a one-night stand. I ended up using men in the way they used me—for sex and companionship when I wanted it.

While I was busy with my community activities, I got involved in the black arts movement in Detroit. I was working with members of a cultural house, a theater group, and Project BAIT, a black radio program. I began to dress in what was called an Afro-chic style, mixing professional clothes with African accessories. I felt because I was a professional, I had to be thin, and because I was black, I had to embrace an African orientation to beauty. I can remember the peace I felt going to Africa when I was fat. It was the first time in my life I felt feminine (without having to put on makeup or trying to act like a "white girl"). West Africans valued large dark women.

The combination of having a lot of money, no responsibilities, and very little confidence in myself as a female sent me to the extremes of Afro-chic on weekdays and being a generic nonwoman on the weekend. I also was in fear that I had to identify publicly with some kind of popular female image (black or white), so that no one would think I was a lesbian. I recognized I had privileges as a "straight" woman in a society that was antiblack, where to be a lesbian was to be in triple jeopardy. I traveled constantly, hoping to find a place in the nonwhite world where I could be comfortable, beautiful, and feel good about myself.

In the next few years I traveled within the states and to Europe, Asia, and Africa several times. I was chasing some illusive need to be doing something important with important people. I used my money as a form of "I can do anything I want" card. I was trying to nurture the awful tension I felt being young and black and beautiful and having a good job— and having all this outside of an organized black movement. I felt guilty. I felt privileged. I felt scared to do anything different.

This was about the time I had a blind date in the Bahamas (of all places) with a doctor from Pakistan. When we got back to the States we were inseparable. Rangul and I moved in together within a month. He was rich and lonely and I was driven and confused. I used to take him to nuclear disarmament and China–United States Friendship meetings, and he would take me to boring dinner parties in the suburbs with his snobbish Indian friends. He was impressed with my rage and I was impressed by the way he challenged his racist friends. Once we went to an afternoon tea where I was the only black woman and someone mistook me for the maid. Rangul went into a rage. That night, Rangul and I drank wine and talked about racism while in my mind I knew we ourselves were playing race games. I was his exotic experience. He was my interracial dating partner, and I was flaunting that fact. When he did eventually ask me to marry him, I realized I could date and sleep nonblack, but I did not want to marry nonblack.

After Rangul, I hung out with my friends at the latest

Detroit hot singles spot. When I was there, I could feel myself withdrawing and when I was home alone on the weekends, I ached to be with people. Other times, my mother would call needing money to pay some debt she had acquired or eager for us to go to lunch together. She had always been a compulsive spender and I had always felt responsible for her. We had grown up like peers. Sometimes she was the mother and sometimes she was the sister. When we went to bars, people often thought she looked younger than I did. We would smile and I would feel awkward and not particularly pleased. I did not always enjoy the blurred boundaries between our mother and daughter identities.

Pressured by a definition of black womanhood that includes marriage, motherhood, and the tradition of "fixing up men," each of us in different ways suffered blows to our self-esteem. The blurred boundaries between our family and female identities did not fulfill the gaps created by our unconditional giving. For Marilyn, Gwen, and I tried to cover up our ugly reality with more shortlived geographical cures. Alternatively, Sara and Elaine, now married to men they considered beyond "fixing," rationalized that job promotions would answer their psychic hungers. Several of us sought to suppress our personal pains by hiding in our parental roles, diving into more community work, or turning to God.

Six months after my great-grandfather pronounced at Thanksgiving dinner that I could get college degrees and go around the world but I could not "get a husband," I went out and got me one. I was twenty-four and Butch had been an old militant high school friend. I met him in a shopping mall one Saturday afternoon. We had nothing in common except sex, old militant high school stories, and the fact that I knew I could dominate him. We had a large African wedding and I was three months pregnant. It was 1977.

Motherhood was a lovely thought to me, and, good scholar

that I was, I started reading Dr. Spock's *Baby and Child Care* almost immediately after the pregnancy test. Some radical I was—I had decided not to have the baby alone because I feared the stigma of illegitimacy and the difficulty of being a single parent. I knew I was in too deep to get out. I anchored myself in the idea that I was going to be a mother and that the child's well-being was of paramount importance. Naturally, my family was relieved that I was at last settling down. I started playing house. We painted. We put up shelves. We bought things on credit. We never talked. Butch got high and I did community improvement work. And I focused on being a mother because I knew it was something I could control.

Suddenly, one morning, just a few days after our daughter was born, my husband said he was too politically black to wear a white shirt and a tie at work. I was on maternity leave and we had no income. I lost all respect for him because he left his job and then refused even to help with household chores. I accused him of not being a man. Our battles over his chauvinism became serious. In revenge, I withheld my affection and sex. Any sense of power I derived from this tactic shriveled when he began hanging out with the "boys," leaving me alone with the bill collectors and the baby. When our first child was a year old, I decided to file for divorce. Although I was economically independent, I still feared being a single black mother. To make matters worse, I discovered during the separation that I was pregnant. Again, I surprised myself. I fancied myself "liberated," but my ambivalence over the abortion left me very depressed. In rapid succession, I entered therapy, got pregnant again, gave birth to another child, had my tubes tied, and again planned to go through with the divorce.

Although I was obsessed with body image after the abortion, continuing to see myself as an object, there was some consolation at the time in my relationship with other women; we formed a kind of Saturday night "niggers ain't shit" club. We thought we were not like our mothers, but just like them we bitched about men's failings as fathers, companions, and financial helpmates. The difference was that, unlike our mothers, we all had high-paying jobs and money in the bank, that is, some measure of at least financial security. With the divorce final, I formed a new triangle of power. My life was now about me and the kids and my work.

After the divorce in 1982, when I was twenty-nine, I had my kids, my job, my political groups, and my women friends, and I thought I was happy, happiness being defined as not having to put up with shit from a man. In reality, I was tired, overextended, and battling everyone and everything—burnt out without feeling or noticing it. A professional friend of mine moved in in order to save money. She shared the bills and helped with child care when I attended evening meetings. I was, in fact, back in my public service mode, working in my local block club and churches to reverse neighborhood problems (drugs, violence, decaying housing). I wasn't willing to give anything up and I wasn't going to slow down the pace of my life. I was in the warrior mode in full swing. As I saw it, everything I did was important, and I just couldn't stop.

The dating scene in Detroit was a nightmare, and the new AIDS scare made it even worse. Leaving my kids temporarily with their grandparents, I escaped to Egypt and Libya. For the first time in years, I slowed down and I had a chance to think, free of the pressures of family and racial expectations or judgment from my political peers or my women friends. And for the first time I asked myself the really difficult questions about what I wanted from life. Alone one afternoon, I visited the Roman ruins of Sabratha in Libya, and I was hypnotized by the blue Mediterranean water and swishing sounds on the rock. As if I had stepped outside myself, I noticed it was noon, with the sun beating directly overhead, and I began to remove my clothes to combat the heat. I felt a warm tear course down my cheek and heard a low hum come from my throat, like a child crying for her mother. I was noticing me grab myself in a hug and I rocked myself like a child. As I watched the wind brushing sand onto my toes, I saw a large seashell being uncovered in front of me. I picked it up and put it to my ear. And I swear I heard it speak.

Many black women trapped in the cultural myth of superwomanhood have found themselves forced by health problems to admit their own vulnerability. Each of us denied that our political and personal lives were unbalanced. Like Marilyn, Sara, Gwen, and Elaine, I took educational detours to evade the pain, deluding myself that I could find some time for reflection, change of direction, and new definitions. Each of us, in different ways, had to feed her internal hunger in order to face her fears. Conquering our fears through making spiritual connections made it possible for us to finally be ok with ourselves.

I returned to Detroit and decided to give up "dealing to be dealing," or the fighting I was doing without a clear rest period. The only way I knew to get a rest, I thought, was to return to school. I was thirty and I wanted to get a Ph.D. That is, at least, what I told my family when I went off to the University of Iowa. During an earlier campus visit, I had walked down the halls, and they had spoken to me, like the shell in Libya. In 1983, I left my Detroit roots, family, and comrades and took off for the land of corn and pigs. I remember driving over the state line at 4:00 A.M. and the sign reading "Welcome to Iowa, A Place to Grow," and those warm Libyan tears returned. I knew I had been fighting to go home for the first time to a place in me I had missed and that had no name. I looked over at my sleeping children in the front seat of the U-Haul truck and wondered why in heaven they picked me as their mother. I stopped the truck when my tears blinded me. I was overwhelmed. Iowa pig farms are beautiful at dawn.

Graduate school for the second time and in an all-white community was very difficult. I felt more displaced than ever because I was older and I was a mother. It was not difficult to enjoy the isolation and anonymity, however; I felt like a child again. I took the time to go to parks and skate and listen to music and play. I was unwinding. I could walk around at night without looking over my shoulder or being harassed and I really loved the absence of the traffic jams of the Motor City. I remember how paranoid I was, coming to Iowa. Strangers in the street used to say hello and I'd be thinking, "What the fuck do they want?"

After about six months in Iowa, I joined a theater group, a women's returning-to-school support group, and met Douglas. He was an administrator at the university. I had not gotten along well with him on my initial campus visit so I avoided him in social situations with other blacks. I thought he was a stiff black bureaucrat. When I joined a theater collective, I found that he was involved in it as well. What a change in his personality when he was doing theater. We had long, long, talks about our families and about our previous pains and about our dreams. He told me about how he worked on his male chauvinism and I told him how I gave up the "niggers ain't shit" club. Coffee breaks led to lunches and lunches to garage sales and Saturday afternoon car washes, and then he and I decided after several months to date exclusively. We had not been intimate yet because we had both come from previous marriages that were nightmares. We just took it slow.

I began to go to the university's Women's Resource and Action Center's brown bag lunch series from week to week, and then the evening programs. I was learning a lot about parenting, feminist psychology, women in the global factory, women's coalitions, and sexuality. A new circle of exciting and political women entered my life. Lunches between class or swimming dates were full of feminist politics. I took my first women's studies course and decided that I would write my dissertation on black women in America. I felt myself becoming centered and recognized why I had been so drained in my community work in Detroit. I had lost touch with women's energies and issues.

I was thrown off that new emotional center as I began to

challenge academic racism, which rewarded whites (especially white women) for writing outside their cultural context but trivialized and (in some cases) demoted blacks for writing about their own culture. Because of these standards, I felt I was in a no-win situation, being a black and a woman. It was too politically dangerous to overtly challenge my professors. After completing the Ph.D. comprehensives, I lost my motivation to put so much of myself into school. Instead, I began taking trips to the mall, shopping, or stayed on the phone all day. I also began overeating. I became obsessed with food. This began to frighten me. I began to buy large amounts of food. I began to sneak food and, of course, I gained twenty pounds. I lost twenty pounds. I entered counseling for bulimia, because I was turning my anger inwards. Just when I was close to having it all—the politics, the Ph.D., the happy home, and a good relationship—I could not understand why I was eating so destructively.

I thought of going back home, but I was on an academic leave from my job for three years and I had sold my house. Bulimia structured my days and nights. Kids to school. Class. Binge. Purge. Study. Pick up kids. Dinner. Binge. Purge. Sleep. The only relief from this new anxiety was the diet club I joined. I dieted and read diet books. Douglas was completely oblivious to all this. Actually, he never made a single comment about my weight losses and gains. I did not like his disinterest in my weight at all. Asking him once, "Why?" He told me that he did not care what I weighed. He cared about me. I thought he was a creature from another planet and kept on eating another year. By this time, I felt controlled by school and in desperate need to have something in my life be "perfect." The battle to control my eating, my body, and my diet was all I thought I could manage to win. In the back of my mind, I was not sure people like me were allowed to be happy. I needed something to be right in my life.

As a distraction to writing my dissertation, I reacted immediately to a school board letter. Before completing my comprehensives, I had organized a group of parents to protest the Iowa City School Board changing black history month to ground hog month. The TV people came to the meetings and I yelled and demanded that they change it back. My involvement in this issue drew me into community politics that ultimately developed a black school board advisory committee and elected a black school board member. I won a community human rights award for these activities and I ended up in the emergency room with chest pains at four in the morning. Hearing my children crying and asking me if I was going to die, I realized that I was "dealing" again. I was feeling like a victim. I was in pain. My women's group was no comfort because the white women kept saying how strong I was and the black women kept saying how much more we have to do. I just wanted to run away. Douglas provided me with an excuse.

In 1986, we moved to Grinnell (a college town of eight thousand, a few of whom are blacks), and three months later were married. I had stalled him long enough. I knew my children and I loved this man, but I was terrified of making a commitment. Numb through the ceremony, the honeymoon, and the first year, I woke up mornings and did not know where I was. The unreality was reinforced when I went downtown, feeling like I was on a stage, performing the black woman role for native Iowans. People would approach me and ask if they had seen me somewhere I had not been—all (the few) black women in town were interchangeable as far as they were concerned. I buried myself in my house and in my work.

The children and I drove to Iowa City every weekend for some black culture and to see my women friends. Douglas was happily preoccupied with his work and rarely joined us. I felt a persistent quiet and confusion, as if my private happiness absolved me of my need to be political. That is when I turned seriously to creative writing. Recognizing that I was stuck— although in constant movement, I was going nowhere—I saw that it might be possible to rejuvenate myself without fleeing to foreign places. I needed to work on my art at home, where I lived, and not only my writing but also my politics, parenting, love relationship, and my work for my communities (black and women) and country. And I had to keep it in the forefront of my consciousness that I did not have to physically or emotionally sacrifice myself at every turn.

I began to express my new identity through writing about myself, my pain, my contradictions, my culture. I began to heal. The bottom line was that I was seeing that my own survival had not been liberation. I was learning that liberation is about having choices. I completed a book and my dissertation, and graduated in 1988. We bought an old red house and we have turned it into a home. I recognized that I did not know *how* to measure liberation for me. The challenge of allowing myself to be happy is politics too, and in this society, it is also a privilege. For now, I am content to have gotten back to listening to the voice in the seashell.

CONCLUSION

THE lessons to be drawn from the habits of surviving are like the chores Mama passed on to me each year as I got older. First, I had to wash the dishes and then later make dinner. Each new chore built my self-worth and skills, and at the same time, filled, first the tiny pockets on my school dresses, and still the purse I now carry, full of all the hopes and needs of my own family. Yet, today my "pocketbook" is more full of the crisis of black womanhood in America than it is of my mother's gifts. The power of black women to make culture, to keep a people alive, is crumbling. The New Left and black macho politics have failed, Reagan and now Bush have slashed welfare programs, and middle-class black and white feminist movements have withered—and all this has robbed my purse of what I treasured from my mama.

I am not poor, but the majority of my twelve million sisters are. No one respects our cultural power anymore. Our habits enact themselves over bare plates, and our power to influence the purpose and direction of our culture is largely immobilized. What do we do with our open arms when no one wants to fill them, especially when we are ourselves unable to resist the imperialism that destroys us from within? The present crisis of black women's identities "manifests itself as genocide, fratricide, homicide, drug addiction and suicide."[1] And we few, privileged by education and burnt out from community service, more and more manifest the crisis by abdicating our responsibility for others and ourselves. The habit of surviving that we mistakenly thought made us whole makes no sense to us now. We are confused by the comfortable yet somehow irresponsible and contradictory lives we were told to live. There is a spiritual and human mandate to try to protect the planet, but we feel alienated from it. It seems impossible not to be overwhelmed by the enormity of the problems that confront us and by all the conflicting "isms." We are identifying and rejecting our male-centered values. Sometimes we yell loudly in protest—yet too often we muffle those cries.

These muffled protests, Mama's and mine, and now my two daughters'—haunt me. I have collected them like a language that is becoming extinct. I have copied down the alphabet, listed the vocabulary, pieced out the grammar. It remains then only to make of these the sentences that will speak our new future.

We heard the front door open. It was Mama. We had not washed the dishes. She entered the kitchen, took a look at the sink, and went off. Mama flung dishes from one side of the kitchen to the other. My brothers and I ducked under the table. She was panting and screaming and swinging her arms like a mad woman. When the sound of broken dishes stopped, we peeked out and saw our mother curled up like a baby.

"I'm sorry, Ms. Scott, but we can't find anything wrong on your EKG. Your blood and lungs are normal. Maybe you're just tired. Have you been under any stress recently?" As the doctor awaited my answer, I turned my head to the side of the emergency room table to glance a few feet past the door to see my two children in bright pink and blue bunny pajamas with webbed feet, crying on my husband's shoulders. He sat looking

bewildered. Tears ran down his face as he lied, "Mommy will be ok. She is just a little tired this time. We'll take her back and make her rest." My own tears blurred the arm of the clock which read 4:28 A.M. Just twenty-four hours ago, I was receiving the Iowa City Human Rights award, saying, "Thank you, it was really nothing."

I will never forget seeing my mother break down that day. I worry that my daughters will never be free of their memory of my tears. Studying habits of surviving has challenged me to question whether my mother could have been as invincible as she seemed. It has also challenged me to answer the questions my daughters now put to me. The complex web of oppression my mother and I shared still has the potential to capture my daughters. Unlike me, however, they seem to know that this need not be. At the least, they seem to know that they have the right to ask me "how not to be caught!"

I do not know why my daughters were able to break ranks and dare to ask, "Mommy, how do we *not* be caught?" I was quite surprised when they did. At first, I felt threatened. Unconsciously, I had assumed that my life—with its highs and lows, its forever fast-forward movement, its precious tried-and-true warrior legacy—was example enough. I had gone along without much thought, somewhat automatically teaching them what my mother had taught me. Clearly, with *much* thought, they were asking me for something different. Somehow they had stepped out of the chorus line to make up a new dance step of their own, and I was unprepared for this.

My second thought was to be worried and angered that by asking the question they were saying they wanted to abandon the black woman's legacy and turn their backs on our race. (I have seen this behavior among the youth of the post–civil rights era.) Finally, I realized that far from turning away from our traditions, they were trying to improve upon them—by going beyond mere survival. I realized that I had tried to forestall this kind of question, to pass the legacy on as I had received it, as if it were the only dance that black women should or could do. But there it was: the question that neither my mother nor I had ever asked ourselves. Once I realized the full significance of the question, I could not dismiss it. I had to face it, and facing the question meant facing pain: the pain of consciously recognizing my own habits of survival for what they are, the pain of seeing myself through my children's eyes, the pain of seeing them dance a new dance, away from me and the chorus line I still feel linked to. But on the other side of the pain is hope.

The question blows my mind. Over and over I ask it again to myself. It makes me feel tense, upside down. I know I do not have an answer, but I do have a clue. It lies in knowing that black women's culture still places us in a no-win situation because when we try to lead full personal lives, we experience guilt for turning our backs on our community. Conversely, if we devote ourselves to the myriad needs of that community, we give up our personal lives.

In my life, these forces have operated something like a pendulum. I swing from one extreme to the other, my private life and personal sanity slowly fading in and out of focus. Just as slowly and relentlessly, the other women pay the costs in their own ways. I know, because I know that we warrior black women cannot stand to be too many in a room together. We remind each other of what we do not show. We cannot publicly express—we silently accept—the double bind of our lives, and we know that our final liberation from this cultural contradiction is either false life or real death. I know this sounds extreme—but it cannot be an accident that we cry so loudly, "Lordy, Jesus . . . carry me home." We realize that we may speak only in church or on our deathbeds, because, finally, we black women do not control the context of our lives. We react to the world. We do not control it. In our silences, we are tragically doomed to create "habits of survival," always to adapt ourselves to the temporal and changing guises of ongoing racial, sexual, and class oppression.

The power of my daughters' question is another clue to its answer. That they can ask means that we can answer. The strategy for winning is in that recognition, and in the teaching, of ourselves, to risk dialogue. I opened up dialogue between myself and my girls. In order to do that, I had to dialogue with my own sisters, and in order to do that, I had to dialogue with my mother and my grandmother. Only then could I make a language from Marilyn's, Sara's, Elaine's, Gwen's, my grandmother's, my mother's, my own, and my daughter's words. There are no guarantees that this strategy for winning through sharing our dialogues will succeed. But the lack of change so far suggests that opportunities have been missed in each generation because mothers and daughters have not talked. It suggests that we should at least try a new pathway. To do otherwise—to think that we do one another favors by not reminding each other of how difficult it has been to be black and women and daughters and mothers—is to opt for mere survival over liberation.

When did it get to feel like all we were doing as black women was passing pain from woman to woman, from woman to child? Did it happen when habits became easier than the work needed to push the generations of pain out of our lives? Maybe my daughters' question comes out of the naiveté of childhood. (We black women were all once children, weren't we?) They only hesitated for a moment, when I asked them to tell me what I had taught them about surviving.

I know now how mistakenly easy dialogue can seem. I almost shut theirs off. And if I had shut off their questioning, they and we would have no new possibilities for learning what each of us has discovered about the balance we seek.

Still, breaking our silence is not enough. Collecting stories—however important—is only the first task in finding black women who have been hidden. Their pains and glories made it possible "for me to call my name out loud" and acknowledge my limitations.[2] The crisis of black womanhood must be acknowledged, analyzed, and dismantled.

Mobilizing and inspiring black women to share their hurt is a political act. This kind of sharing must include exploration, as well, of the internalization of racism, sexism, heterosexism, and classism. We must have these discussions among ourselves in order to create a safe place in which we no longer need to hide our power by "hiding our pain."[3]

We must reject outright the evolution from "tuff sister" to superwoman to bionic woman. It is not our true birthright. It is a slow death sentence from within. It is modeling the wrong messages to other Americans and to women of color around the world. Admiration for survival and strength is just that— admiration. It cannot be a bus ticket home. It is not a transforming ideology that will bring world peace. The question is not simply one of feminism or black liberation. The question is of the basic tools we need to dismantle our individual and group oppression—the basic tools we need to break habits.

The beginning of the task is to reconsider the way we think about gender-based analysis of the social, cultural, racial, sexual, and heterosexist exploitation of black women as blacks, women, and Americans. The beginning of the task is to acknowledge the limitations of conventional thought in these areas. The beginning of the task is to create the safety for black women to cry, to make the movement inside, to jar the survival instincts and spiritual intuition. Then we can model for other women a truly revolutionary process and frame our own social action around our own agenda for personal and political change. It is imperative that we do this necessary "internal work." Before "we can act like we got some sense," we have first got to feel what we have been through; to feel what we are doing and have done.[4] Human beings need to be listened to and understood by other human beings, and the interchange is the gift black women must begin to give each other.

The conceptualization of this book required of me scholarly and personal growth. The task begun here will continue all of my life. I know that the healing can take place within myself, my mother, my family, and my country. I began with a simple question to my mama, "How did you do it?" Then the question was turned on me: "Kesho, why do you continue to do it?" And finally I heard my daughters ask, "Mommy, how shall we do it now?"

My First Daughter's Dance:
Jameka, Age Eleven

Mom, I was about five years old when I realized I was a black woman. You told me. When we moved to Iowa, I especially knew I was black because I felt something else was expected of me by you. I didn't like that feeling. Sometimes, I just don't want to deal with it. I know you are strong. I remember when that kid on the bus said something racist and you made him and the principal apologize. I admired you, but I didn't feel I could do something like that yet. I know I have to. I watch how you stand up for the people you love and everything like that. You have taught me I can do something about everything. I can see you say whatever you want and do whatever you think is right, openly. I wonder, Mom, does it bother you? I see a lot of black women covering something up. You know, Mom, I don't think it is good to cover up what's hurting you.

I think you do a lot, Mom. You help me and Monté [her sister], help the family, and help black people, but you don't show us how you feel. That is weird. And you really seem to hurt when other people don't listen to you. But you keep that inside and you wait and wait for another chance to let out your feelings.

You are different from other people's parents. You teach me to do something, but tell me to experiment by doing it different ways. You tell me to stand up for myself, then you tell me to get right back up and fight. You have taught me so many ways to fight, before the fight, I just say forget it. I know it isn't stupid what you say but I don't want to deal with it.

Mom, you taught me not to take no crap, especially from men. Because you say, what if they leave you or you don't want them? You taught me to depend on myself. I try. It is not always a happily-ever-after ending, you know, like Cinderella or Snow White. I guess I know I'll always have to struggle as long as the first thing people see is that I'm a black female. I just don't want to make racism out of every tiniest conversation. I hate it! And when I tell you I disagree about politics, you start talking me down about the women of our family's tradition and what Martin Luther King, Jr., did. (I don't always tell you when something emotionally is going on with me because you always turn it into a political thing.) And most times, I'm scared because I know you're right. You act like a book, Mom, that tells me how I should feel and act.

I guess I have feelings about political things. And I appreciate the way you don't judge me in other things. I can talk to you about anything, even about what was in my diary. But one thing I don't like about you is your sexism. Why do you cook for men? I don't like it. I feel stabbed in the back. You make a lot of excuses about this when I bring it up. Maybe you want to be what you think is the "ultimate wife"—I don't know. I'm going to hate being a wife if this is what it is like. I'm supposed to feel comfortable with a person, not like a cook.

I've learned, Mom, from you that black women can do anything and improve their lives. You taught me that nobody can really make you do something—and that you're the one who makes the final decision. Black women are heroic because of what they set out to do. I feel like I have to do heroic things. It seems like you're pushing me. It's like there is no limit for you, Mom, just keep on, keep on, but there is a limit, Mom. You got to cool down sometimes, even when people depend on you. I see this especially with men who always depend on you, Mom. I think you help them too much. Three times is enough. I think they have to figure things out for themselves. And if we black women stop helping black men, then, I think pretty soon they will do something. That way they can stop thinking we're always gonna be there for them.

When I grow up I want to be a fashion designer, lawyer, and singer. I want to be political, but not talk about it all the time. I want to be a black woman, but I don't want to end up like most of them—feeling responsible for everyone—and never being my own self and feeling like we always have to change something to make it better for our culture. It is too much pressure. I won't give in to it. I won't always try to change things. I may change one or two things, you know, but not like change the democracy or seventy thousand black people. I'm not going to go out looking for change, I'll wait until it comes. I don't think it is right for it to mean that being a black woman is like saying you are a freedom fighter.

I guess, Mom, I feel like I owe you something. I owe you to keep on fighting for others, but I think I should pay you in another way. And when I grow up and have a daughter, I hope people won't be dependent on black women. Mom, I guess it seems like you're other people's God, controlling things because people want to be controlled. I don't want to be controlled and responsible for other people. I may help the homeless or do things for the church or maybe help against apartheid in South Africa. But I won't be a robot and you be the programmer. I don't really think, Mom, you're really helping them unless you are teaching them to work it out themselves. It is like, I'm too dependent on you if someone called me a bad name in school, then I should do something about it. I can tell you. But I should act.

I don't believe black women were put on this earth to fight, fight, fight. I believe black women have got to learn when it is over. I guess I need to teach you, Mom, that you have to be satisfied with yourself even when you are not fighting. It isn't fair when I don't want to be a freedom fighter and get accused of not being a black woman. It makes me feel like I am nothing. Mom, fighting all the time is an addiction. I don't see any way ever to be satisfied with yourself.

MY SECOND DAUGHTER'S DANCE:
MONTÉ, AGE NINE

You taught me about street smarts, when to say yes and no and to know when something is right or wrong. I think when I'm grown up because I'm not a woman yet, I'll know how to stand up for myself. I think what it means to be a black woman is to get a job, go to get a college education, be a writer or doctor, and that I won't live with you. I'll have bigger responsibilities. I feel like being a black woman you have to help people although it [their problems] isn't my fault. I think it is a nice thing to do.

You also taught me not to let anyone take control of me and to know my black history. (When you came to my class to talk about black history month in February, the white children thought you were going to sue them or kick them out of class. But they saw that you were a nice black mother.) I want to be like you in politics, but I'm afraid because I might get assassinated like all the other black people. I'm afraid of the Ku Klux Klan. It's sort of hard to be a black person because you don't know what might happen to you.

I'm a tomboy and I have a lot of girl friends. They are my friends and you taught me that there is no girl or boy stuff. That is sexist to think boys should play with trucks and girls play with dolls. I think everybody should play with robots or transformers.

I want to be equal in a marriage like you and daddy. You were both poor and got an education and got arrested in college and know how to stand up for your rights. I know how to protest when someone won't wait on me in the restaurant. First of all, I'd do what Martin Luther King, Jr., did, I go out and I'd get a couple of my friends (black and white) and I'd protest until they served me. He protested for five hours until they finally served him. And when someone calls me a bad name, I'll just get into a lecture and keep screaming at the person, saying that they are wrong. I'll call them a bad name in their culture. That is what leaders do, Mom. Mostly all the leaders that I've heard of that fought for all rights was always black people. I don't know of any white people who get up and speak about how everyone should be free. There was Kennedy, of course, he was our president. I never known a black person is gonna become president, it just never happened. He'll probably get assassinated on the first day. I don't know if Martin Luther King, Jr., was alive if he'd probably make it to the president.

I don't think black people should do all the leading. White people should have a chance to lead. No matter where you grow up you still have to stand up for yourself. I don't even know what a ghetto is actually. I thought it was a kind of apartment building where they give you a little room and you have cockroaches and dark alleys. No matter, you still have to fight for your rights. Mom, you came from a ghetto, and it affected you because you are always trying to make everything perfect. You didn't have a chance to have fun or live your life. But you did do right things. Maybe that is why you have bad health.

I want to be powerful and beautiful like my sister and fight back like you, Mom, and wear makeup and have a religion like Grandie [her grandmother]. And I also want to be a writer like you, Mom. I like to go to your readings. I love how you speak and when you go places. When I grow up like your age I'm gonna go to Africa like you. I think it is really heroic to go to Africa.

I think the one thing you should do more is sleep a lot. It scares me when you say you're tired and then when a friend comes over to talk politics you perk up and act like nothing was wrong. You are trying to hide things. I don't want to hide these kinds of things as a leader when I grow up. I don't think I have to if I don't want to. I wonder is there a place where there isn't a lot of racism. I know there is some in Africa,

United States, and Alabama. It is even in Grinnell. And even if there was no more racism in the world, we would still have problems. You'd still have sexism and ageism and all sorts of child abuse. Mom, I don't know if it will ever be a good world or not.

NOTES

INTRODUCTION

1. Lena Horne and Richard Schickel, *Lena* (New York: Limelight Editions, 1965), p. 293.
2. Sheila Radford-Hill, "Considering Feminism as a Model for Social Change," *Feminist Studies, Critical Studies,* ed. Teresa de Lauretis (Bloomington: Indiana University Press, 1986), pp. 161–165.
3. Doris Kearns, "Angles of Vision," *Telling Lives: The Biographer's Art,* ed. Marc Patcher (Washington, D.C.: New Republic Books, 1979), p. 93.
4. Barbara Smith, ed., *Home Girls* (New York: Kitchen Table Press, 1982), p. xxviii.
5. Suzanne Pharr, *Homophobia: A Weapon of Sexism* (Inverness, Calif.: Chardon Press, 1988), pp. 45–49.
6. Catharine A. MacKinnon, "Feminism, Marxism, Method and the State," *Signs* 7 (Spring 1982): 535–543.
7. Ellen Cantarow, *Moving the Mountain* (Old Westbury, N.Y.: Feminist Press, 1980), p. xiv.
8. Rickey Sherover-Marcuse, "Liberation Theory: A Working Framework." Classroom handout, 1987.

9. Suzanne Lipsky, "Internalized Oppression," *Black Re-Emergence,* Vol. 2, ed. Joyce Duncan (Seattle, Wash.: Rational Island Publishers, 1978), pp. 148–152.

10. Barbara Love, "Internalized Oppression and the Participation of Black People in the Re-Evaluation Counseling Communities," *Black Re-Emergence,* Vol. 4, ed. Jenny Yamato (Seattle, Wash.: Rational Island Publishers, 1987), pp. 1–2.

11. Gerda Lerner, ed., *Black Women in White America* (New York: Vintage Books, 1973), pp. 26–27.

12. Catherine Foster, "Forgotten Women: A Century of Narratives by Black Writers," *The Christian Science Monitor* (Feb. 5, 1988), p. B-1.

13. James Clifford, "On Ethnographic Authority," *Representations* 1:2 (Spring 1983): 118–146.

14. Kesho Scott, Cherry Muhanji, and Egyirba High, *Tight Spaces* (San Francisco, Calif.: Spinsters/Aunt Lute Books, 1987), Introduction.

15. Audre Lorde, "Who Said It Was Simple," *From a Land Where Other People Live* (Detroit: Broadside Press, 1973), p. 39.

16. Bell Hooks, *Feminist Theory: From Margin to Center* (Boston: South End Press, 1984), p. 43.

17. Barbara Tuchman, "Biography as a Prism of History," *Telling Lives,* Patcher, ed., p. 145.

CHAPTER 1. THE PREVIOUS GENERATION

1. Paula Giddings, *When and Where I Enter* (New York: Bantam Books, 1984), p. 244.

2. Giddings, *When and Where,* pp. 222–223.

3. Susan M. Hartmann. *The Home Front and Beyond* (Boston: Twayne Publishers, 1982), p. 1.

4. Jacqueline Jones, *Labor of Love, Labor of Sorrow* (New York: Basic Books, 1985), pp. 2–6.

5. Jones, *Labor of Love,* p. 233.

6. Jones, *Labor of Love,* p. 234.

7. Barbara Christian. *Black Feminist Criticism* (Elmsford, N.Y.: Pergamon Press, 1985), p. 27.

8. Hartmann, *Home Front,* pp. 15–27.

9. Giddings, *When and Where,* p. 232.

10. Jones, *Labor of Love,* p. 262.

11. Marion Cuthbert, "Problems Facing Negro Young Women," *Opportunity* (Feb. 2, 1936): 48.

12. Hartmann, *Home Front*, p. 78.
13. Hartmann, *Home Front*, pp. 5–6.
14. Giddings, *When and Where*, p. 237.
15. Jones, *Labor of Love*, p. 252.
16. Jones, *Labor of Love*, p. 237.
17. Jones, *Labor of Love*, p. 240.
18. Giddings, *When and Where*, p. 229.
19. Jones, *Labor of Love*, pp. 265–267.
20. Hartmann, *Home Front*, p. 81.
21. Jones, *Labor of Love*, p. 253.
22. Hartmann, *Home Front*, p. 86.
23. Jones, *Labor of Love*, p. 260.
24. Jones, *Labor of Love*, p. 263, and see Jean Smith's story "Frankie Mae" in *Black-Eyed Susans*, edited by Mary Helen Washington (Garden City, N.Y.: Anchor Books, 1975).
25. Hartmann, *Home Front*, pp. 88, 190.
26. Giddings, *When and Where*, pp. 229–230.
27. Giddings, *When and Where*, pp. 252–253, 270.
28. Hartmann, *Home Front*, pp. 190, 201–202.
29. Zora Neale Hurston, *Their Eyes Were Watching God* (Chicago: University of Illinois Press, 1937), p. 29.
30. Jones, *Labor of Love*, p. 273.
31. Hartmann, *Home Front*, p. 193.
32. Horne and Schickel, *Lena*, pp. 293–300.
33. Jones, *Labor of Love*, p. 271.
34. Hurston, *Their Eyes*, p. 29.
35. Angela Y. Davis, "Reflections on the Black Woman's Role in the Community of Slaves," *Black Scholar* 3 (Dec. 1971): 7.
36. Giddings, *When and Where*, p. 247.
37. Hartmann, *Home Front*, p. 165.
38. Washington, *Black-Eyed Susans*, p. xxi.
39. Jones, *Labor of Love*, pp. 263–271.
40. Giddings, *When and Where*, p. 242.
41. Maya Angelou, *I Know Why the Caged Bird Sings* (New York: Bantam Books, 1969), p. 265.
42. See Washington, *Black-Eyed Susans*, p. xvi.
43. Giddings, *When and Where*, p. 252.
44. Washington, *Black-Eyed Susans*, p. xxvii.
45. Angela Y. Davis, *Women, Race and Class* (New York: Random House, 1981), pp. 209–215.
46. Hartmann, *Home Front*, p. 171.
47. Giddings, *When and Where*, p. 248.

48. Christian, *Black Feminist Criticism*, p. 223.

49. Hartmann, *Home Front*, p. 172.

50. Hartmann, *Home Front*, p. 177.

51. Giddings, *When and Where*, pp. 251–256.

52. Hartmann, *Home Front*, p. 179.

53. James A. Goodman, "Institutional Racism: The Crucible of Black Identity," *Black Self-Concept*, eds. James A. Banks and Jean D. Grambs (New York: McGraw-Hill, 1972), pp. 117–140.

54. James P. Comer, M.D., and Alvin F. Poussaint, M.D., *Black Child Care* (New York: Simon & Schuster, 1975), pp. 1–11.

55. Toni Morrison, *Sula* (New York: Alfred A. Knopf, 1974), p. 69.

56. Hartmann, *Home Front*, p. 179.

57. Davis, "Reflections," p. 7.

58. Ann Allen Shockley, "Black Lesbian Images in American Literature," *Home Girls*, Smith, ed., pp. 83–93.

59. Hartmann, *Home Front*, p. 180.

60. Audre Lorde, *Zami: A New Spelling of My Name* (Watertown, Mass.: Persephone Press, 1982), p. 255.

61. Christian, *Black Feminist Criticism*, p. 197.

62. Jones, *Labor of Love*, p. 232.

63. Hartmann, *Home Front*, pp. 210–211.

64. The term *thick description* (a term from cultural anthropology that relates to interpreting a cultural trait in its context) comes from Clifford Geertz's *Interpretation of Culture* (New York: Basic Books, 1973).

65. Audre Lorde, *Sister Outsider* (Trumansburg, N.Y.: Crossing Press, 1984), p. 39.

Chapter 6. A Black Woman's Chorus Line

1. Jones, *Labor of Love*, p. 320.

2. Jones, *Labor of Love*, p. 315.

3. Rhetough Groves Pumas, "Dilemmas of Black Females in Leadership," *The Black Woman*, ed. La Frances Rodgers-Rose (Beverly Hills: Sage, 1980), p. 205.

4. Cheryl Townsend Gikes, "Holding Back the Ocean with a Broom: Black Women and Community Work," *The Black Woman*, Rodgers-Rose, ed., p. 223.

5. Giddings, *When and Where*, p. 316.

6. Radford-Hill, "Considering Feminism," *Feminist Studies*, de Lauretis, ed., pp. 165–166.

7. Hattie Gosset, "Why We Need to Give Up Feminist Bashing," *Emerge Magazine* (Jan. 1990), pp. 37–39.

8. Joyce Ladner, "Racial Oppression and the Black Girl," *Tomorrow's Tomorrow* (Garden City, N.Y.: Anchor Books, 1971), pp. 77–124.

9. Robert Staples, *Introduction to Black Sociology* (New York: McGraw-Hill, 1976), pp. 89–90.

10. Jacqueline Trescott and Dorothy Gilliam, "The Black Woman," *Washington Post* (Dec. 28, 1986), p. 6.

11. Pumas, "Dilemmas of Black Females," pp. 206–207.

12. Trescott and Gilliam, "The Black Woman," Dec. 29, 1986, p. 6.

13. Jones, *Labor of Love*, p. 10.

14. Jones, *Labor of Love*, p. 10.

15. Gloria Wade-Gayles, "She Who Is Black and Mother: In Sociology and Fiction, 1940–1970," *The Black Woman*, Rodgers-Rose, ed., p. 90.

16. Betty Friedan, *The Feminine Mystique* (New York: Dell, 1963), p. 28.

17. Janice Hall, "The Black Woman and Child Rearing," *The Black Woman*, Rodgers-Rose, ed., pp. 81–82.

18. Harriette Pipes McAdoo, "Black Mothers and the Extended Family Support Network," *The Black Woman*, Rodgers-Rose, ed., p. 126.

19. James A. Banks and Jean D. Grambs, eds., *Black Self-Concept* (New York: McGraw-Hill, 1972), p. 120.

CONCLUSION

1. Radford-Hill, "Considering Feminism," *Feminist Studies*, de Lauretis, ed., p. 169.

2. Cheryl Clarke, "Lesbianism: An Act of Resistance," *Feminist Studies*, de Lauretis, ed., p. 157.

3. Lorde, *Sister Outsider* p. 36.

4. Smith, ed., *Home Girls*, p. xxiv.

BIBLIOGRAPHY

Angelou, Maya. *I Know Why the Caged Bird Sings.* New York: Bantam Books, 1969.

Aptheker, Bettina. "Strong Is What We Make Each Other: Unlearning Racism Within Women's Studies." *Women's Studies Quarterly* (Winter 1981): 13–16.

Aptheker, Bettina. *Women's Legacy.* Amherst: University of Massachusetts Press, 1982.

Banks, James A., and Grambs, Jean D., eds. *Black Self-Concept.* New York: McGraw-Hill, 1972.

Barnett, Ida B. Wells. *Crusade for Freedom.* Edited by Elfreda Ouster. Chicago: University of Chicago Press, 1970.

Beale, Frances. "Double Jeopardy." In *The Black Woman,* ed. Toni Cade. New York: Signet, 1970.

Bellah, Robert N.; Madsen, Richard; Sullivan, William M.; Swidler, Ann; Tipton, Steven M. *Habits of the Heart.* Berkeley and Los Angeles: University of California Press, 1985.

Bennett, Lerone, Jr. *Before the Mayflower.* Baltimore: Penguin Books, 1962.

Berry, Mary, and Bassingame, John. *The Long Memory: The Black Experience.* New York: Oxford Press, 1982.

Billingsley, Andrew. *Black Families in White America.* Englewood Cliffs, N.J.: Prentice-Hall, 1966.

Bogle, Donald. *Brown Sugar: Eighty Years of America's Black Female Superstars.* New York: Harmony Books, 1980.

Boyd, Melba J. "The Salt in the Sugar: A Comparative Analysis of the Novel and Film *The Color Purple.*" Paper presented at the African-American World Studies Faculty Seminar, Afro-American Studies Department, University of Iowa, Iowa City, April 2, 1986.

Boyd-Franklin, Nancy. "Black Family Life-Styles: A Lesson in Survival." In *Class, Race and Sex: The Dynamics of Controls,* eds. Amy Severdeow and Hanna Lessinger. Boston: G. K. Hall, 1980.

Brooks, Gwendolyn. *Maude Martha.* New York: Harper & Row, 1953.

Burnham, Linda. "Has Poverty Been Feminized in Black America?" *Black Scholar* 16:2 (March/April, 1985): 14–24.

Caldren, Erma, and Teel, Leonard Ray. *Erma: A Black Woman Remembers.* New York: Random House, 1981.

Capanzano, Vincent. "Life Histories." *American Anthropologist* 86 (1984): 953–960.

Cantarow, Ellen. *Moving the Mountain.* Old Westbury, N.Y.: Feminist Press, 1980.

Chester, P. *Women in Madness.* New York: Doubleday, 1972.

Chisholm, Shirley. *Unbought and Unbossed.* Boston: Houghton Mifflin, 1970.

Christian, Barbara. *Black Feminist Criticism.* Elmsford, N.Y.: Pergamon Press, 1985.

Clark, Cheryl. "Lesbianism: An Act of Resistance." In *Feminist Studies, Critical Studies,* ed. Teresa de Lauretis. Bloomington: Indiana University Press, 1986.

Clifford, James. "On Ethnographic Authority." *Representations* 1:2 (Spring 1983): 118–146.

Comer, James P., M.D., and Poussaint, Alvin F., M.D. *Black Child Care.* New York: Simon & Schuster, 1975.

Coser, L. *Sociology Through Literature.* Englewood Cliffs, N.J.: Prentice-Hall, 1963.

Cuthbert, Marion. "Problems Facing Negro Young Women." *Opportunity* (Feb. 2, 1936): 48.

Davis, Angela Y. *If They Come in the Morning: Voices of Resistance.* New York: Third Press, 1971.

Davis, Angela Y. "Reflections on the Black Woman's Role in the Community of Slaves." *Black Scholar* 3 (Dec. 1971): 2–15.

Davis, Angela Y. *Women, Race and Class.* New York: Random House, 1981.

de Lauretis, Teresa, ed. *Feminist Studies, Critical Studies.* Bloomington: Indiana University Press, 1986.

Dill, Bonnie Thornton. "Race, Class and Gender: Prospects for an All-Inclusive Sisterhood." *Feminist Studies* 9:1 (1983): 131–150.

Du Bois, W. E. B. *The Souls of Black Folks.* New York: Signet, 1982.

Du Bois, Carol Ellen. *Feminism and Suffrage: The Emergence of an Independent Women's Movement in America.* Ithaca, N.Y.: Cornell University Press, 1978.

Epstein, C. F. "Black and Female: The Double Whammy." *Psychology Today* (Aug. 1973): 57–61.

Evans, Sara. *Personal Politics.* New York: Vintage Books, 1980.

Foster, Catherine. "Forgotten Women: A Century of Narratives by Black Writers." *The Christian Science Moniter* (Feb. 5, 1988), p. B-1.

Franklin, John Hope. *From Slavery to Freedom: History of the Negro American.* New York: Alfred A. Knopf, 1980.

Freedom, Jo. *The Politics of Women's Liberation.* New York: McKay, 1975.

Freire, Pablo. *Education for Critical Consciousness.* New York: Seabury Press, 1973.

Friedan, Betty. *The Feminine Mystique.* New York: Dell, 1963.

Geertz, Clifford. *Interpretation of Culture.* New York: Basic Books, 1973.

Geiger, Susan N. G. "Women's Life Histories." *Signs* 1 (1986): 334–351.

Giddings, Paula. *When and Where I Enter.* New York: Bantam Books, 1984.

Gikes, Cheryl Townsend. "Holding Back the Ocean with a Broom: Black Women and Community Work." In *The Black Woman,* ed. La Frances Rodgers-Rose. Beverly Hills, Calif.: Sage, 1980.

Goodman, James A. "Institutional Racism: The Crucible of Black Identity." In *Black Self-Concept,* eds. James A. Banks and Jean D. Grambs. New York: McGraw-Hill, 1972.

Gosset, Hattie. "Why We Need to Give Up Feminist Bashing," *Emerge Magazine* (Jan. 1990): 37–39.

Gwaltney, John. *Drylongso.* New York: Vintage Books, 1981.

Hall, Janice. "The Black Woman and Child Rearing." In *The Black Woman,* ed. La Frances Rodgers-Rose. Beverly Hills, Calif.: Sage, 1980.

Harding, Vincent. *There Is a River.* New York: Harcourt Brace Jovanovich, 1981.

Hartmann, Susan M. *The Home Front and Beyond.* Boston: Twayne Publishers, 1982.

Heron, H. *Black Suicide.* New York: Basic Books, 1969.

Hilgrad, E. R. *Primitive Culture.* London: Murry Press, 1913.

Hill, Robert. *The Strength of Black Families.* New York: Emerson Hall, 1972.

Holiday, Billie, and Duffy, William. *Lady Sings the Blues.* New York: Lancer Books, 1972.

Hooks, Bell. *Ain't I a Woman.* Boston: South End Press, 1981.

Hooks, Bell. *Feminist Theory: From Margin to Center.* Boston: South End Press, 1984.

Horne, Lena, and Schickel, Richard. *Lena.* New York: Limelight Editions, 1965.

Horwitz, Richard P. *The Strip.* Lincoln: University of Nebraska Press, 1985.

Hull, Gloria T.; Scott, Patricia Bell; and Smith, Barbara. *But Some of Us Are Brave.* Old Westbury, N.Y.: Feminist Press, 1982.

Hurston, Zora Neale. *Their Eyes Were Watching God.* Chicago: University of Illinois Press, 1937.

Jones, Jacqueline. *Labor of Love, Labor of Sorrow.* New York: Basic Books, 1985.

Joseph, Gloria I., and Lewis, Jill. *Common Differences: Conflicts in Black and White Feminist Perspectives.* New York: Doubleday Anchor, 1981.

Katzman, David, and Turtle, William. *Plain Folks.* Urbana: University of Illinois Press, 1982.

Kearns, Doris. "Angles of Vision." In *Telling Lives: The Biographer's Art,* ed. Marc Patcher. Washington, D.C.: New Republic Books, 1979.

Kessing, Rodger M. "Theories of Culture." *Annual Review of Anthropology* 3 (1974): 73–97.

Ladner, Joyce. *Tomorrow's Tomorrow.* Garden City, N.Y.: Anchor Books, 1971.

LaFeber, Walter. *The American Century.* New York: John Wiley & Sons, 1975.

Langness, Lewis L. *The Life History in Anthropological Science.* New York: Holt, Rinehart & Winston, 1965.

Langness, Lewis L. *The Study of Culture.* San Francisco, Calif.: Chandler & Sharp, 1974.

Lerner, Gerda, ed. *Black Women in White America.* New York: Vintage Books, 1973.

Lipsky, Suzanne. "Internalized Oppression." In *Black Re-Emergence,* Vol. 2, ed. Joyce Duncan. Seattle, Wash.: Rational Island Publishers, 1987.

Lorde, Audre. *Sister Outsider*. Trumansburg, New York: Crossing Press, 1984.

Lorde, Audre. "Who Said It Was Simple." In *From a Land Where Other People Live*. Detroit: Broadside Press, 1973.

Lorde, Audre. *Zami: A New Spelling of My Name*. Watertown, Mass.: Persephone Press, 1982.

Love, Barbara. "Internalized Oppression and the Participation of Black People in the Re-evaluation Counseling Communities." In *Black Re-Emergence*, Vol. 4, ed. Jenny Yamato. Seattle, Wash.: Rational Island Publishers, 1987.

McAdoo, Harriette Pipes. "Black Mothers and the Extended Family Support Network." In *The Black Woman*, ed. La Frances Rodgers-Rose. Beverly Hills, Calif.: Sage, 1980.

MacKinnon, Catharine A. "Feminism, Marxism, Method and the State," *Signs* 7 (Spring 1982): 535–543.

Mandelbaum, David G. "The Study of Life History." *Current Anthropology* 14:3 (June 1973): 177–196.

Memmi, Albert. *Portrait of a Jew*. New York: Orion Press, 1962.

Morrison, Toni. *Sula*. New York: Alfred A. Knopf, 1974.

Moses, Yolanda T. "Black American Women and Work: Historical and Contemporary Strategies for Empowerment." *Women's Studies International Forum* 8:4 (1985): 351–359.

Noble, Jean. *Beautiful, Also, Are the Souls of My Black Sisters*. Englewood Cliffs, N.J.: Prentice-Hall, 1978.

Pharr, Suzanne. *Homophobia: A Weapon of Sexism*. Inverness, Calif.: Chardon Press, 1988.

Pumas, Rhetough Groves. "Dilemmas of Black Females in Leadership." In *The Black Woman*, ed. La Frances Rodgers-Rose. Beverly Hills, Calif.: Sage, 1980.

Radford-Hill, Sheila. "Considering Feminism as a Model for Social Change." In *Feminist Studies, Critical Studies,* ed. Teresa de Lauretis. Bloomington, Ind.: Indiana University Press, 1986.

Rich, Adrienne. *On Lies, Secrets and Silence: Selected Prose, 1966–1978*. New York: W. W. Norton, 1979.

Rodgers, Carolyn. *How I Got Ovah: New and Selected*. New York: Doubleday/Anchor, 1975.

Rodgers-Rose, La Frances, ed. *The Black Woman*. Beverly Hills: Sage, 1980.

Schultz, D. *Coming Up Black: Patterns of Ghetto Socialization*. Englewood Cliffs, N.J.: Prentice-Hall, 1969.

Scott, Kesho; Mahunji, Cherry; and High, Egyirba. *Tight Spaces*. San Francisco: Spinsters/Aunt Lute Books, 1987.

Shockley, Ann Allen. "Black Lesbian Images in American Literature." In *Home Girls*, ed. Barbara Smith. New York: Kitchen Table Press, 1982.

Slater, Jack. "Suicide: A Growing Menace to Black Women." *Ebony* 28 (September 1973): 152–160.

Smith, Barbara, ed. *Home Girls*. New York: Kitchen Table Press, 1982.

Stack, Carol. *All Our Kin: Strategies for Survival in a Black Community*. New York: Harper & Row, 1974.

Stanley, Liz, and Wise, Sue. *Breaking Out: Feminist Consciousness and Feminist Research*. London: Routledge & Kegan Paul, 1983.

Staples, Robert. *The Black Woman in America*. Chicago: Nelson Hall, 1973.

Staples, Robert. *Introduction to Black Sociology*. New York: McGraw-Hill, 1976.

Stone, Albert. *American Autobiography*. Englewood Cliffs, N.J.: Prentice-Hall, 1981.

Tate, Cecil F. *The Search for a Method in American Studies*. Minneapolis: University of Minnesota Press, 1973.

Tate, Claudia. *Black Women Writers at Work*. New York: Continuum Publishing, 1983.

Terrell, Mary Church. *A Colored Woman in a White World*. Washington, D.C.: Ransdell Publishers, 1940.

Trescott, Jacqueline, and Gilliam, Dorothy. "The New Black Woman." *The Washington Post* (Dec. 28, 29, 30, 1986), p. A-1 (each issue).

Tuchman, Barbara. "Biography as a Prism of History." In *Telling Lives: The Biographer's Art*, ed. Marc Patcher, Washington, D.C.: New Republic Books, 1979.

Wade-Gayles, Gloria. "She Who Is Black and Mother: In Sociology and Fiction, 1940–1970." In *The Black Woman*, ed. La Frances Rodgers-Rose. Beverly Hills: Sage, 1980.

Walker, Alice. *In Search of Our Mothers' Gardens*. San Diego: Harcourt Brace Jovanovich, 1983.

Wallace, Michelle. *Black Macho and the Myth of the Superwoman*. New York: Dial Press, 1978.

Washington, Mary Helen. *Black-Eyed Susans*. Garden City, N.Y.: Anchor Books, 1975.

Wise, Gene. "Some Elementary Axioms for an American Culture Studies." *Prospects* 4 (1979): 517–547.